# small
# GASOLINE
# engines

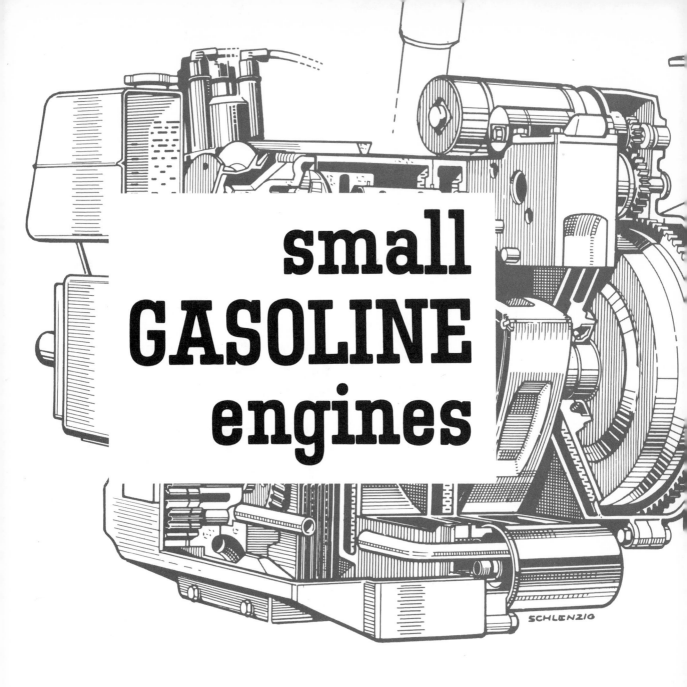

# small GASOLINE engines

SCHLENZIG

DELMAR PUBLISHERS
COPYRIGHT ©1973
BY LITTON EDUCATIONAL PUBLISHING, INC.

LIBRARY OF CONGRESS CATALOG CARD NUMBER:  72-13390

Printed in the United States of America
Published Simultaneously in Canada by
Delmar Publishers, A Division of
Van Nostrand Reinhold, Ltd.

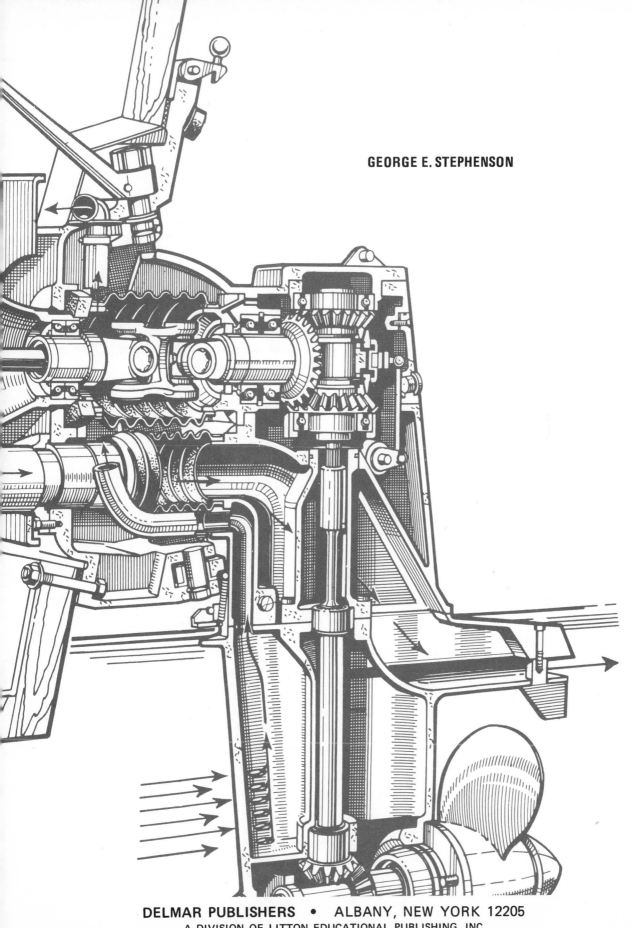

GEORGE E. STEPHENSON

**DELMAR PUBLISHERS** • ALBANY, NEW YORK 12205
A DIVISION OF LITTON EDUCATIONAL PUBLISHING, INC.

# Preface

SMALL GASOLINE ENGINES explores the use of a power source that has shown a remarkable growth in helping man to do his work. Along with replacing muscle power, small gasoline engines have found many recreational applications. To mention only a few of the more common applications, these engines serve as the source of power for lawnmowers, chain saws, portable pumps, power tools and equipment, boats, and motorcycles.

For those who intend to qualify as mechanics of small engines and for others who merely wish a general understanding of this common source of power, SMALL GASOLINE ENGINES provides basic instruction. It is the aim of this text to provide instructional material on the construction, operation, care and maintenance, and application of small two-cycle and four-cycle gas engines.

Now in its *second* edition, SMALL GASOLINE ENGINES continues to keep pace with the technological advances which are so rapidly changing our style of living. With more in-depth coverage and the inclusion of many recent developments, the following topics summarize the changes made in this latest edition:

- solid-state ignition

- recent quality designations and viscosity classification for oil

- horizontal and vertical crankshaft engine designs

- fractional distillation of petroleum and characteristics of gasoline

- crankcase ventilation

- spark plug characteristics and problems

- latest specifications for small gas engines from various manufacturers

- *new unit* on the rotating combustion engine, including its construction, operation, and application

The author of this publication, George E. Stephenson, is a graduate of Stout State University (BS) and Colorado State University (MEd). He has also authored *Power Technology* and *Drawing for Product Planning*. Mr. Stephenson is a past president of the Illinois Power Mechanics Association. In 1967 he received the AIAA Outstanding Teacher of the Year Award – state of Illinois. For several years, the author has served as a supervising teacher for the Western Illinois University student teaching program. Mr. Stephenson is currently a power mechanics and general industrial arts teacher in school district No. 205, Galesburg, Illinois.

Each unit of SMALL GASOLINE ENGINES is treated as a single, coherent block of instruction and is concluded with pertinent study questions, discussion topics, and suggested instructor demonstrations.

Of special significance is the inclusion of laboratory experiences which follow each of the units of study. These are designed to guide the student in the procedures of assembly and disassembly and direct his work in an orderly fashion while he investigates the workings of the small gasoline engine. The lab experiences are closely correlated to the appropriate units so that the combination of theory and practice provides for a logical and unified instructional program. The procedures given in these sections are fundamental and apply to all makes of small gasoline engines.

The first ten units which comprise SMALL GASOLINE ENGINES are identical to the first ten units of *Power Technology* by the same author, except that the latter publication does not include the laboratory experiences. *Power Technology* also goes far beyond instruction in small gasoline engines; the content includes all major sources of energy application. For those students who desire a broader or continuing presentation of energy sources and their applications, the latter title is recommended. Other titles in the Automotive/Power Mechanics series include:

BASIC AUTOMOTIVE SERIES (9 books)

Automobile Engine — Basic Parts

The Brake System

The Cooling and Exhaust System

The Differential

The Fuel System

The ignition system, cranking and charging circuits

The Lubricating System

The Steering System

The Standard Transmission

AUTOMOTIVE OSCILLOSCOPE

GENERAL REPAIR TOOLS FOR AUTOMOTIVE MECHANICS

AUTOMOTIVE DRAWING INTERPRETATION

RELATED SCIENCE — AUTOMOTIVE TRADES

PRACTICAL PROBLEMS IN MATH FOR AUTOMOTIVE TECHNICIANS

AUTOMOTIVE STEERING SYSTEMS

AUTOMOTIVE STARTING AND CHARGING SYSTEMS

AUTOMOTIVE AIR CONDITIONING

A series of full-color transparencies correlated to the SMALL GASOLINE ENGINES units can be obtained from DCA Educational Publications, Inc., 4865 Stenton Avenue, Philadelphia, Pennsylvania 19144. These transparencies can be employed as instructional aids to clarify and enrich the course content. A suggested procedure for the presentation of each transparency is included in the *Instructor's Guide* of this text.

The author and editorial staff at Delmar Publishers are interested in continually improving the quality of this instructional material. The reader is invited to submit constructive criticism and questions. Responses will be reviewed jointly by the author and source editor. Send comments to:

Editor-in-Chief
Box 5087
Albany, New York 12205

# Contents

## Unit 1

## MAN'S STRUGGLE TO HARNESS ENERGY

Prehistoric man knew power. He observed its existence in the force of the wind, the heat of the sun, in flowing water, fire, and even in the wild animals that preyed on him and on one another. These forces were sometimes a blessing but very often, a real danger: heat, cold, hurricane, flood, predatory animals could threaten his existence.

When man began to think in terms of "How can I get this power to work for me?", the mechanics of power was born. Slowly through the centuries, man developed machines and devices that harnessed this energy to do his work.

Nature has provided the energy sources, and man's ingenuity has provided the machines, a happy combination that is responsible for a high degree of civilization. But man's application of nature's sources of energy has been a long and gradual evolution. Without his intellect and nature's help, man today would still be in his cave, hunting animals with a spear and praying that the forces of nature would be gentle.

For the general purposes of our introduction, we shall use the term "power" in its general sense, interchangeably with "force" and "energy". Later in our discussion, however, these and other terms will be defined in their true, technical descriptions.

### THE SUN, MAJOR SOURCE OF POWER

Almost all sources of power can be traced to the sun. Coal was formed through the ages as plant life died and was accumulated in the swampy areas of the earth. This plant life grew through the sun's energy. When coal is burned this energy is released, energy that has been stored for perhaps millions of years.

The story of petroleum is similar. It is believed that petroleum was formed ages ago where large amounts of plant and animal life accumulated. The petroleum fuels we burn release stored energy. Wood, of course, possesses energy and releases its energy when it is burned. Without the sun, no plants or animals could have lived.

Wind and water power are also traceable to the sun. Wind is the circulation of air caused by the sun's heat. Water power is harnessed from a flowing stream, which is filled by rainfall. The rain is caused by the sun evaporating the earth's water. In a short time the water condenses and rain falls, filling the streams.

With the exception of atomic power, all of our power sources can be traced quite directly to the sun.

## EARLY ATTEMPTS TO CONTROL POWER

Surely one of man's first attempts at controlling power was to use fire for warmth and cooking.

Another early step forward was the domestication of wild animals. The taming of the horse and his use as a beast of burden provided man with new power, horse power to be exact.

Of course, the beast of burden's load was lightened with the evolution of the wheel. The wheel enabled the animal to "carry" a larger load with less effort. Again, it further increased man's power, or rate of doing work. Men used animals for land transportation for centuries and in some parts of the world animals are still the main form of transportation.

For most of the world it has only been within the last century that the beast has been taken out of harness and the engine put in its place. The oxen, donkey and horse have been replaced by the truck, tractor and automobile. No doubt our grandfathers remember the "horse and buggy days" of not so long ago.

Another early force that was harnessed was wind. The use of sailboats can be traced back 5000 years or more. For centuries the exploration and conquest of the world was done with the aid of the sailing ship. Ancient traders and merchants sent their wares around the world in sailing ships. The first colonists in America were brought to our shores by sail.

## DEVELOPMENT OF STEAM POWER

In 1765 James Watt of Scotland produced a successful steam engine. Although others had worked on steam engines earlier, Watt's engine was vastly more efficient. It really consisted of three parts; boiler, cylinder and piston, and condenser. When steam was let into the cylinder the piston was forced to the top of the cylinder. The steam was then shut off and the condenser opened. The condenser turned the steam back into water; when this happened a vacuum was created pulling the piston down. This cycle produced useful work and was repeated over and over. Watt's engine was first used to power water pumps in the coal mines of England.

Quite naturally Watt's steam engine became an extremely efficient and refined machine through the years and was the key to rapid industrial growth. Steam engines could be built anywhere, the factory was no longer tied to the river and water power. The steam engine provided the power for the newly developing factories of the era. Workers and craftsmen were brought from their small shops into the more efficient factories. Steam-powered machinery increased the productivity of workers. England attempted a monopoly on the use of steam engines, but in 1789 Samuel Slater came to America with memorized plans. By 1807, fifteen steam powered cotton mills were operating successfully in America.

On August 18, 1807, Robert Fulton boarded his new ship, the Clermont, fired the stokers of a steam engine and, in the midst of flying sparks and thick smoke, the first successful steamship voyage was made. Fulton traveled from New York to Albany in a record time of 32 hours.

Steam engines were soon used to power railroads in the U. S. Although the race between Peter Cooper's Tom Thumb and a horse-drawn train in 1830 failed due to mechanical difficulties, the steam engine DeWitt Clinton followed by making a successful run from Albany, New York to nearby Schenectady.

Another type of steam engine, the turbine, was developed toward the end of the 19th century. In this engine a jet of steam directed against the turbine blade rotated the blade, producing power, much the same as a windmill. The steam turbine was used mainly for powering large ships and producing electrical power. Today the steam turbine is still widely used.

## THE DEVELOPMENT OF THE INTERNAL COMBUSTION ENGINE

Steam power was dominant as a power source until the advent of the internal combustion engine. The internal combustion engine has taken over many steam engine jobs and has found a multitude of new jobs on its own. The smaller, internal combustion engine was ideally suited for land vehicles and the development of automobiles, trucks, tractors, etc.

One of the earliest attempts to produce an internal combustion engine was made by Christian Hygenes late in the 17th century. In his engine a piston was forced down a cylinder by an explosion of gunpowder. Many other persons continued working through the years to produce a successful engine in which fuel could be burned directly, right inside the engine itself.

The first practical internal combustion engines were produced in 1878, less than 100 years ago. These engines were made by the Otto and Langan firm at Deutz, Germany. They burned the vapor from oil for fuel and, though successful, they were crude and cumbersome by present standards. The engines weighed about 1,110 pounds per horsepower. Today, engines are manufactured that weigh as little as three pounds per horsepower.

Smaller internal combustion engines such as the "Small Gasoline Engine" also have earned their place in advancing our civilization. They, too, have been helping man to do his work for many years. And in recent years small engines have found a tremendous popularity both for work and recreation. It is toward a thorough understanding of the small gasoline engine that we shall direct our study in this manual. We shall begin with a review of terms basic to an understanding of mechanical power; then proceed to study construction of the small gasoline engine; fuel systems, carburetion and governors; lubrication; cooling systems; ignition systems; care and maintenance; troubleshooting and tune-up; and, finally, specifications and buying considerations.

---

## STUDY QUESTIONS

1. What is the original source of nearly all power? Explain.

2. What sources of power were used before the steam engine?

3. In what ways did the development of the steam engine affect society?

4. Who is credited with producing the first practical internal combustion engine? How long ago?

5. Compare the weight per horsepower of early engines with the weight per horsepower of present day engines.

6. How has the internal combustion engine affected our modes of travel, economy, and way of life?

7. List several uses of small gasoline engines, both for work and pleasure.


## CLASS DISCUSSION TOPICS

● Discuss how machines evolved slowly through the centuries.

● Discuss the rapid technological developments of the 19th and 20th centuries.

● Discuss the steam engine and the Industrial Revolution.

● List the common types of heat engines.

● Discuss the occupations in which small gasoline engines are regularly used.

● Discuss how friends, relatives and others use small gasoline engines occasionally during the year.

Unit 2

# WORK, ENERGY, POWER

In Unit 1 we briefly reviewed man's attempts to control sources of power from his earliest awareness of such sources to the present day. Before getting into a detailed study of the elements of small gasoline engines, however, it is necessary for us to review some of the terms which are basic to an understanding of mechanical power. What is power? What is energy? What is work? Are these terms all the same and, if not, how do they differ? It is the purpose of this unit to define and explain these terms, so that as they are used in later units their meaning will be clear.

## WORK

Work is a scientific term as well as an everyday term. To the man on the street, work means engaging in an occupation. One person may work hard at an office while another person may work hard carrying bricks on a construction job. Both men may come home exhausted but, scientifically speaking, only the man carrying bricks has done much work.

Work involves moving things, and more than that, moving things by applying a force. Work, then, is applying a force to cause motion or in other words, motion caused by applying a force.

## Measurement of Work

The common unit for measuring work is the foot-pound. Raising one pound, one foot is one foot-pound of work. A man carrying 50 pounds of bricks up a 10-foot ladder does 500 foot-pounds of work. Work is, therefore, applying a force through a distance.

Work = Force × Distance

(Ft.-lbs.) = (Pound) × (Feet)

As a simple example, calculate the work involved in lifting a 20-pound weight 5 feet.

Work = Force × Distance

Work = 20 lbs. × 5 ft. = 100 ft.-lbs.

By scientific definition, the man who struggles to move a boulder but fails to budge it is not doing work because there is no "distance moved". Of course all engines can do work because they are capable of applying force to move machines, loads, implements, and so forth, through distances.

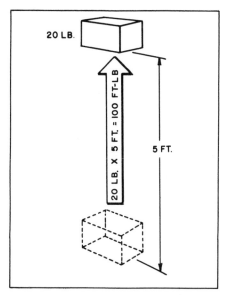

Fig. 2-1 A Twenty-pound Weight Lifted Five Feet in the Air.

## ENERGY

Energy is the ability to do work. The energy stored in our bodies, for instance, gives each of us a potential to do work. A person can work for a long period of time on his stored energy before he needs "refueling" with food. The human body is a good example of one major energy form: potential energy.

## Potential Energy

Potential energy is scientifically stated as the energy a body has due to its position, its condition, or its chemical state: position, water at the top of a waterfall; condition, a tightly wound watch spring; chemical state, fuels such as gasoline, coal, etc., or foodstuffs to be burned in the body.

5

Stored or potential energy is measured in the same way as work, in foot-pounds. How much potential energy is there when a 20-pound weight is lifted 5 feet?

Potential Energy = Force × Distance

Potential Energy = (weight) × (height)

Potential Energy = 20 lbs. × 5 ft.

Potential Energy = 100 ft.-lbs.

With the weight at the five-foot height, there is 100 foot-pounds of potential energy.

### Kinetic Energy

Kinetic energy is the energy of motion, the energy of a thrown ball, the energy of water falling over a dam, the energy of a speeding automobile. Kinetic energy is, in effect, "released potential energy".

Consider a thrown ball, the work of throwing it, and what becomes of it. If a 3/4-pound ball is thrown by applying a force of 8 pounds through 6 feet, how much work is done?

Work = Force × Distance

Work = 8 lbs. × 6 ft.

Work = 48 ft.-lbs.

What becomes of this energy? It exists as energy of motion of the ball, kinetic energy. The ball in flight has 48 ft.-lbs. of energy which it will deliver to whatever it hits.

Turning back to the example of potential energy, when the 20-pound weight which rests 5 feet above the floor is allowed to fall, its potential energy of 100 ft.-lbs. becomes 100 ft.-lbs. of kinetic energy, energy of motion.

Energy can change form but it cannot be destroyed. This is the Law of the Conservation of Energy. Energy can take the form of light, sound, heat, motion, and electricity. Consider the potential chemical energy of gasoline in an engine. Upon ignition, its energy is converted mainly into heat energy. The heat energy is used to push the pistons down and now can be seen as the kinetic energy of the rotating crankshaft.

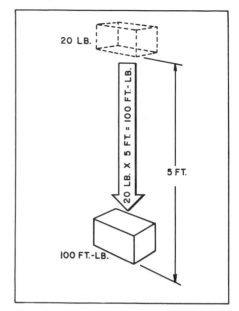

Fig. 2-2 A Twenty-pound Weight Dropped to the Floor from a Height of Five Feet Delivers 100 ft.-lbs. of Kinetic Energy.

Again refer back to the 20-pound weight poised at a 5-foot height. When the weight falls to the floor its energy is not lost, but, rather, it is transformed into other types of energy. The floor would become slightly warmer at the point of impact due to the creation of heat energy. There would be an audible sound at the moment of impact, an indication of the presence of sound energy. Of course, the floor would give slightly, thus absorbing some energy.

The Efficiency of Machines that transform energy is not 100 percent. That is to say, some used energy does not perform a useful purpose. It literally may be wasted in moving the machine parts to overcome friction inherent in all machines. The efficiency of a machine is the ratio of the work done by the machine to the work put into it.

Stated as a formula:

$$Efficiency = \frac{Output}{Input} \times 100$$

or

$$Efficiency = \frac{Input - Losses}{Input} \times 100$$

or

$$Efficiency = \frac{Output}{Output + Losses} \times 100$$

The figure "100" in these formulas is a way of converting the fraction to a percentage.

## POWER

In everyday language people use the word "power" to mean a variety of things: "political power", "financial power", etc. However, in the language of scientists and engineers, "power" refers to how fast work is done, or how fast energy is transferred. "Power is the rate of doing work" and "Power is the rate of energy conversion" are two useful definitions of the term.

How fast a machine can work is an important consideration for engineers, and for consumers too. For example, when gasoline is purchased the person buys potential energy. The "size" of the engine will determine how fast this energy can be converted into power. A 10-horsepower engine can work only half as fast as a 20-horsepower engine.

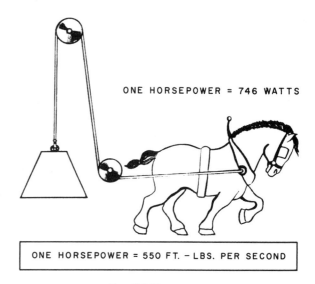

ONE HORSEPOWER = 746 WATTS

ONE HORSEPOWER = 550 FT. – LBS. PER SECOND

Fig. 2-3 Horsepower.

### Measurement of Power

Power is measured in foot-pounds per second or in foot-pounds per minute. Referring again to the 20-pound weight that was lifted 5 feet, how much power was required to lift the weight if it were done in 5 seconds?

Work = Force × Distance

Work = 20 lbs. × 5 ft. = 100 ft.-lbs.

$$\text{Power} = \frac{\text{Work}}{\text{Time}}$$

$$\text{Power} = \frac{100 \text{ ft.-lbs.}}{5 \text{ seconds}}$$

Power = 20 ft.-lbs./second

As another example: if an elevator lifts 3500 pounds a distance of 40 feet and it takes 25 seconds to do it, what is the rate of doing work?

Work = Force × Distance

Work = 3500 lbs. × 40 ft. = 140,000 ft.-lbs.

$$\text{Power} = \frac{\text{Work}}{\text{Time}}$$

$$\text{Power} = \frac{140{,}000 \text{ ft.-lbs.}}{25 \text{ sec.}} = 5600 \text{ ft.-lbs./sec.}$$

Power can also be expressed in foot-pounds per minute. If a pump needs 10 minutes to lift 5000 pounds of water 60 feet, it is doing 300,000 ft.-lbs. of work in 10 minutes, which is a rate of 30,000 foot-pounds per minute.

### Horsepower

The power of most machinery is measured in horsepower. The unit originated many years ago when James Watt, attempting to sell his new steam engines, had to rate his engines in comparison with the horses they were to replace. He found that an average horse, working at a steady rate, could do 550 foot-pounds of work per second. This rate is the definition of one horsepower.

The formula for horsepower is:

$$\text{Horsepower} = \frac{\text{Work}}{\text{Time (in seconds)} \times 550}$$

If Time in the formula above is expressed in minutes, it is multiplied by 550 × 60 (seconds) or 33,000. The formula, then, may be expressed as:

$$\text{Horsepower} = \frac{\text{Work}}{\text{Time (in minutes)} \times 33{,}000}$$

What horsepower motor would the elevator previously referred to have?

$$\text{Horsepower} = \frac{\text{Work}}{\text{Time (in seconds)} \times 550}$$

$$\text{Horsepower} = \frac{140{,}000 \text{ ft.-lbs.}}{25 \text{ sec.} \times 550}$$

Horsepower = 10 +

SUMMARY

We have now discussed those terms which are basic to an understanding of the applications of mechanical power which will follow in later units. The measurements which these terms involve have been shown as formulas. To review, the following formulas are a means of expressing each of the terms we have covered:

a.  WORK = FORCE × DISTANCE

b.  $\text{EFFICIENCY} = \dfrac{\text{OUTPUT}}{\text{INPUT}} \times 100$

c.  $\text{POWER} = \dfrac{\text{WORK}}{\text{TIME}} = \dfrac{\text{FORCE} \times \text{DISTANCE}}{\text{TIME}}$

d.  $\text{HORSEPOWER} = \dfrac{\text{WORK}}{\text{TIME (in sec.)} \times 550}$

$= \dfrac{\text{WORK}}{\text{TIME (in min.)} \times 33000}$

---

## STUDY QUESTIONS

1.  Give a definition of work.

2.  What is the unit of measurement for work?

3.  A 100-pound boy climbs a 16-foot stairway.  How much work has he done?

4.  Define energy.

5.  Explain the difference between kinetic and potential energy.

6.  Explain the conservation of energy.  What are some common forms of energy?

7.  Explain why a machine cannot be 100 percent efficient.

8.  Define power.

9.  What is the unit of measurement for power?

10. How much power is needed to lift a 100-pound bag of cement onto a 3-foot truck bed in 2 seconds?

11. What is the formula for horsepower?

12. How much horsepower does an engine on a grain elevator deliver if it can load 705 pounds of corn into a 25-foot storage bin in 55 seconds?

## CLASS DISCUSSION TOPICS

● Have a student lift a given weight a definite height and calculate the work.

● Discuss the difference between "scientific work" and other kinds of work.

● Discuss and list many potential and kinetic energy sources.

● Discuss the origin of the term horsepower.

## CLASS DEMONSTRATION TOPICS

◆ Demonstrate how the horsepower developed by an average student might be calculated.

◆ Demonstrate the transformation of energy by striking and burning a match.

◆ Demonstrate potential and kinetic energy sources.

◆ Demonstrate the conservation of energy.

◆ Demonstrate losses due to friction and how they affect the efficiency of a machine.

## Unit 3
### CONSTRUCTION OF THE RECIPROCATING ENGINE

The internal combustion engine is classified as a <u>heat</u> engine; in other words, its power is produced by <u>burning</u> a fuel. The power stored in the fuel is released when it is burned. The word "internal" means that the fuel is burned inside the engine itself. Our most common fuel is gasoline. Of course, if gasoline is to burn inside the engine there must be oxygen present to support the combustion. Therefore, the fuel actually needs to be a mixture of gasoline and air. When ignited, a fuel mixture of gasoline and air burns ferociously; it almost explodes. The engine is designed to harness this power.

The engine block is fitted with a cylindrical shaft. This is the <u>cylinder</u>. A plate fits over the head of the block, sealing off the top of the cylinder, the <u>cylinder head</u>. The cylinder contains a <u>piston</u>, a cylindrical fitting which fits the cylinder exactly. The piston is free to slide up and down within the cylinder. The fuel mixture is brought into the cylinder; then the piston moves up and compresses the fuel into a small space called the combustion chamber. When the fuel is ignited and burns, tremendous pressure builds up. This pressure forces the piston back down the cylinder; thus the untamed energy of combustion is harnessed to become useful mechanical energy. The basic motion within the engine is that of the piston sliding up and down the cylinder, a reciprocating motion.

There are still many problems, however. How can the up-and-down motion of the piston be converted into useful rotary motion? How can exhaust gases be removed? How can new fuel mixture be brought into the combustion chamber? Let us look at the engine's basic parts.

### BASIC ENGINE PARTS

The internal combustion engine parts discussed on the next few pages are those of the four-stroke cycle gasoline engine, our most common type. The most essential of these parts are briefly listed below.

- Cylinder: hollow; stationary; piston moves up and down within cylinder.
- Piston: fits snugly into cylinder but still can be moved up and down.
- Crankshaft: converts reciprocating motion into more useful rotary motion.
- Connecting rod: connects piston and crankshaft.
- Valves: "doors" for admitting fuel mixture and releasing exhaust.
- Crankcase: the body of the engine, it contains most of engine's moving parts.

### CYLINDER

The cylinder is a finely machined, high quality cast iron part in which the piston slides up and down. Even though an engine may be basically made from aluminum, the cylinder itself will usually be made of cast iron. Normally the aluminum body of the engine is cast around the cylinder and the two are inseparable.

However, on some engines the cylinder section can be removed. This is particularly true of very large engines. In engine specifications the diameter of the cylinder is an important measurement. It is referred to as the "bore" of the engine.

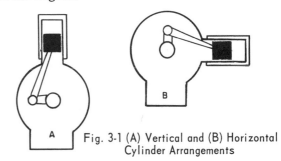

Fig. 3-1 (A) Vertical and (B) Horizontal Cylinder Arrangements

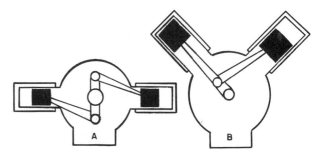

Fig. 3-2 (A) Opposed and (B) V-type Cylinder Arrangements

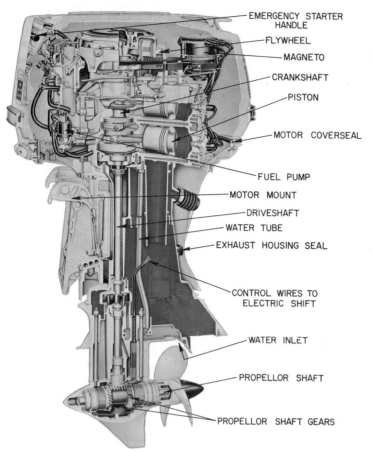

EMERGENCY STARTER HANDLE

FLYWHEEL

MAGNETO

CRANKSHAFT

PISTON

MOTOR COVERSEAL

FUEL PUMP

MOTOR MOUNT

DRIVESHAFT

WATER TUBE

EXHAUST HOUSING SEAL

CONTROL WIRES TO ELECTRIC SHIFT

WATER INLET

PROPELLOR SHAFT

PROPELLOR SHAFT GEARS

Fig. 3-3 Cross-section of a Typical
Johnson Outboard Motor.

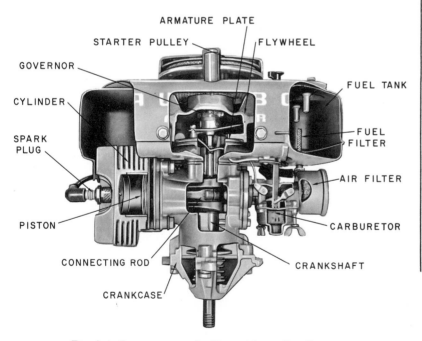

ARMATURE PLATE

STARTER PULLEY

FLYWHEEL

GOVERNOR

FUEL TANK

CYLINDER

SPARK PLUG

FUEL FILTER

AIR FILTER

PISTON

CARBURETOR

CONNECTING ROD

CRANKSHAFT

CRANKCASE

Fig. 3-4 Cross-section of a Typical Lawn-Boy Engine.

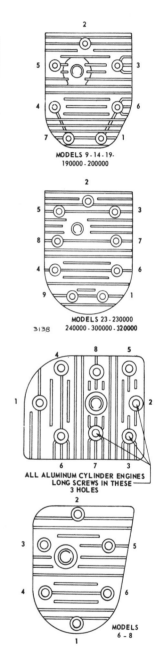

MODELS 9-14-19-
190000-200000

MODELS 23-230000
240000-300000-320000

ALL ALUMINUM CYLINDER ENGINES
LONG SCREWS IN THESE
3 HOLES

MODELS
6-8

Fig. 3-5 A Typical Cylinder Head.
Note the Sequence for Tightening
the Head Bolts.

## CYLINDER HEAD

The cylinder head forms the top of the combustion chamber and it is bolted tightly to the cylinder. It is important to tighten all cylinder head bolts with an even pressure and in their correct order so that uneven stresses will not set up in the cylinder walls. A gasket between the two metal surfaces makes an airtight seal. The cylinder head also contains the spark plug.

Fig. 3-7 Pistons Cast of Aluminum.

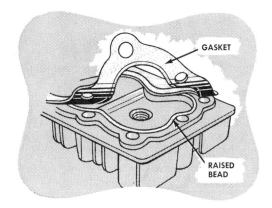

Fig. 3-6 The Cylinder Head Gasket Provides an
Airtight Seal.

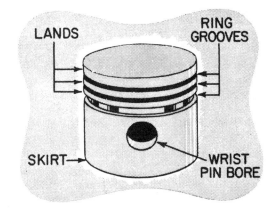

Fig. 3-8 The Nomenclature of the Piston

## PISTON

The piston slides up and down in the cylinder. It is the only part of the combustion chamber that can move when the pressure of the rapidly burning fuel mixture is applied. The piston may be made of cast iron, steel, or aluminum; aluminum is commonly used for small engines because of its light weight and its ability to conduct heat away rapidly.

There must be clearance between the cylinder wall and the piston to prevent excessive wear. The piston is .003 to .004 of an inch smaller than the cylinder. To check this clearance, a special feeler gage is necessary.

The piston top, or "crown" may be flat, convex, concave, or any of many other shapes. Manufacturers select the shape that will cause turbulence of the fuel mixture in the combustion chamber and that will promote smooth burning to the fuel mixture. The piston has machined grooves near the top to accommodate the piston rings.

The distance the piston moves up and down is called the "stroke" of the engine. The uppermost point of the piston's travel is called its top dead center position (TDC). The lowest point of the piston's travel is called its bottom dead center (BDC). Therefore, "stroke" is the distance between TDC and BDC.

## PISTON RINGS

Piston rings provide a tight seal between the piston and the cylinder wall. Without the piston rings much of the force of combustion would escape between the piston and cylinder into the crankcase. Primarily the piston rings act as a "power seal", ensuring that a maximum amount of the combustion power is used in forcing the piston down the cylinder. Of course, by having the piston rings between the piston and cylinder wall there is a small area of metal sliding against the cylinder wall. Therefore, the piston rings reduce friction and the accompanying heat and wear that are caused by friction. Another function of the piston ring is to control the lubrication of the cylinder wall.

11

The job of the piston rings might appear rather simple but the piston rings may have to work under several harsh conditions such as, (1) distorted cylinder walls, due to improper tightening of head bolts, (2) cylinder out of round, (3) worn or scored cylinder walls, (4) worn piston, and (5) conditions of expansion due to intense heat. The important job of providing a power seal can become difficult if the engine is worn or has been abused.

Piston rings are made of cast iron or steel and are finely machined. Sometimes their surfaces are plated with other metals to improve their action. There are many designs of piston rings and some rings, especially oil rings, consist of more than one piece.

Two serious problems, (1) blow-by and (2) oil pumping, can be caused by bad piston rings, bad piston, warped cylinder, distortion, and/or scoring. In blow-by, the pressures of combustion are great enough to break the oil seal provided by the piston rings. When this happens, the gases of combustion force their way into the crankcase. The result is a loss in engine power and contamination of the crankcase.

Piston rings that are not fitted properly may start pumping oil. This pumping action will lead to fouling in the combustion chamber, excessive oil consumption, and poor combustion characteristics. The rings have a side clearance which can cause a pumping action as the piston moves up and down.

A piston will usually have three or four piston rings. The top piston ring is a compression ring which exerts a pressure of 8-12 pounds on the cylinder wall. The ring has a clearance in its groove; it can move slightly up and down and expand slightly in and out. The second ring from the top is also a compression ring. These two rings form the power seal.

The third ring down, and fourth if one is present, is an oil control ring. The job of this piston ring is to control the lubrication of the cylinder wall. These rings spread the correct amount of oil on the cylinder wall, scraping the excess from the wall and returning it to the crankcase. These rings are slotted and grooves are cut into the piston behind the ring. This enables much of the excess oil to be scraped

"through" the piston and it then drips back into the crankcase. It should be noted that compression rings have a secondary function of oil control.

Fig. 3-9 Typical Compression Ring.

Fig. 3-10 Typical Oil Control Ring.

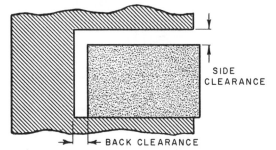

Fig. 3-11 Cross-section Showing a Piston Ring in its Groove. Notice Back Clearance and Side Clearance.

Two clearances or tolerances that are important in piston rings are, (1) end gap and (2) side clearance. The end gap is the space between the ends of the piston ring, measured when the ring is in the cylinder. The gap must be large enough to allow for expansion due to heat but not so large that power loss due to blow-by will result. Often .004″ is allowed for each inch of piston diameter (top ring), .003″ is allowed for rings under the top ring. Since the second and third rings are exposed to less heat their allowance can be smaller.

Side clearance or ring groove clearance is also provided for heat expansion. Often .0025″ is allowed for the top ring and .003″ is allowed on the second and third rings.

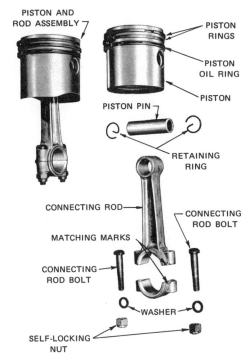

Fig. 3-12 A Typical Piston, Piston Pin, Connecting Rod, and Associated Parts.

## PISTON PIN OR WRIST PIN

The piston pin is a precision ground steel pin that connects the piston and the connecting rod. This pin may be solid or hollow; the hollow piston pin has the advantage of being lighter in weight. Because piston pins are subjected to heavy shocks when combustion takes place, high tensile strength steel is used. To keep noise at a minimum, the piston pin fits to a very close tolerance in the connecting rod. The piston pin does not rotate. It has a rocking motion similar to the action of a man's wrist as he holds a bar tightly and swings it back and forth: hence the name "wrist pin." Heavy shocks, close tolerances, and the rocking motion make the lubrication of this part difficult. In most engines, lubricating oil is squirted or splashed on it.

## CONNECTING ROD

The connecting rod connects the piston (with the aid of the piston pin) and the crankshaft. Many small engines have cast aluminum connecting rods; larger engines may have steel connecting rods. Generally the cross section of the connecting rod is an "I" beam shape. The

lower end of the connecting rod is fitted with a cap. Both the lower end and the cap are accurately machined to form a perfect circle. This cap is bolted to the rod, encircling the connecting rod bearing surface on the crankshaft. Many connecting rods are fitted with replaceable bearing surfaces, especially on heavy-duty or more expensive engines.

## CRANKSHAFT

The crankshaft is the vital part that converts the reciprocating motion of the piston into rotary motion. One end of the crankshaft has a provision for power takeoff and the other is machined to accept the flywheel.

Crankshafts are carefully forged and machined steel. Because they must accept a great amount of force; their bearing surfaces are large, and because they revolve at high speeds, they must be well balanced.

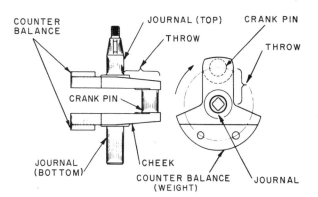

Fig. 3-13 Single Throw Crankshaft: One Crankpin for One Cylinder.

Engines designed with <u>vertical</u> crankshafts are excellent for applications such as rotary power lawnmowers where the blade is bolted directly to the end of the crankshaft. Most wheeled applications such as motor bikes and go-karts use <u>horizontal</u> crankshaft engines which enable the power to be delivered to an axle through belts or chains. Multiposition engines such as chain saws are another variation. The crankshafts themselves are much the same but other changes in engine design are necessary to meet the requirements of crankshaft position. An engine may also have clockwise or counterclockwise crankshaft rotation.

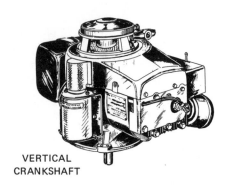

VERTICAL
CRANKSHAFT

HORIZONTAL
CRANKSHAFT

Fig. 3-14 Two Types of Small Engine Design.

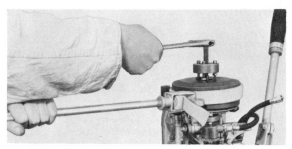

Fig. 3-15A Pulling the Fly Wheel of an Outboard Engine.

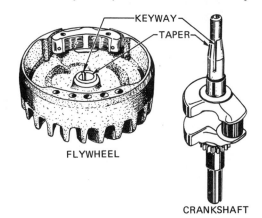

KEYWAY

TAPER

FLYWHEEL

CRANKSHAFT

Fig. 3-15B A Key "Locks" the Fly Wheel and Crank Shaft Together.

## CRANKCASE

The crankcase is the "body" of the engine. It houses the crankshaft and has bearing surfaces on which the crankshaft revolves. Many other parts are located within the crankcase: connecting rod, cam gear and camshaft, lubrication mechanism. The cylinder and bottom of the piston are exposed to the crankcase. On four-cycle engines a reservoir of oil is found within the crankcase. This lubricating oil is splashed, pumped, or squirted onto all the moving parts located in the crankcase.

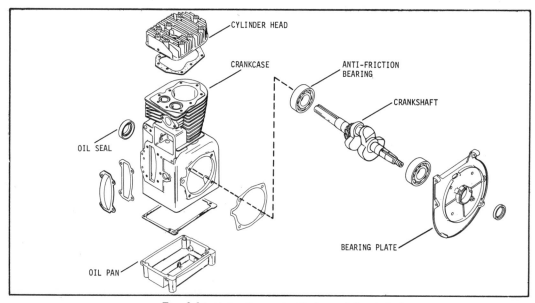

CYLINDER HEAD

CRANKCASE

ANTI-FRICTION
BEARING

CRANKSHAFT

OIL SEAL

BEARING PLATE

OIL PAN

Fig. 3-16 Major Parts of a Horizontal Crankshaft.

## FLYWHEEL

The flywheel is mounted on the tapered end of the crankshaft. A key keeps the two parts solidly together and they revolve as one part. The flywheel is found on all small engines. It is relatively heavy and helps to smooth out the operation of the engine. That is, after the force of combustion has pushed the piston down, the momentum of the flywheel helps to move the piston back up the cylinder. This tends to minimize or eliminate sudden jolts of power during combustion. The more cylinders the engine has, the less important this "smoothing out" action becomes.

The flywheel may also be a part of the engine's cooling system by having air vanes to scoop air as the flywheel revolves. This air is channeled across the hot engine to carry away heat.

Most flywheels on small gasoline engines are part of the ignition systems, in that they have permanent magnets mounted in them. These permanent magnets are an essential part of the magneto ignition system.

## VALVES

The most common valves used today are called poppet valves. With these valves, exhaust gases can be removed from the combustion chamber and new fuel mixture can be brought in. To accomplish this, the valve actually pops open and snaps closed. In the normal four-cycle combustion chamber there are two valves, one to let the exhaust out (Exhaust) and one to allow the fuel mixture to come in (Intake).

Quite possibly, the two valves will look almost identical, but they are different. The exhaust valve must be designed to take an extreme amount of punishment and still function perfectly. Not only is it subjected to the normal heat of combustion (about 4500° F), but when it opens, the hot exhaust gases rush by it and when the valve returns to its seat, a small area touches, making it difficult for the valve's heat to be conducted away. This rugged valve opens and closes 1800 times a minute if the engine is operating at 3600 r.p.m.

Exhaust valves are made from special heat-resisting alloys and are hollow, being filled with metallic sodium. This metallic sodium melts at about the boiling point of water and helps to rapidly conduct the heat from the valve head down the valve stem. Some exhaust valves, however, are made from solid steel.

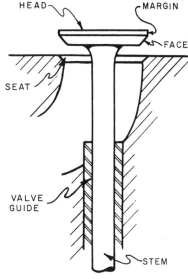

Fig. 3-17 A Typical Valve.

Intake valves operate in the same manner as exhaust valves except they are not subjected to the extreme heat conditions. Each time they open new fuel mixture rushes by, helping to cool the intake valve.

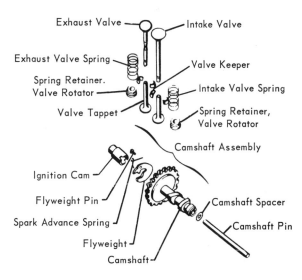

Fig. 3-18 Complete Valve Train and Camshaft Assembly.

Operation of the valve requires the help of associated parts or "valve train." The valve

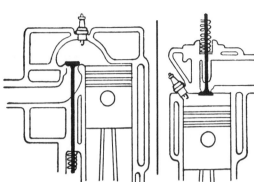

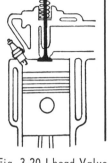

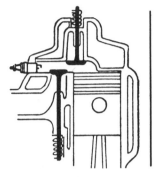

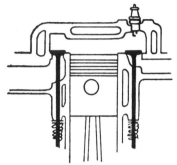

Fig. 3-19 L-head Valve Arrangement

Fig. 3-20 I-head Valve Arrangement.

Fig. 3-21 F-head Valve Arrangement.

Fig. 3-22 T-head Valve Arrangement.

train consists of the valve (intake or exhaust), valve spring, tappet or valve lifter, and cam. The valve spring closes the valve, holding it tightly against its seat. The tappet rides on the cam and there is a small clearance between the tappet and the valve stem; some tappet clearances are adjustable especially on larger and more expensive engines. The cam or lobe pushes up on the tappet; the tappet pushes up on the valve stem; and the valve opens when the high spot on the cam is reached. Of course the opening and closing of the valves must be carefully timed in order to get the exhaust out at the correct time and the new fuel mixture in at the correct time.

## VALVE ARRANGEMENT

Engines may be designed and built with one of several valve arrangements.

● The L-head: both valves open up on one side of the cylinder. This is the most common arrangement in small gasoline engines

● The I-head: both valves open down over the cylinder.

● The F-head: one valve opens up and one valve opens down; both are on the same side of the cylinder.

● The T-head: one valve is on one side of the cylinder and the other valve is on the opposite side; both valves open up.

## CAMSHAFT

The camshaft and its associated parts control the opening and closing of the valves.

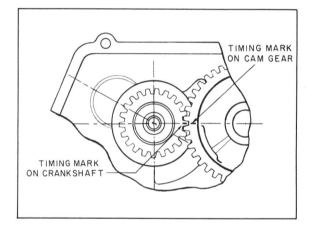

Fig. 3-23 Aligning Timing Marks on the Crankshaft Gear and Camshaft Gear. Notice the Larger Camshaft Gear Revolves at One-half Crankshaft Speed.

The cams on this shaft are eggshaped. As they revolve, their noses cause the valves to open and close. A tappet rides on each cam and when the nose of the cam comes under the tappet the valve is pushed open, admitting new fuel mixture or allowing exhaust to escape, depending on which valve is opened.

The camshaft is driven by the crankshaft, and on four-cycle engines the camshaft operates at one-half the crankshaft speed. (If the engine is operating at 3400 r.p.m., the camshaft will be revolving at 1700 r.p.m.) The crankshaft and camshaft must be in perfect synchronization, so most engines have timing marks on the gears to insure the correct reassembly of the gears.

## FOUR-STROKE CYCLE OPERATION

All of these parts and many others must be assembled to operate as a smooth functioning, powerful team; the gasoline engine. The most common method of engine operation is the four-stroke cycle. Most small gasoline engines operate on this principle as do their larger brothers, automobile engines.

Four-stroke cycle means that it takes four strokes of the piston to complete the operating cycle of the engine. The piston goes down the cylinder, up, down, and back up again to complete the cycle. This takes two revolutions of the crankshaft; each stroke is one-half revolution.

When the piston travels down the cylinder, this is Intake; fuel mixture enters the combustion chamber. Reaching the bottom of its stroke, the piston comes up on Compression and the fuel mixture is pressed into a small space at the top of the combustion chamber. Power comes when the fuel mixture is ignited, pushing the piston back down. The piston moves up once more pushing the exhaust gases out of the combustion chamber. This is Exhaust. These four strokes complete the engine's cycle and require two revolutions of the crankshaft. As soon as one cycle is complete, another begins. If an engine were operating at a speed of 3600 r.p.m., there would be 1800 cycles each minute.

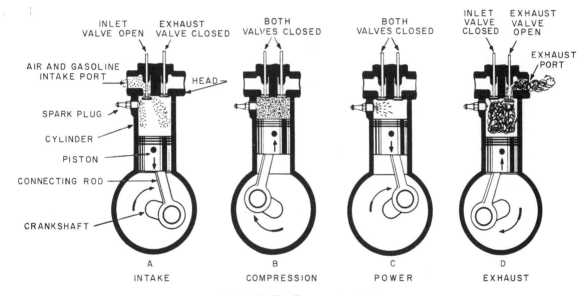

Fig. 3-24 The Four-stroke Cycle.

It would be a good idea to take a closer look at the four strokes of the four-stroke cycle.

### INTAKE STROKE

If the fuel mixture is to enter the combustion chamber, the intake valve must be open, the exhaust valve must be closed. With the intake valve open and the piston traveling down the cylinder, the fuel mixture rushes in easily.

All around us and pushing down on everything is an atmospheric pressure of 14.7

lbs. per sq. in. at sea level. When the piston is at the top of its stroke there is normal atmospheric pressure in the combustion chamber, but when the piston travels down the cylinder there is more space for the same amount of air and the air pressure is reduced; a partial vacuum is created. The intake valve opens, the normal atmospheric pressure rushes in to equalize this lower air pressure in the combustion chamber. The fuel mixture is actually pushed into the combustion chamber, even though we think of it as being sucked in by the partial vacuum.

## COMPRESSION STROKE

When the piston reaches the bottom of its stroke and the cylinder is filled with fuel mixture, the intake valve closes and the exhaust valve remains closed. The piston now travels up the cylinder compressing the fuel mixture into a smaller and smaller space. When the fuel mixture is compressed into this small space it can be ignited more easily and it will expand very rapidly.

The term "Compression Ratio" applies to this stroke. If the piston compresses the fuel mixture into one-sixth of the original space the compression ratio is 6:1. An engine whose piston compresses the fuel mixture into one-eighth the original space has a compression ratio of 8:1. The higher the compression, the more powerful the force of combustion will be.

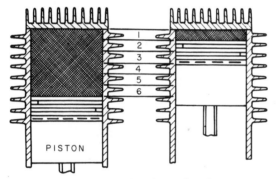

Fig. 3-25 An Engine with a Six to One Compression Ratio.

## POWER STROKE

When the piston reaches the top of its stroke, and the fuel mixture is compressed, a spark jumps across the spark plug igniting the fuel mixture. The fuel mixture burns very rapidly, the next thing to an explosion, and the burning, expanding gases exert a great pressure in the combustion chamber. The combustion pressure is felt in all directions, but only the piston is free to react. This it does by being pushed rapidly down the cylinder. This is the power stroke: rapidly burning fuel creates a pressure that pushes the piston down, turning the crankshaft and producing usable rotary motion.

Of course both intake and exhaust valves must be closed for this stroke. The force of combustion must not leak out the valves. Also, this force should not "blow-by" the piston rings.

Correctly fitting piston rings prevent this. All gaskets, namely the cylinder head gasket and spark plug gasket, must be airtight. The power must be transmitted to the top of the piston and not lost elsewhere.

## EXHAUST STROKE

When the piston reaches the bottom of its power stroke the momentum of the flywheel and crankshaft bring the piston back up the cylinder. This is the exhaust stroke. Now the exhaust valve opens, the intake valve remains closed, and the piston pushes the burned exhaust gases out of the cylinder and combustion chamber.

The four-stroke cycle engine is an efficient and entirely successful producer of power.

## TWO-STROKE CYCLE ENGINE

Another common operating principle for gasoline engines is the two-stroke cycle. This engine is also entirely successful and in common use today, especially for outboard motors, chain saws, and many lawnmowers. The two-stroke cycle engine is constructed somewhat differently from the four-stroke cycle engine.

Two-stroke cycle means that it takes two strokes of the piston to complete the operating cycle of the engine. The piston goes down the cylinder and back up again and the cycle is completed. This takes only one revolution of the crankshaft.

With the piston at the top of its stroke, the fuel mixture tightly compressed in the combustion chamber, the engine is ready for its first stroke, the Power stroke. A spark ignites the fuel mixture and the great pressure pushes the piston rapidly down the cylinder. As the piston nears the bottom of its stroke, the exhaust ports begin to uncover and the exhaust gases, which are still hot and under pressure, start to rush through the ports and out of the engine. Just after the exhaust ports begin to uncover, the piston uncovers the intake ports. Fuel mixture rushes into the cylinder, being deflected to the top of the cylinder first and

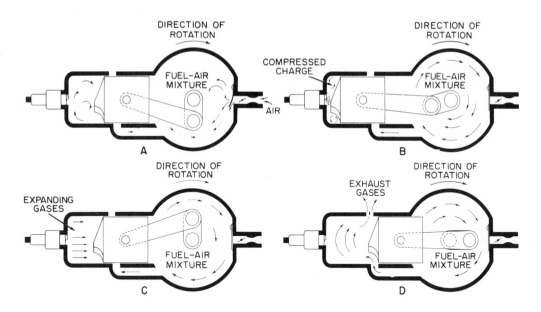

Fig. 3-26 Two-cycle Engine Operation.

finally scavenging out the last bit of exhaust. By this time the piston has reached the bottom of its stroke and is on its way back up the cylinder; the ports are sealed off, trapping the fuel mixture. Therefore, this stroke is Compression, the piston pushing the fuel mixture into a smaller and smaller space. The two strokes, then are Power and Compression, with Intake and Exhaust taking place between the two.

One question remains to be answered: why does the fuel mixture rush through the intake ports into the combustion chamber? First of all, not because there is a partial vacuum in the combustion chamber as in the four-stroke cycle engine. With the exhaust ports open, the combustion chamber soon would be at atmospheric pressure. The answer lies in the crankcase and reed valves. As the piston moves up the cylinder, a low pressure, or partial vacuum, is created in the crankcase; there is a larger space for the same amount of air. The greater atmospheric pressure outside "sees" this low pressure and rushes through the carburetor, pushing open the springy reed valves, filling the crankcase with fuel mixture. When the pressure in the crankcase and the atmospheric pressure are just about equal, the leaf valves spring shut.

As the piston moves back down the cylinder on its power stroke, the fuel mixture, trapped in the crankcase is put under a slight pressure; the same amount of mixture being pushed into a smaller space. The leaf valve can open in only the opposite direction. When the piston nears the bottom of its stroke, the exhaust ports uncover allowing the exhaust to escape. The intake ports open slightly after the exhaust ports and the pressure in the crankcase pushes through the intake ports and into the cylinder, filling it with new fuel mixture.

This cycle would then be repeated. If the engine operates at 4000 r.p.m. the cycle will be completed 4000 times each minute. There is a power stroke for each revolution of the crankshaft.

CRANKCASE

The crankcase of a two-stroke cycle engine is designed to be just as small in volume as possible. The smaller the volume, the greater the pressure created as the piston comes back down the cylinder. The greater the crankcase pressure, the more efficient the transfer of fuel from the crankcase through the transfer ports into the cylinder.

## INTAKE AND EXHAUST PORTS

Intake and exhaust ports are holes drilled in the cylinder wall to allow exhaust gases to escape and new fuel mixture to enter. They are located near the bottom of the cylinder and are covered and uncovered by the piston. By using ports, many parts seen in the four-cycle engine are eliminated: valves, tappets, valve springs, cam gear, camshaft. The remaining major moving parts are the piston, connecting rod, and crankshaft.

## PISTON

The piston still serves the same function in the cylinder, but for two-cycle engines the top is designed differently. On the intake side there is a sharp deflection that sends the incoming fuel mixture to the top of the cylinder. On the exhaust side there is a gentle slope so that exhaust gases have a clear path to escape. The loop scavenged two-cycle engine does, however, have a flat top piston; it will be discussed in a later section.

## REED OR LEAF VALVES

These valves are located between the carburetor and crankcase. The valve itself is a thin sheet of springy alloy steel. It springs open to allow fuel mixture to enter the crankcase, and springs closed to seal the crankcase.

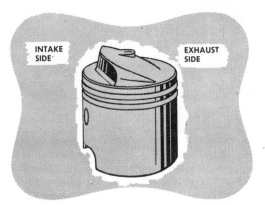

Fig. 3-27 A Piston for a Two-cycle Engine Showing the Exhaust Side and the Intake Side.

There may be only one reed valve or there may be several reed valves working together. By far the greatest number of small gasoline engines operating on the two-cycle principle use reed valves even though it is possible to use a poppet valve in the crankcase.

## OTHER TWO-CYCLE OPERATION

There are other methods of two-cycle operation; not all two-cycle engines use reed or leaf valves. These other engines would still have the two strokes, Compression and Power, with intake and exhaust taking place between the two, but different valves are used to achieve the result.

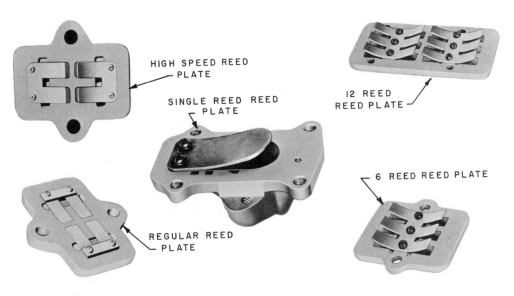

Fig. 3-28 Reed Plates.

## ROTARY VALVE

Some two-cycle engines will be found that use a rotary valve for admitting fuel mixture. The rotary valve is a flat disc, with a section removed, that is fastened to the crankshaft. It normally seals the crankcase, but as the piston nears the top of its stroke and there is a slight vacuum in the crankcase, the valve is rotated to its open position, allowing fuel mixture to travel from the carburetor through the open valve and into the crankcase.

## POPPET VALVES

Also, there are some two-cycle engines that use poppet valves to admit new fuel mixture into the crankcase. These poppet valves may be spring loaded and operated by differences in crankcase pressure. They open when the partial vacuum in the crankcase overcomes a slight spring tension. This happens when the piston is on its upward stroke. With the poppet valve open, fuel mixture rushes into the crank-

case. The poppet valve may also be operated by cam action. In this case a crankshaft cam opens the valve for the piston's upward stroke.

## LOOP SCAVENGING

The loop scavenged two-cycle engine is basically the same in operation as other two-cycle engines. However, its piston is different in that it has large bores on either side of the piston skirt and the top is flat. The piston is forced down the cylinder on the power stroke. Exhaust ports are uncovered near the bottom of the stroke and exhaust starts out. Also, the large bores in the cylinder line up with intake passages and ports in the cylinder permitting new fuel mixture to rush in. The fuel mixture comes in from both sides, looping up to the top of the cylinder and then back down to scavenge out the remaining exhaust. Loop scavenging provides a more complete removal of exhaust gases and produces somewhat more horsepower per unit weight.

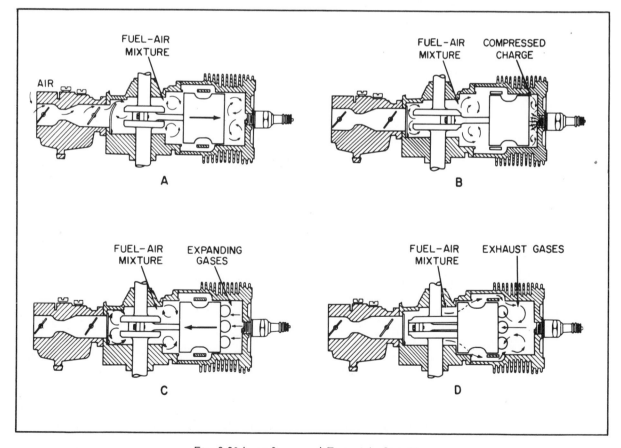

Fig. 3-29 Loop Scavenged Two-cycle Operation.

## GENERAL STUDY QUESTIONS

1. Explain the term "Internal Combustion".
2. List the most essential parts of the engine.
3. Of what metal is the cylinder made?
4. What purpose does a gasket serve?
5. What is a combustion chamber?
6. What purpose do piston rings serve?
7. What is the function of the crankshaft?
8. What does the flywheel accomplish?
9. Explain how the valves are operated.
10. At what speed does the camshaft revolve relative to the crankshaft?

## FOUR-STROKE CYCLE STUDY QUESTIONS

1. Explain what causes the fuel mixture to rush into the cylinder during the intake stroke.
2. What is accomplished on the compression stroke?
3. Explain the power stroke.
4. How many revolutions are required for the complete cycle?
5. Explain compression ratio.

## TWO-STROKE CYCLE STUDY QUESTIONS

1. What parts are replaced by the intake and exhaust ports?
2. How is the two-stroke cycle piston different from the four-stroke cycle piston?
3. Explain the action of the reed or leaf valves.
4. Explain how intake and exhaust take place on a two-cycle engine.
5. What part does the crankcase play in regard to the fuel mixture?
6. How many revolutions are required for the complete cycle?

## CLASS DISCUSSION TOPICS

● What other "systems" does an engine need in addition to the basic moving parts?
● Discuss the basic differences in two- and four-cycle engines.
● Discuss advantages and disadvantages of two- and four-cycle engines.
● Discuss how parts can be damaged by careless handling.

## CLASS DEMONSTRATION TOPICS

▶ Inspect the basic parts of the two-cycle and four-cycle engine.

▶ Remove the cylinder head of a four-cycle engine, rotate the crankshaft, and observe the action of the valves.

▶ Remove the valve spring cover of a four-cycle engine, rotate the crankshaft, and observe the action of the valve lifters and valve springs.

▶ Remove the carburetor of a two-cycle engine, turn the engine over rapidly, and observe the action of the leaf valves. Note: this action is not pronounced and must be carefully observed.

▶ Using a disassembled engine, connect piston, connecting rod, and crankshaft to illustrate how reciprocating motion is converted to rotary motion.

▶ Using a camshaft and crankshaft, point out timing marks.

▶ Using a camshaft and crankshaft, count the gear teeth to illustrate the speed relationship of the two gears.

# LABORATORY EXPERIENCES

Laboratory Experience 1

ENGINE DISASSEMBLY (Four-Stroke Cycle)

## OBJECTIVES

▶ To learn to identify the basic engine parts.

▶ To learn how basic parts work together in an engine.

## REFERENCE

● Review Pages 9 - 21

## INTRODUCTION

The gasoline engine consists of many parts that function together as a smooth power team. It is important to be able to identify these parts and know how they fit and work together. Every student should have an appreciation of the precision workmanship that goes into an engine. The intelligent student will want to preserve the integrity of the engine's precision as he disassembles and reassembles the parts.

NOTE: Laboratory Experiences 1 and 2 are well suited for a class demonstration, especially if the students are "beginners". If, however, students have a background in engine disassembly, it can be accomplished at the end of Unit 2 in the text. Another alternative is to "teacher demonstrate" the work with Unit 2 and then have the students do Laboratory Experiences 1 and 2 while they study Unit 8 on Simple Repairs.

## STUDENT ASSIGNMENT

You are to disassemble a typical four-stroke cycle engine, study the basic parts and then reassemble the engine. Remember, speed in engine disassembly is <u>not</u> the important thing. What is important is a careful, workmanlike approach to the job. It is essential that you record your work in the work record box on the following page as you complete each step of the disassembly procedure.

### Disassembly Procedure

Your instructor may supplement or revise specific steps of the procedure which follows since there are many makes of engines. The following disassembly procedure is your general guide.

1. Drain oil from crankcase.

2. Disconnect spark plug cable and remove spark plug.

3. Drain gas tank, disconnect fuel line, remove gas tank.

4. Remove air cleaner. (Use care if it contains oil.)

5. Drain carburetor, remove throttle and governor connections, remove carburetor from engine.

6. Remove metal air shrouding.

7. Remove crankshaft nut; also grass screens, starter pulleys, etc.

8. Remove flywheel.

9. Remove the magneto plate assembly. (The main bearing is on the flywheel side of this plate.)

10. Remove cylinder head.

11. Remove the crankcase from the engine base. (This may not be necessary if the engine has an inspection plate.)

12. Unbolt the connecting rod cap and push the piston and rod up and out of the cylinder.

13. Remove the crankshaft by pulling it out. (The main bearing plate may have to be loosened to do this.)

## WORK RECORD BOX

| Part | Disassembly (nuts, bolts, etc.) | Operation performed | Tool used |
|------|--------------------------------|---------------------|-----------|
|      |                                |                     |           |
|      |                                |                     |           |
|      |                                |                     |           |
|      |                                |                     |           |
|      |                                |                     |           |
|      |                                |                     |           |
|      |                                |                     |           |
|      |                                |                     |           |
|      |                                |                     |           |
|      |                                |                     |           |
|      |                                |                     |           |
|      |                                |                     |           |
|      |                                |                     |           |
|      |                                |                     |           |
|      |                                |                     |           |
|      |                                |                     |           |
|      |                                |                     |           |
|      |                                |                     |           |

## Reassembly Procedure

Reverse the disassembly procedure.  Listed below are some points to remember in reassembly.

1.  Tighten all machine screws and bolts securely.

2.  Be certain the piston is reinstalled exactly as it came out.

3.  Line up timing marks on crankshaft with timing mark on camshaft.

4.  Line up match mark on connecting rod cap with match mark on connecting rod.

5.  Be certain flywheel keyway slips into the key on the crankshaft.

6.  Check all gaskets; replacement may be necessary, especially if the engine is to be operated.

7.  Refill crankcase with oil if engine is to be operated.

8.  Refill gas tank if engine is to be operated.


## GENERAL STUDY QUESTIONS

1.  Why should most gaskets be replaced when the engine is reassembled?

2.  Explain the value of match marks on the connection rod and cap.

3.  Why is uniform tightening of cylinder head bolts important?

4.  Explain why timing marks are used on the crankshaft and camshaft.

5.  How many piston rings are on the piston?  What type are they?

Laboratory Experience 2

VALVE TRAIN AND CAMSHAFT (Four-Stroke Cycle)

OBJECTIVES

◆ To learn to identify the parts of the valve train and camshaft.

◆ To learn how the valve train and camshaft work together.

REFERENCE

● Review Pages 9 - 21

INTRODUCTION

The engine's valves, exhaust and intake, provide a route for exhaust gases to escape and a route for new fuel mixture to enter. The valves are of the poppet type, being raised off their seats when they are opened. They are subjected to severe punishment in the combustion chamber but still must function perfectly, opening at exactly the right instant and closing to make an airtight seal. The parts that work with the valves are referred to as the valve train and camshaft.

NOTE: This laboratory experience may be done at the completion of disassembly on Laboratory Experience 1 or it may be done starting with a fully assembled engine. If students start with a fully assembled engine they should follow the disassembly procedure for Laboratory Experience 1; then continue on with the disassembly of the valve train and camshaft.

STUDENT ASSIGNMENT

You are to remove the valves, the valve springs, and the valve spring retaining parts. Then remove the camshaft and valve lifters. Study these parts and then reassemble them correctly. It is essential that you record your work in the work record box on the following page as you complete each step of the disassembly procedure.

Disassembly Procedure

Your instructor may supplement or revise specific steps of the procedure which follows since there are many makes of engines. The following disassembly procedure is your general guide:

1. Remove the valve plate exposing the valve springs, valve lifters, and valve stems.

2. Compress the valve spring with a valve spring compressor.

3. Remove the valve spring retainers by slipping or flipping them out.

4. Pull the valve out of the engine.

5. Remove the valve spring, still compressed.

6. Remove the camshaft. If the camshaft is held in the crankcase with a camshaft support pin it must be driven out with a blunt punch. In most cases, drive the punch from the takeoff side toward the flywheel side.

   NOTE: Other engines may be constructed with a one-piece camshaft that comes out when the crankshaft is removed.

7. Pull out the camshaft.

8. Remove the valve lifters; they will probably fall out when the camshaft is removed.

## WORK RECORD BOX

| Part | Disassembly (nuts, bolts, etc.) | Operation performed | Tool used |
|---|---|---|---|
|  |  |  |  |
|  |  |  |  |
|  |  |  |  |
|  |  |  |  |
|  |  |  |  |
|  |  |  |  |
|  |  |  |  |
|  |  |  |  |
|  |  |  |  |
|  |  |  |  |
|  |  |  |  |
|  |  |  |  |
|  |  |  |  |
|  |  |  |  |
|  |  |  |  |
|  |  |  |  |
|  |  |  |  |

### Reassembly Procedure

Reverse the disassembly procedure. Here are some points to remember.

1. Reinstall the intake and exhaust valves in their correct places.

2. A special tool is needed to aid in the installation of valve spring retainers on some engines.

3. Reinstall the camshaft support pin correctly: from flywheel side to the power takeoff side, in most cases.

## GENERAL STUDY QUESTIONS

Study the valves and associated parts and answer the following questions.

1. Why are exhaust valves and intake valves made differently?

2. When you examine the two valves, how can you tell them apart?

3. What is the function of the valve spring?

4. Why does the camshaft rotate at one-half the crankshaft speed?

5. How many degrees are the intake and exhaust cams apart? Why?

Laboratory Experience 3

EXHAUST AND INTAKE PORTS (Two-Stroke Cycle)

OBJECTIVES

▶ To learn the construction and location of the exhaust ports.

▶ To observe how the ports are covered and uncovered by the piston.

REFERENCE

● Review Pages 9 - 21

INTRODUCTION

The exhaust ports and intake ports replace the valves of the four-stroke cycle engine. The ports are the "doors" for exhaust gases and new fuel mixture. The ports are actually holes bored in the cylinder wall. The action of the piston moving up and down the cylinder seals off and opens the ports.

STUDENT ASSIGNMENT

You are to remove the exhaust baffle plate, muffler, or exhaust manifold (different terms, all pertaining to the same area) and examine the ports. Then turn the engine over, observing how the ports are covered and uncovered by the piston. It is essential that you record your work in the work record box on the following page as you complete each step of the disassembly procedure.

Disassembly Procedure

Your instructor may supplement or revise specific steps of the procedure which follows since there are many makes of engines. The following disassembly procedure is your general guide:

1. Drain the gas tank.

2. Drain the carburetor.

3. Remove the spark plug cable from the spark plug.

4. Remove the spark plug from the cylinder.

5. Remove any metal shrouding that is around the exhaust area.

6. Remove the exhaust baffle plate, muffler, or exhaust manifold; exposing the exhaust ports.

## WORK RECORD BOX

| Part | Disassembly (nuts, bolts, etc.) | Operation performed | Tool used |
|------|--------------------------------|---------------------|-----------|
|      |                                |                     |           |
|      |                                |                     |           |
|      |                                |                     |           |
|      |                                |                     |           |
|      |                                |                     |           |
|      |                                |                     |           |
|      |                                |                     |           |
|      |                                |                     |           |
|      |                                |                     |           |
|      |                                |                     |           |
|      |                                |                     |           |
|      |                                |                     |           |
|      |                                |                     |           |

Reassembly Procedure

Reverse the disassembly procedure.

GENERAL STUDY QUESTIONS

Study the exhaust ports and their operation and answer the following questions.

1. If your engine has been "in operation", did you observe any carbon deposits around the exhaust ports? Describe these deposits.

2. Explain why the engine "turned over" easily when the spark plug was removed.

3. How many ports make up the exhaust port team?

4. Is the exhaust side of the piston a gentle slope or a sharp deflection? Why?

Laboratory Experience 4

REED VALVES (Two-Stroke Cycle)

## OBJECTIVES

▶ To learn to identify the reed valves.

▶ To gain an understanding of how the reed valves operate.

## REFERENCE

● Review Pages 9 - 21

## INTRODUCTION

The reed valves open to allow fuel mixture to rush into the crankcase and close to trap the fuel mixture in the crankcase. The part is made of a thin springy metal sheet that will react to small differences in air pressure. It has no comparable part on the four-stroke cycle engine.

## STUDENT ASSIGNMENT

You are to remove the reed valve plate, study the reed valves, and then reassemble the parts removed. It is essential that you record your work in the work record box on the following page as you complete each step of the disassembly procedure.

Observation of the opening and closing of the reed valves can usually be done by removing the carburetor, leaving the reed valve plate installed on the crankcase. Then, turn the engine over rapidly. The action of the reed valves is not pronounced, therefore, they must be watched very closely. If the spark plug is removed from the cylinder the engine can be turned over more easily.

### Disassembly Procedure

Your instructor may supplement or revise specific steps of the procedure which follows since there are many makes of engines. The following disassembly procedure is your general guide:

1. Drain gas tank.

2. Remove any metal shrouding from the carburetor area.

3. Drain carburetor.

4. Remove throttle and governor connections.

5. Remove carburetor.

6. Remove spark plug from cylinder.

7. Rotate flywheel rapidly and observe reed valve action.

8. Remove reed valve plate from crankcase.

9. Remove individual reed valves for inspection only if the engine is not to be operated again. The reed valves may be damaged through unnecessary handling.

## WORK RECORD BOX

| Part | Disassembly (nuts, bolts, etc.) | Operation performed | Tool used |
|---|---|---|---|
| | | | |
| | | | |
| | | | |
| | | | |
| | | | |
| | | | |
| | | | |
| | | | |
| | | | |
| | | | |
| | | | |
| | | | |
| | | | |
| | | | |
| | | | |
| | | | |

## Reassembly Procedure

Reverse the disassembly procedure.

## GENERAL STUDY QUESTIONS

Study the reed valves and answer the following questions.

1. The reed valves are between what two main parts?

2. What condition in the crankcase causes the reed valves to be pulled open?

3. What condition in the crankcase causes the reed valves to spring closed?

4. How many individual reed valves work together as a team on "your" engine?

5. Trace the path of the fuel mixture in a two-cycle engine, beginning with the gasoline tank, continuing to the combustion chamber.

Unit 4

## FUEL SYSTEMS, CARBURETION AND GOVERNORS

The fuel system must maintain a constant supply of gasoline for the engine, and the carburetor must correctly mix the gasoline and air together to form a combustible mixture which will burn rapidly when ignited in the combustion chamber.

A typical fuel system contains a gasoline tank (the reservoir for gasoline); a carburetor (a mixing device for gasoline); the fuel line (tubes made of rubber or copper through which the gasoline passes from the gas tank to the carburetor); and an air cleaner (a device for filtering air brought into the carburetor). In addition, the system may have a shutoff valve (a valve at the gas tank that can cut off the gasoline supply when the engine is not in use); a fuel pump (a pump that supplies the carburetor with a constant supply of gasoline); a sediment bowl (a small glass bowl attached to the fuel line where dirt and other foreign matter can settle out); and a strainer (a fine screen in the gas tank to prevent leaves and dirt from entering the fuel line).

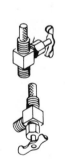

Fig. 4-1 Fuel Shutoff Valve

Fig. 4-2 Sediment Bowl with Built-in Fuel Shutoff Valve.

It should be realized that not all fuel systems will contain all eight of the basic parts: shutoff valves, sediment bowls, fuel pumps, and air cleaners are not common to all engines.

A constant supply of gasoline must be available at the carburetor. To provide this supply, four methods are in common use today: (1) Suction, (2) Gravity, (3) Fuel Pump, (4) Pressurized Tank.

SUCTION SYSTEM

The suction system is probably the simplest. With this method the gas tank is located below the carburetor and the gasoline is simply sucked up into the carburetor. However, the gas tank cannot be very far away from the carburetor or the carburetor action will not be strong enough to pull the gasoline from the tank.

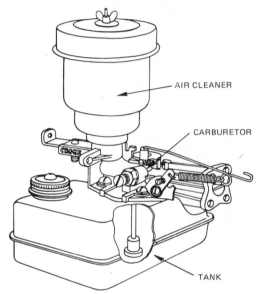

AIR CLEANER

CARBURETOR

TANK

Fig. 4-3 Suction Feed Fuel System.

GRAVITY SYSTEM

With the gravity system the gas tank is located above the carburetor and the gasoline runs down hill to the carburetor. To prevent gasoline from continuously pouring through the carburetor, the carburetor has incorporated within it a float and float chamber. This float chamber provides a constant level of gasoline without flooding the carburetor. When gasoline is used, the float goes down, opening a valve to admit more gasoline to the float chamber; the float rises and shuts off the gasoline when it reaches its correct level. In actual practice the float and float valve do not rapidly open and close, but "assume a position" allowing the correct amount of fuel to constantly enter the float chamber. If the engine were speeded up, a new position would be assumed by the float and float valve, supplying an increased flow of gasoline.

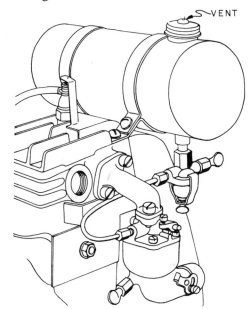

Fig. 4-4 Gravity Feed Fuel System.

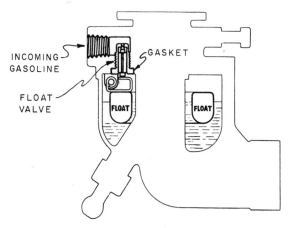

Fig. 4-5 Cutaway of a Carburetor, Showing Float and Float Valve.

## FUEL PUMP

On many engines it is necessary to place the gas tank some distance from the carburetor, and, therefore, the fuel must be brought to the carburetor by some other means than gravity or suction. One method is by using a fuel pump. The automobile engine uses a fuel pump; among smaller engines, the outboard motor with a remote fuel tank is a good example of an engine that commonly uses a fuel pump.

The fuel pump used on many two-stroke cycle outboard motors is quite simple, consisting of a chamber, inlet and discharge valve, a rubber diaphragm, and a spring. This fuel pump is operated by the crankcase pressure. As the piston goes up, low pressure in the crankcase pulls the diaphragm toward the crankcase, sucking gasoline through the inlet valve into the fuel chamber. As the piston comes down, pressure in the crankcase pushes the diaphragm away from the crankcase. When this happens, the intake valve closes and the discharge valve opens, allowing the trapped fuel to be forced to the carburetor.

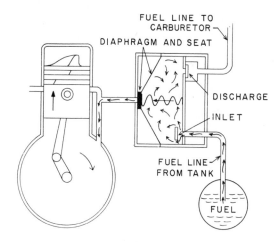

(A) Low Pressure in the Crankcase Allows the Fuel Chamber to be Filled.

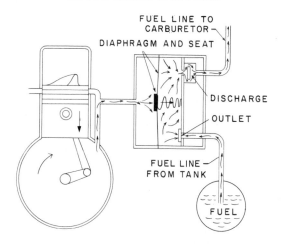

(B) High Pressure in the Crankcase Forces the Trapped Fuel on to the Carburetor.

Fig. 4-6 Effects of Low and High Pressure in Crankcase.

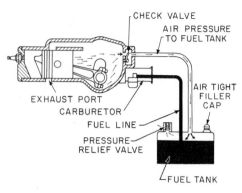

Fig. 4-7 Pressurized Fuel Systems can be Found on Many Outboard Engines.

## PRESSURIZED FUEL SYSTEM

Another method for forcing fuel to travel long distances to the carburetor is the pressurized fuel system. This method is often used with outboard motors. Engines using this system will have two hoses or lines between the gas tank and the engine: one brings gasoline to the carburetor; the other brings air, under pressure, from the crankcase to the gas tank. If this method is used, the gas tank must be airtight so that sufficient air pressure can build up to force the gasoline to flow to the carburetor.

## THE CARBURETOR

The carburetor must prepare a mixture of gasoline and air in the correct proportions for burning in the combustion chamber. The carburetor must function correctly under all

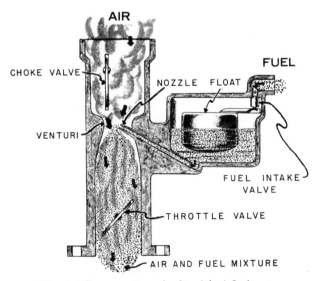

Fig. 4-8 Cross-section of a Simplified Carburetor.

engine speeds, under varying engine loads, in all weather conditions, and at all engine temperatures. To meet all these requirements, carburetors have many built-in parts and systems and may be quite complex.

Before studying the carburetor's operation in detail, an examination of the basic carburetor parts and their functions will be helpful.

Throttle or Butterfly: The throttle controls the speed of the engine by controlling the amount of fuel mixture that enters the combustion chamber. The more fuel mixture admitted, the faster the engine speed.

Choke: The choke controls the air flow into the carburetor. It is used only for starting the engine. In starting the engine, the operator closes the choke, cutting off most of the engine's air supply. This produces what is called a "rich mixture" (one containing a higher percentage of gasoline) which ignites and burns readily in a cold engine. As soon as the engine starts, the choke is opened.

Needle Valve: The needle valve controls the amount of gasoline that is available to the carburetor. It controls the richness or leanness of the fuel mixture.

Idle Valve: The idle valve also controls the amount of gasoline that is available to the carburetor but it functions only at low speeds or idling. Some carburetors have what is called a Slow-Speed Needle Valve which performs essentially the same job as the idle valve.

Float and Float Bowl: The float and float bowl will be found on all carburetors except the suction-fed carburetor and diaphragm carburetors (to be discussed later). The float and float bowl maintain a constant gasoline level in the carburetor.

Venturi: The venturi is a section of the carburetor that is constricted, or has a smaller cross-sectional area for the air to flow through. In the venturi, the gasoline and air are brought together and here their mixing begins.

<u>Jets</u>: Carburetor jets are small openings through which gasoline passes within the carburetor.

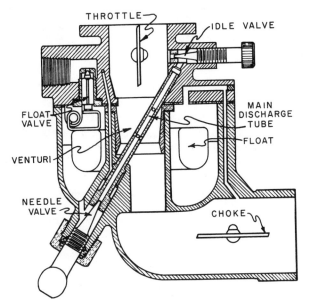

Fig. 4-9 A Gravity Fed Briggs-Stratton Carburetor.

In the beginning, air flows through the carburetor because there is a partial vacuum or suction in the combustion chamber as the piston travels down the cylinder. Normally we think of the air being sucked into the engine by the piston action. Atmospheric pressure outside the engine actually pushes the air through the carburetor to equalize the lower pressure that is in the combustion chamber.

Air flows rapidly through the carburetor as the piston moves down, and in the carburetor the air must pass through a constriction called the "venturi". For the same amount of incoming air to pass through this smaller opening, it must travel faster, and this it does. Here a principle of physics comes into use: the greater the velocity of air passing through an opening, the lower the static air pressure exerted on the walls of the opening. The venturi creates a low-pressure area within the carburetor.

Also the principle of the air foil is used to gain lower pressure conditions in the venturi section. A fuel supply tube or jet is placed in the venturi section. The action of the incoming air causes a high pressure on the front of the jet but a very low pressure on the back of the jet. Gasoline is available in this jet and streams

out of the jet because a low-pressure area has been created by the action of the venturi and the air foil, and because the gasoline is under atmospheric pressure which is greater. Greater pressure pushes the gasoline out of the discharge jet into the air stream.

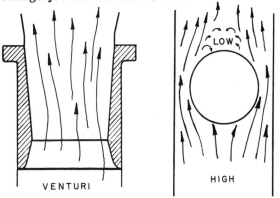

Fig. 4-10 (A) The Venturi Creates a Low Pressure in the Carburetor. (B) The Principle of the Air Foil Also Helps Create a Low Pressure.

As gasoline streams into the air flow, it is mixed thoroughly with the air. The best mixture of gasoline and air is 14 or 15 parts of air to 1 part of gasoline, by weight. This air to gasoline ratio can be changed for different operating conditions; heavy load and fast acceleration require more gasoline (richer mixture). The needle valve is used to change this ratio; it controls amount of gasoline that is available to be drawn from the discharge jet.

The throttle or butterfly is mounted on a shaft beyond the venturi section. The operator of the engine controls its setting to control the engine speed. When the throttle is wide open the butterfly does not restrict the flow of air; air flows easily through the carburetor; the engine is operating at its top speed. As the operator closes the throttle, the flow of air is restricted. A smaller amount of air can rush through the carburetor, therefore, the air pressures at the venturi section are not as low and less gasoline streams from the discharge holes. With less fuel mixture in the combustion chamber, the piston is pushed down with less force during combustion; power and speed are reduced.

The ratio of air to fuel remains approximately the same through the different throttle settings. However, when the throttle is closed and the engine begins to idle, very little air is drawn through the carburetor and the difference between atmospheric pressure and venturi air is slight. Little gasoline is drawn from the discharge jet. In fact, the mixture of gasoline is so "lean" that a special idling device must be built into the carburetor to provide a "richer" mixture for idling.

In some carburetors, the main discharge jet is continued on up past the venturi section to the area of the throttle. It discharges fuel into a small well and jet that are behind the throttle butterfly when it is closed. The air pressure behind the butterfly is very low. Therefore, gasoline streams from the idle jet readily and mixes with the small amount of air that is coming through the carburetor and a "rich" fuel mixture is provided for idling. A threaded needle valve called the "idle valve" controls the amount of gasoline that can be drawn from the idle jet.

When a cold engine is to be started, an extremely rich mixture of gasoline and air must be provided if the engine is to start easily. The choke will provide this rich mixture. It is a butterfly placed in the air horn before the venturi section. For starting, the choke is closed, shutting off most of the carburetor's air supply. When the engine is turned over slowly, usually by hand, little air is drawn through the carburetor but the air pressure within the carburetor is very low and gasoline streams from the main discharge jet, mixing with the air that does get by the choke. As soon as the engine starts, the choke is opened. The fuel mixture provided when the engine is choked is actually so rich that all the gasoline may not vaporize with the air and "raw" liquid gasoline may be drawn into the combustion chamber. Continued operation with the choke closed may cause crankcase dilution, i.e., the raw gasoline seeps into the crankcase diluting the lubricating oil.

This is now the complete carburetor: (1) Float and float bowl, maintaining a constant reservoir of gasoline in the carburetor; (2) Venturi section, producing a low-pressure area; (3) Needle valve, controlling the richness or leanness of fuel mixture; (4) Main discharge jet, squirting gasoline into airstream; (5) Idle valve, providing a rich mixture for idling conditions; (6) Choke, producing an extremely rich mixture for easy starting.

## DIAPHRAGM CARBURETOR

This type of carburetor has come into wide use, especially on chain saws. It is also found on other applications where the engine may be tipped at extreme angles. The diaphragm supplies the carburetor with a constant supply of gasoline.

The diaphragm carburetor may be gravity fed. Crankcase pressure moves the diaphragm and associated linkages to allow gasoline to enter the fuel chamber. The gasoline is available by gravity and the in and out motion of the diaphragm meters out fuel in the correct amount.

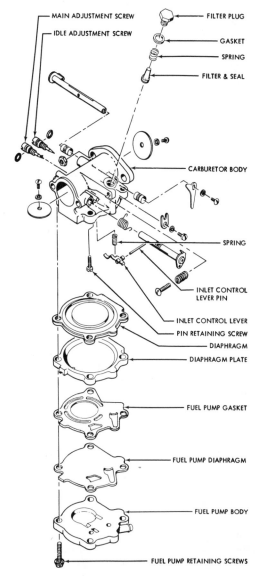

Fig. 4-11 An Exploded View of a Diaphragm Carburetor with Built-in Fuel Pump.

Diaphragm carburetors are also built which operate with a built-in fuel pump. The fuel pump operates on crankcase pressure and its action is virtually the same as that of the outboard fuel pump previously discussed. Diaphragm carburetors have found wide acceptance in the small engine field.

I    HIGH SPEED MIXTURE ADJUSTING SCREW

2    IDLE SPEED MIXTURE ADJUSTING SCREW

3    IDLE SPEED REGULATING SCREW

Fig. 4-12 Diaphragm Carburetor Installed on a McCulloch Chain Saw.

## HIGH-SPEED — LOW-SPEED CONTROLS

Many carburetors, especially those on outboard motors, have what is termed "high-speed" and "low-speed" controls. The high-speed control corresponds to the main needle valve while the slow-speed control corresponds to the idle valve. The carburetors used on Johnson motors, as well as those used on other manufacturers' motors, have these controls. When the throttle butterfly is closed or just about closed, the motor is idling or operating at slow speeds. Now the fuel comes from the slow-speed jet because it is located in the area of greatest suction. As the butterfly opens, the low-pressure or suction effect is felt more and more on the high-speed jet located in the venturi until the low-speed jet becomes ineffective. Now the great bulk of the fuel is coming from the high-speed jet.

It would not be correct to say that the two controls are independent of each other. Rather, there is a shifting of control throughout the speed range. One does not abruptly "cut-out" and the other "cut-in". Even at full throttle, a small amount of gasoline can be entering through the slow-speed jet.

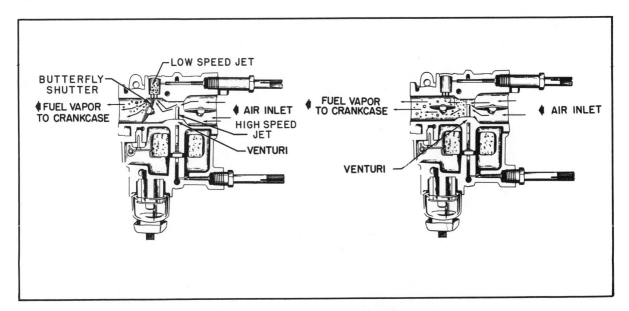

(A) Showing Butterfly Shutter Set for Slow Speed Operation (Closed). Note Maximum Fuel Vaporization at Slow Speed.

(B) Butterfly Shutter Full Open for High Speed Performance. Note Maximum Fuel Vaporization at High Speed Jet with Minimum of Vaporization at the Slow Speed Jets.

Fig. 4-13 Sectional View of a Mixing Chamber

## AIR BLEEDING CARBURETORS

There is a tendency for carburetors to supply too rich a fuel mixture at high speeds; the ratio of gasoline to air increases as the velocity of the air passing through the carburetor increases. One method that is commonly used to correct this condition is Air Bleeding. The Zenith carburetor shown below uses the principle of air bleeding.

A small amount of air is introduced into the main discharge well vent to restrict the flow of gasoline from the main discharge jet. As engine speeds are increased, greater amounts of air are brought into the main discharge well vent, placing a greater restriction on the gasoline flow, thereby overcoming the carburetor's natural tendency to provide too rich a mixture at high speeds. This action maintains the proper ratio of fuel and air between a throttle setting of one-fourth to wide open.

The air that enters the discharge well vent does mix with the gasoline and is drawn through the main discharge jet into the main air stream.

## ACCELERATING PUMP

Another problem inherent in all carburetors is a response lag when the throttle is quickly opened. Air can react very quickly to an increased demand but gasoline lags behind. The result is too lean a mixture and acceleration is sluggish. Carburetors equipped with an accelerating pump provide instant response for rapid acceleration.

The main parts of the accelerating pump are the spring, vacuum piston, and fuel cylinder. At idling and low operating speeds, the vacuum piston is drawn to the top of the fuel cylinder by the engine vacuum, which is strong enough to overcome the force of the spring, holding the piston at the top of its stroke. Now the fuel cylinder is filled with gasoline.

If the throttle is suddenly opened, the engine vacuum drops enough for the piston spring to overcome the force of the vacuum, pushing the pump piston down the fuel cylinder. This reserve amount of gasoline in the fuel cylinder is forced into the main discharge jet and on into the carburetor venturi.

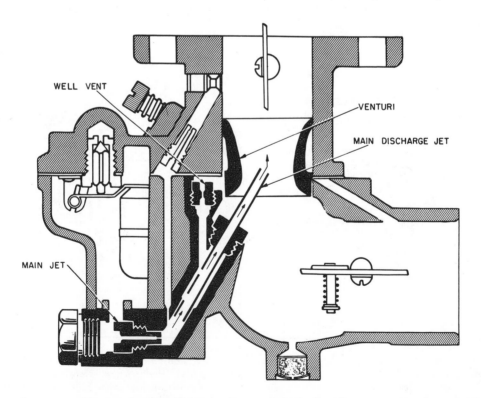

Fig. 4-14 Air Brought into the Well Vent Bleeds into the Main Discharge Jet, Maintaining Correct Air-Fuel Ratio throughout Throttle Range.

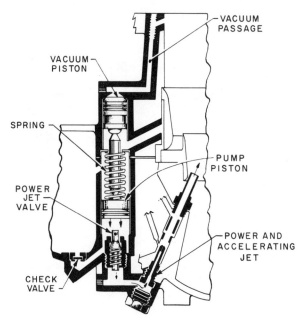

Fig. 4-15 Cross-section of an Accelerating Pump.

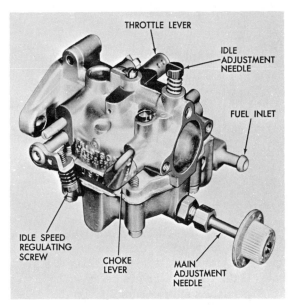

Fig. 4-16 Tillotson MD Float Feed Type Carburetor.

## CARBURETOR ADJUSTMENTS

The engine manufacturer will set the carburetor adjustments at the factory. These settings will cover normal operation. However, after a long period of usage, or under special operating conditions, it may be necessary to adjust the carburetor. In adjusting the carburetor, the main needle valve and the idle valve are both reset to give the desired richness or leanness of fuel mixture. Too lean a mixture can be detected by the engine missing and backfiring, while too rich a mixture can be detected by heavy exhaust and sluggish operation.

Here is a typical procedure for adjusting a carburetor for maximum power and efficiency.

1. Close the main needle valve and idle valve "finger tight". Excessive force can damage the needle valve. Turn clockwise to close.

2. Open the main needle valve one turn. Open the idle valve 3/4 turn. Turn counterclockwise to open.

3. Start the engine, open the choke, and allow the engine to reach operating temperature.

4. Run engine at operating speed (2/3 to 3/4 of full throttle). Turn the main needle valve in (clockwise) until the engine slows down, indicating too lean a mixture. Note the position of the valve. Turn the needle valve out (counterclockwise) until the engine speeds up and then slows down, indicating too rich a mixture. Note the position of the valve. Reposition the valve halfway between the rich and lean settings.

5. Close the throttle so the engine runs slightly faster than normal idle speed. Turn the idle valve in (clockwise) until the engine slows down, then turn the idle valve out until the engine speeds up and idles smoothly. Adjust the idle-speed regulating screw to the desired idle speed.

NOTE: Idle speed is not the slowest speed at which the engine will operate; rather, it is a slow speed that maintains good air flow for cooling and a good takeoff spot for even acceleration. A tachometer and the manufacturer's specifications regarding proper idle speed are necessary for the best adjustment.

6. Test the acceleration of the engine by opening the throttle rapidly. If acceleration is sluggish, a slightly richer fuel mixture is usually needed.

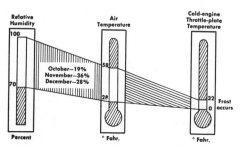

Fig. 4-17 Humidity and Temperature Conditions Which May Lead to Carburetor Icing.

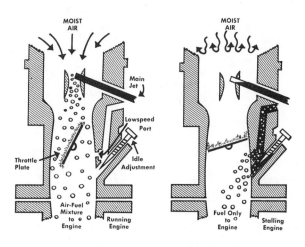

Fig. 4-18  Under Carburetor Icing Conditions, Ice Forms on the Throttle Plate, Cutting off Air to the Engine When Throttle Closes.

## CARBURETOR ICING

Carburetor icing is an annoying phenomenon that may occur when the engine is cold and certain atmospheric conditions are present. If the temperature is between 28°F. and 58°F., and the relative humidity is above 70%, carburetor icing may take place.

Fuel mixture of gasoline and air rushes through the carburetor and the rapid action of evaporating gasoline chills the throttle plate to about 0°F. Moisture in the air will condense and freeze on the throttle plate when the relative humidity is high. This formation of ice restricts the air flow through the carburetor and at low or idle settings the ice may completely block off the air flow, stalling the engine.

When this condition is present, the engine can be restarted but will stall again at low or idle speeds. As soon as the carburetor is warm enough to prevent ice formation, normal operation can take place.

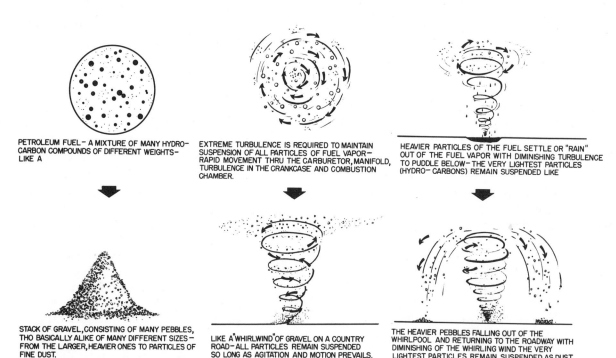

PETROLEUM FUEL – A MIXTURE OF MANY HYDRO-CARBON COMPOUNDS OF DIFFERENT WEIGHTS – LIKE A

EXTREME TURBULENCE IS REQUIRED TO MAINTAIN SUSPENSION OF ALL PARTICLES OF FUEL VAPOR – RAPID MOVEMENT THRU THE CARBURETOR, MANIFOLD, TURBULENCE IN THE CRANKCASE AND COMBUSTION CHAMBER.

HEAVIER PARTICLES OF THE FUEL SETTLE OR "RAIN" OUT OF THE FUEL VAPOR WITH DIMINISHING TURBULENCE TO PUDDLE BELOW – THE VERY LIGHTEST PARTICLES (HYDRO-CARBONS) REMAIN SUSPENDED LIKE

STACK OF GRAVEL, CONSISTING OF MANY PEBBLES, THO BASICALLY ALIKE OF MANY DIFFERENT SIZES – FROM THE LARGER, HEAVIER ONES TO PARTICLES OF FINE DUST.

LIKE A "WHIRLWIND" OF GRAVEL ON A COUNTRY ROAD – ALL PARTICLES REMAIN SUSPENDED SO LONG AS AGITATION AND MOTION PREVAILS.

THE HEAVIER PEBBLES FALLING OUT OF THE WHIRLPOOL AND RETURNING TO THE ROADWAY WITH DIMINISHING OF THE WHIRLING WIND THE VERY LIGHTEST PARTICLES REMAIN SUSPENDED AS DUST

Fig. 4-19 Turbulence is Necessary to Keep the Gasoline Molecules Suspended in the Air.

## VAPOR LOCK

Vapor lock can occur anywhere along the fuel line, fuel pump, or in the carburetor when temperatures are high enough to vaporize the gasoline. Gasoline vapor in these places will cut off the liquid fuel supply, stalling the engine. If vapor lock occurs, the operator must wait until the carburetor, gas line, and fuel pump cool off and the gasoline vapor returns to liquid before the engine will restart. Vapor lock usually occurs on unseasonably hot days and is more troublesome at high altitudes.

## GASOLINE

Most internal combustion engines burn gasoline as their fuel. Gasoline comes from petroleum, also called crude oil. Crude oil is actually a mixture of different hydrocarbons; gasoline, kerosene, heating oil, lubricating oil, and asphalt. These chemicals are all hydrocarbons, but they have characteristics that are quite different. Hydrogen is a light, colorless, odorless gas; carbon is black and solid. Different combinations of carbon and hydrogen give the different characteristics of hydrocarbon products.

The various hydrocarbons are separated by distillation of the crude oil. Crude oil is first heated to a temperature of 700° to 800° F. and then released into a fractionating or bubble tower, Fig. 4-20. The tower contains 20 to 30 trays through which hydrocarbon vapors can rise from below. When the heated crude oil is released into the tower, most of it flashes into vapor. As the vapors rise, they cool, and each type of hydrocarbon condenses at a different tray level. Heavier hydrocarbons condense first at relatively high temperatures. The lighter hydrocarbons, such as gasoline, condense high in the tower at relatively low temperatures. Gasoline is then further processed to improve its qualities.

Good gasoline must have several characteristics. It must vaporize at low temperatures for good starting. It must be low in gum and sulfur content. It must not deteriorate during storage. It must not knock in the engine. It must have proper vaporizing characteristics for the climate and altitude. It must burn cleanly to reduce air polution.

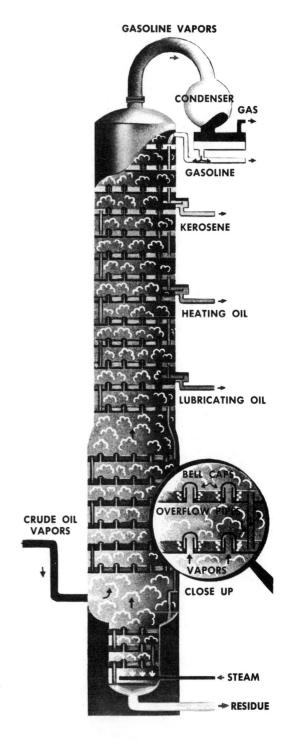

Fig. 4-20 Distillation of Petroleum in the "Bubble Tower."

The vaporizing ability of gasoline is the key to its success as a fuel. In order to burn inside the engine, the hydrocarbon molecules of the gasoline must be mixed with air since oxygen is also necessary for combustion. To mix the gasoline and air, there must be rapid motion and turbulence to keep the molecules suspended in the air. Of course, there is rapid motion and turbulence in the carburetor, and this turbulence continues on into the combustion chamber. In fact, combustion chambers are designed to create the maximum turbulence so that gasoline molecules will stay suspended in the air until they are ignited. A thorough mixture insures smooth and complete burning of gasoline, delivering maximum power.

Although the vaporizing ability of gasoline makes it an excellent fuel, it also presents a considerable fire and explosion hazard. When vaporized, a gallon of gasoline produces 21 cubic feet of vapor. If this vapor were combined with air in a mixture of 1.4 to 7.6 percent gasoline by volume, it would explode when ignited. Therefore, only one gallon of gasoline properly vaporized would completely fill an average living room with explosive vapor. The safety rules given in unit 8 for the use and storage of gasoline should always be followed.

In engines the compression of the fuel mixture of gasoline and air results in high combustion pressures and the force necessary to move the piston. This compression may also cause the gasoline to explode (detonate) in the engine instead of burning smoothly.

Detonation is also called knocking, fuel knock, spark knock, carbon knock, and ping. To understand it, one has to think in slow motion. The spark plug ignites the fuel mixture, and a flame front moves out from this starting point. As the flame front sweeps across the combustion chamber, heat and pressure build. The as-yet-unburned portion of the fuel mixture ahead of the flame front is exposed to this heat and pressure. If it self-detonates, two flame fronts are created which race toward each other. The last unburned portion of fuel caught between the two fronts explodes with hammerlike force. Detonation causes a knocking sound in the engine and power loss. Repeated detonation can damage the piston, Fig. 4-21.

Preignition causes the same undesirable effects as detonation, including engine damage, Fig. 4-22. The cause of preignition, however, is somewhat different. Hot spots, or red carbon deposits, actually ignite the fuel mixture and begin combustion before the spark plug fires.

Fig. 4-21 Detonation Damage.

Fig. 4-22 Preignition Damage.

The antiknock quality of a gasoline, or its ability to burn without knocking, is called its octane rating. Gasoline that has no knocking characteristics at all is rated at 100. Usually, tetraethyl lead is added to gasoline to give it the proper antiknock quality. If lead is not used, as in nonleaded gasoline, then special aromatic compounds are used to obtain smooth burning.

*Spark occurs.....*      *Spark occurs.....*      *Ignited by hot deposit..*

*...continues rapidly...*      *......continues......*      *..regular ignition spark..*

*.. combustion begins..*      *.. combustion begins..*      *.. ignites remaining fuel.*

*...and is completed.*      *......detonation.*      *..flame fronts collide.*

Fig. 4-23A   Normal Combustion      Fig. 4-23B   Detonation      Fig. 4-23C   Preignition

The higher the compression ratio of the engine, the higher the octane requirements for the engine's fuel. Low-grade gasoline with an octane rating of 70-85 is suitable for compression ratios of 5-7 to 1. Regular grade gasoline with an octane rating of 88-94 is suitable for compression ratios of 7-8.5 to 1. Most small engine manufacturers recommend the use of regular gasoline. High-octane, premium gasoline does not improve the performance of small engines. Premium gasoline with an octane rating of about 100 is suitable for compression ratios of 9-10 to 1. Super premium has an octane rating of over 100 and is good for engines with compression ratios of 9.5-10.5 to 1.

---

### ENGINE SPEED GOVERNORS

Speed governors are used to keep engine speed at a constant rate regardless of the load. For instance, a lawnmower is required to cut tall as well as short grass. A governor will insure that the engine operates at the same speed in spite of the varying load conditions. Engines on many other applications need this "constant speed" feature too.

Speed governors are also used to keep the engine operating speed below a given, preset rate, so that the engine speed will not surpass this rate. This maximum rate is established and the governor set accordingly by the engineers at the factory. This type of speed governor protects both the engine and the operator from speeds that are dangerously high.

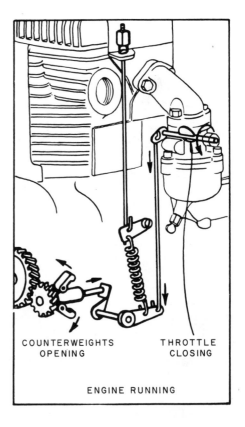

Fig. 4-24 Briggs-Stratton Mechanical Governor Operates on Centrifugal Force.

There are two main governor systems used on small gasoline engines: (1) Mechanical or Centrifugal type and (2) Pneumatic or Air Vane type. Although there are other types of governors, most of the governors used on small engines will fall into one of these categories.

## MECHANICAL GOVERNORS

The mechanical governor operates on centrifugal force. With this method, counter-weights mounted on a geared shaft, a governor spring, and the associated governor linkages, maintain the engine speed at the desired r.p.m.'s. For constant speed operation the action follows this pattern: when the engine is stopped, the mechanical governor's spring will pull the throttle to an open position. The governor spring tends to keep the throttle open, but as engine speed increases, centrifugal force throws the "hinged" counterweights further and further from their shaft. This action puts tension on the spring in the other direction, to close the throttle. At governed speed the spring tension is overcome by the counterweights and the throttle will open no further, a balanced position is maintained; the engine assumes its maximum speed.

If, however, a greater load is placed on the engine, its speed will slow down; the hinged counterweights will swing inward due to lessened centrifugal force; and the governor spring will become dominant, opening the throttle wider. With a wider throttle opening, the engine speeds up until governed speed is reached again. The action described is fast and smooth; little time is needed for the governor to meet "revised" load conditions.

The governed speed can be changed somewhat by varying the tension on the governor spring. The more tension there is on the governor spring, the higher the governed speed.

Another commonly used centrifugal or mechanical governor is the flyball type. With this governor, round steel balls in a spring loaded raceway move outward as the engine speed increases. The centrifugal force applied by these balls increases until it balances the spring tension holding the throttle open. At this point, the governed speed is reached.

Fig. 4-25 A Centrifugal Governor (Mechanical) Used on Certain Wisconsin Engines.

Fig. 4-26 A Mechanical Governor Used on Certain Lauson Engines.

## PNEUMATIC OR AIR VANE GOVERNORS

Many engines will be seen with a pneumatic or air vane governor. Again, the governor works to hold the throttle at the governed speed position, preventing it from opening further. An air vane, which is located near the flywheel blower, controls the speed. As engine speed increases, the flywheel blower pushes more air against the air vane, causing it to change position. At governed speed the air vane position overcomes the governor spring tension and a balance is assumed.

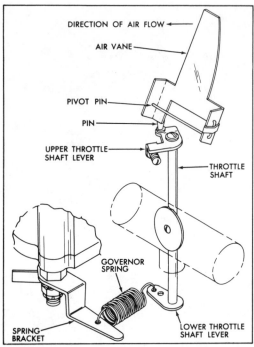

Fig. 4-27 A Pneumatic or Air Vane Governor Used on Certain Lauson Engines.

Engines are often designed so that they may be accelerated freely from idle speed on up to governed speed. If this is the case, the governor spring takes on very little tension at low speeds. The operator has full control. As the throttle is opened further and further, there is more tension on the spring, both from the operator and from the strengthening governor action. At governed speed, the force to close the throttle balances the spring tension to open the throttle.

It should be noted that not all engines are equipped with engine speed governors. Engines that will always be operated under a near constant load will find the governor unnecessary. The load of an outboard engine is a good example of a near constant load. Although different loads are placed on the outboard (number of people in boat, position of people in boat, use of trolling mechanism to decrease boat's speed, etc.), the load is constant at full throttle for a given period of use.

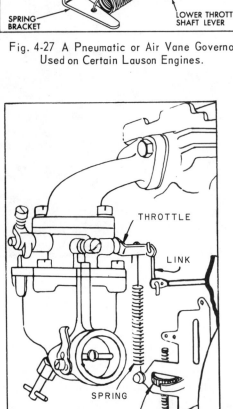

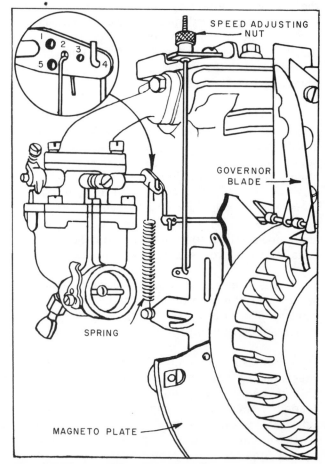

Fig. 4-28 A Pneumatic or Air Vane Governor Used on Certain Briggs-Stratton Engines.

## GENERAL STUDY QUESTIONS

1. Name the basic parts of a typical fuel system.

2. What force is used to operate most outboard fuel pumps?

3. How can a pressurized fuel system be recognized?

4. Briefly describe the task of the carburetor.

5. Name the main parts that make up the carburetor.

6. What causes air to flow through the carburetor?

7. What causes low air pressure in the venturi section of the carburetor?

8. What is the function of the throttle?

9. What is the function of the choke?

10. What is the function of the needle valve?

11. Explain the action of the float in a float-type carburetor.

12. What is the advantage of a diaphragm carburetor?

13. Explain the principle of air bleeding.

14. Explain the operation of the accelerating pump.

15. What is a "rich mixture"?

16. Why is turbulence important inside the combustion chamber?

17. What two main purposes do engine speed governors serve?

18. What are the two main classifications of engine speed governors?

19. Are engines made that do not have engine speed governors?

20. Can the governed speed be changed? How?


## CLASS DEMONSTRATION TOPICS

▶ Using a fully assembled engine, have the students trace the flow of fuel and also identify the parts of the fuel system.

▶ Demonstrate, with an engine operating, how to set a carburetor for maximum power.

▶ Demonstrate, with an operating engine, how "too lean" or "too rich" mixture affects operation and acceleration.

▶ Demonstrate the action of a carburetor with an atomizer or insect sprayer.

▶ Disassemble and inspect a fuel pump (automotive or outboard).

▶ Illustrate vaporization with a small saucer of gasoline beside a small saucer of oil.

▶ Demonstrate, with an operating engine, how the governor maintains governed speed and will not allow the throttle to open to "full".

▶ Demonstrate how governed speed can be changed. Stop engine to readjust governor.

Laboratory Experience 5

BASIC PARTS OF THE CARBURETOR

## OBJECTIVES

▶ To learn to identify the basic parts of the carburetor.

▶ To learn the function of each basic part of the carburetor.

## REFERENCE

● Review Pages 34-48

## INTRODUCTION

The carburetor is a key part of the gasoline engine. By mixing gasoline and air together, it provides the engine with the explosive fuel mixture necessary for ignition and power. Its main parts allow the engine to be operated under different load conditions, different speed conditions, and different starting conditions.

## STUDENT ASSIGNMENT

You are to remove the carburetor from the engine, then: (1) Disassemble the carburetor, (2) Study the basic parts, (3) Reassemble the carburetor. When you have reassembled the carburetor, reinstall it on the engine. It is essential that you record your work in the work record box on the following page as you complete each step of the disassembly procedure.

Disassembly Procedure

Your instructor may supplement or revise specific steps of the procedure which follows since there are many makes of carburetors. The following disassembly procedure is your general guide:

1. Remove metal shrouding to expose carburetor, if necessary.

2. Close fuel shutoff valve at gas tank or drain gas tank.

3. Drain carburetor float bowl, if drain valve is on the float bowl.

4. Remove the air cleaner. (Use care if it contains oil.)

5. Remove gas line from carburetor.

6. Remove throttle and governor connections.

7. Remove carburetor from engine.

8. Disassemble float bowl and inspect the float chamber.

9. Remove the main or high-speed needle valve - counterclockwise.

10. Remove idle screw or slow-speed needle valve - counterclockwise.

CAUTION: Never force needle valves in against their seats - they will be damaged. Do not remove the choke or throttle valves.

## WORK RECORD BOX

| Part | Disassembly (nuts, bolts, etc.) | Operation performed | Tool used |
|------|---------------------------------|---------------------|-----------|
|      |                                 |                     |           |
|      |                                 |                     |           |
|      |                                 |                     |           |
|      |                                 |                     |           |
|      |                                 |                     |           |
|      |                                 |                     |           |
|      |                                 |                     |           |
|      |                                 |                     |           |
|      |                                 |                     |           |
|      |                                 |                     |           |
|      |                                 |                     |           |
|      |                                 |                     |           |
|      |                                 |                     |           |
|      |                                 |                     |           |
|      |                                 |                     |           |
|      |                                 |                     |           |
|      |                                 |                     |           |
|      |                                 |                     |           |
|      |                                 |                     |           |
|      |                                 |                     |           |
|      |                                 |                     |           |

## GENERAL STUDY QUESTIONS

Study the carburetor and answer the following questions:

1. Does the engine have a fuel pump?

2. Is the carburetor suction fed?

3. Is the carburetor gravity fed?

4. Does the carburetor have a float bowl?

5. Does the carburetor have a needle valve?

6. Does the carburetor have an idle valve?

7. Does the carburetor have a choke?

8. Does the carburetor have an air cleaner?

9. What does the carburetor do?

10. What causes air to flow through the carburetor?

11. Did you locate the venturi section?  What does the venturi section do?

12. What is the function of the throttle?

13. What is the function of the choke?

14. Trace the path of fuel and fuel mixture through "your" engine.

Laboratory Experience 6

## ADJUSTING THE CARBURETOR FOR MAXIMUM POWER AND EFFICIENCY

### OBJECTIVE

> To learn how to adjust the carburetor for maximum power and efficiency.

### REFERENCE

● Review Pages 34-48

### INTRODUCTION

The correct carburetor adjustment is vital to top engine performance. An improper mixture of fuel and air can cause sluggish operation, overheating, increased part wear, excessive fuel consumption, fouled spark plugs, and other troubles. The needle valve and idle valve control the ratio of gasoline to air and the valves must be correctly positioned. Normal operation uses a ratio of about 15 parts air to 1 part gasoline (by weight) although the ratio may be richer or leaner to suit conditions.

### STUDENT ASSIGNMENT

You are to adjust a carburetor for maximum power and efficiency. These adjustments should be made with the engine operating and with the carburetor and engine at normal operating temperature. It is essential that you record your work in the work record box on the following page as you complete each step of the procedure.

CAUTION: Do not operate the engine without proper ventilation or exhaust system. Also, be certain that no loose clothing can become involved with the moving parts.

#### Adjustment Procedure

Your instructor may supplement or revise specific steps of the procedure which follows since there are many makes of carburetors and engines. The following adjustment procedure is your general guide:

1. Close the main needle valve and idle valve "finger tight". Excessive force can damage the needle valves. Turn clockwise to close.

2. Open the main needle valve one turn. Open the idle valve 3/4 turn. Turn counterclockwise to open.

3. Start engine, open choke, allow engine to reach operating temperature.

4. Run engine at operating speed (2/3 to 3/4 of full throttle). Turn the main needle valve in (clockwise) until engine slows down, indicating too lean a mixture. Note the position of valve. Turn the needle valve out (counterclockwise) until the engine speeds up and then slows down, indicating too rich a mixture. Note position of valve. Reposition the valve half-way between the rich and lean setting.

5. Close the throttle so the engine runs slightly faster than normal idle speed. Turn the idle valve in (clockwise) until the engine slows down. Then turn the idle valve back out until the engine speeds up and idles smoothly. Now adjust the idle speed regulating screw to desired idle speed.

NOTE: Idle speed is not the slowest speed at which the engine will operate; rather, it is a slow speed that will maintain good air flow for cooling and a good takeoff spot for even acceleration. A tachometer and the known proper idle speed are necessary for the best adjustment.

6. Test the acceleration of the engine by opening the throttle rapidly. If acceleration is sluggish a slightly richer fuel mixture is probably necessary.

## WORK RECORD BOX

| Part | Disassembly (nuts, bolts, etc.) | Operation performed | Tool used |
|------|------|------|------|
|  |  |  |  |
|  |  |  |  |
|  |  |  |  |
|  |  |  |  |
|  |  |  |  |
|  |  |  |  |
|  |  |  |  |
|  |  |  |  |
|  |  |  |  |
|  |  |  |  |
|  |  |  |  |
|  |  |  |  |
|  |  |  |  |

## GENERAL STUDY QUESTIONS

Adjust the carburetor and answer the following questions.

1. What problems will too lean a fuel mixture cause? Too rich?

2. Describe the engine exhaust produced by too rich a fuel mixture.

3. Explain how needle and idle valves can be damaged.

Laboratory Experience 7

FUEL PUMPS

## OBJECTIVES

▶ To learn the basic construction of the diaphragm fuel pump.

▶ To gain an understanding of how the fuel pump operates.

## REFERENCE

● Review Pages 34-48

## INTRODUCTION

The diaphragm fuel pump action is simple and reliable. The flexible diaphragm moves out and gasoline enters the fuel chamber through the inlet check valve. Now the diaphragm moves in and the fuel is forced on to the carburetor through the discharge check valve. Each valve will allow fuel flow in one direction only. In outboard fuel pumps the diaphragm is operated by the differences of crankcase pressure. In the automobile fuel pump the diaphragm is operated by cam action.

NOTE: Outboard fuel pumps are small, fairly intricate, and somewhat delicate. Their disassembly and inspection is not recommended for "beginners". The automobile fuel pump construction and action is basically the same and these pumps are larger and easier for the "beginner" to handle. Discarded automobile fuel pumps are also easy to obtain.

## STUDENT ASSIGNMENT

You are to disassemble and inspect the fuel pump. Be sure to note how the diaphragm can move in and out. Also, note how the inlet and discharge valves will allow fuel flow in only one direction. Trace the flow of fuel through the pump. It is essential that you record your work in the work record box on the following page as you complete each step of the disassembly procedure.

Disassembly Procedure
———————————

Your instructor may supplement or revise specific steps of the procedure which follows since you may be working on either an automotive or outboard fuel pump. The following disassembly procedure is your general guide:

1. Remove fuel lines "from tank" and "to carburetor".

2. Remove fuel pump from engine.

3. Remove machine screws that hold the pump together at the diaphragm.

4. Carefully separate the halves of the pump, exposing the diaphragm.

5. Remove and inspect the inlet and discharge valves (on some pumps this is not possible).

## WORK RECORD BOX

| Part | Disassembly (nuts, bolts, etc.) | Operation performed | Tool used |
|------|----------------------------------|---------------------|-----------|
|      |                                  |                     |           |
|      |                                  |                     |           |
|      |                                  |                     |           |
|      |                                  |                     |           |
|      |                                  |                     |           |
|      |                                  |                     |           |
|      |                                  |                     |           |
|      |                                  |                     |           |
|      |                                  |                     |           |
|      |                                  |                     |           |
|      |                                  |                     |           |

### Reassembly Procedure

Reverse the disassembly procedure.

## GENERAL STUDY QUESTIONS

Study the fuel pump and answer the following questions.

1. Explain what causes the diaphragm to move in and out.

2. Describe the shape of the inlet and discharge valves.

Laboratory Experience 8

AIR VANE GOVERNOR (Disassemble and Inspect)

OBJECTIVE

▶ To learn the basic parts of an air vane governor and how they work together.

REFERENCE

● Review Pages 34-48

INTRODUCTION

The air vane governor is operated by the flywheel air flow which is channeled by it. The faster the engine speed the more the hinged vane is deflected by the air blast. The governor spring works to hold the throttle wide open while the air vane works to close the throttle. Governed speed is reached when the force to open the throttle and the force to close the throttle balance each other. The greater the governor spring tension the higher the governed speed since a bigger air blast from the flywheel is needed to balance the spring tension.

STUDENT ASSIGNMENT

You are to examine the air vane type of engine speed governor in order to identify and become familiar with its various parts. It is essential that you record your work in the work record box on the following page as you complete each step of the disassembly procedure.

Disassembly Procedure

Your instructor may supplement or revise specific steps of the procedure which follows since there are many makes of engines. The following disassembly procedure is your general guide:

1. Remove all air shrouding that covers the flywheel area; expose the engine speed governor.

2. Study the air scoops on the flywheel, the governor spring, the air vane, and the associated linkages.

3. Determine how the tension on the governor spring can be changed to increase or decrease governed speed.

4. Remove the governor parts only if directed to do so by the instructor.

WORK RECORD BOX

| Part | Disassembly (nuts, bolts, etc.) | Operation performed | Tool used |
|------|--------------------------------|---------------------|-----------|
|      |                                |                     |           |
|      |                                |                     |           |
|      |                                |                     |           |
|      |                                |                     |           |
|      |                                |                     |           |
|      |                                |                     |           |
|      |                                |                     |           |
|      |                                |                     |           |
|      |                                |                     |           |

Reassembly Procedure

Reverse the disassembly procedure.   Use great care with the delicate parts.   They must not bind at any point.   Free movement is essential for proper operation.

GENERAL STUDY QUESTIONS

Study the air vane governor and answer the following questions.

1. What are the main parts of the air vane governor?

2. If the air shrouding were removed from the engine would the governor operation be affected?  Why?

3. How can the governor spring tension be changed on "your" engine?

Laboratory Experience 9
ENGINE SPEED GOVERNOR ACTION

OBJECTIVES

▶ To observe the action of the governor on the throttle.

▶ To learn how to adjust the governed speed.

REFERENCE

● Review Pages 34-48

INTRODUCTION

The engine speed governor, on most small engines, is provided to enable the engine to deliver constant r.p.m. regardless of engine load. The engine operating under light load will have quite a bit of reserve throttle opening to enable the engine to maintain constant speed when load is increased. The governed speed can usually be adjusted through a range of several hundred r.p.m.'s to satisfy the particular needs of the engine operator. To increase the governed speed the tension on the governor spring is increased; to decrease speed the spring tension is decreased. On some engines the governor spring is hooked into numbered holes; on others, a nut on a threaded link to the spring is tightened; and on others, a lever arm is repositioned. Many systems are used.

CAUTION: Do not operate the engine without proper ventilation or exhaust system. Also, be certain that no loose clothing can become involved with the moving parts.

STUDENT ASSIGNMENT

You are to study the engine speed governor, either mechanical or air vane type, to become familiar with the action of the governor on the engine throttle. As a part of this study, you will learn how to adjust the governor for the various speed settings. It is essential that you record your work in the work record box on the following page as you complete each step of the procedure.

Procedure

Either mechanical or air vane governors can be used for this laboratory experience. Use an engine that is on a test stand, not one connected to an implement.

1. With the engine stopped, work the throttle and observe the throttle position for idle and the throttle position for wide open.

2. Start the engine, bring the engine to governed speed (many governors do this automatically). Now note the throttle opening. Using a tachometer on the end of the crankshaft, take the engine r.p.m. Record r.p.m. in work record box on the following page.

3.  Stop engine.

4.  Readjust governor spring tension for increased "top" speed or readjust governor spring tension for decreased "top" speed,

5.  Start the engine, bring the engine to new governed speed.  Note the throttle opening. Using a tachometer on the end of the crankshaft take the engine r.p.m.  Record r.p.m. in work record box.

6.  Stop engine.

### WORK RECORD BOX FOR RECORDING R.P.M's

| Part | Disassembly (nuts, bolts, etc.) | Operation performed | Tool used |
|------|------|------|------|
|  |  |  |  |
|  |  |  |  |
|  |  |  |  |
|  |  |  |  |
|  |  |  |  |
|  |  |  |  |
|  |  |  |  |
|  |  |  |  |
|  |  |  |  |
|  |  |  |  |
|  |  |  |  |
|  |  |  |  |
|  |  |  |  |

## GENERAL STUDY QUESTIONS

Upon completion of the adjustment procedure answer the following questions.

1.  Explain the function of the engine speed governor.

2.  How was governor spring tension adjusted on "your" engine?

3.  Was "your" engine speed governor a mechanical or air vane governor?

4.  How does the throttle opening in Procedure Step #5 compare with that in Step 2?

## LUBRICATION

Whenever surfaces move against one another, they cause friction and friction results in heat and wear. Lubricating oils have one main job to perform in the engine; namely, to reduce friction. The lubricating oil provides a film that separates the moving metal surfaces and keeps the contact of metal against metal to an absolute minimum.

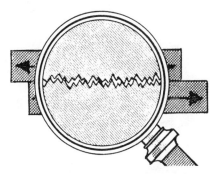

Fig. 5-1 Exaggerated View of Metal Surfaces in Contact.

Without a lubricating oil or with insufficient lubrication, the heat of friction builds up rapidly. Engine parts become so hot that they fail; that is, the metal begins to melt — it gets mushy; bearing surfaces seize, parts warp out of shape, or parts actually break. The common expression is to say the engine "burns up".

As an example of friction, take a book, lay it on the table and then push the book with your hand. Notice the resistance. Friction makes the book difficult to slide. Now place three round pencils between the book and the table top, push the book and notice how easily it moves. Friction has been greatly reduced. Oil molecules correspond to the pencils by forming a coating between two moving surfaces. With oil, the metal surfaces literally roll along on the oil molecules and friction is greatly reduced.

Besides reducing friction and the wear and heat it causes, the lubricating oil serves several other important functions.

### 1. Oil Seals Power

The oil film seals power, particularly between the piston and cylinder walls. The tremendous pressures in the combustion chamber cannot pass by the airtight seal the oil film provides. If this oil film fails, a condition called "blow-by" exists. Combustion gases push by the film and enter the crankcase. Blow-by not only reduces engine power, but also has a harmful effect on the oil's lubricating quality.

### 2. Oil Helps to Dissipate Heat

Oil helps to dissipate heat by providing a good path for heat transfer. Heat conducts readily from inside metal parts through an oil film to outside metal parts that are cooled by air or water. Also, heat is carried away as "new" oil arrives from the crankcase and the "hot" oil is washed back to the crankcase.

### 3. Oil Keeps the Engine Clean

Oil keeps the engine clean by washing away microscopic pieces of metal that have been worn off moving parts. These minute pieces settle out in the crankcase or they are trapped in the oil filter, if one is used.

### 4. Oil Cushions Bearing Loads

The oil film has a cushioning effect since it is squeezed from between the bearing surfaces relatively slowly. It has a shock absorber action. For example, when the power stroke starts, the hard shock of combustion is transferred to the bearing surfaces; the oil film helps to cushion this shock.

### 5. Oil Protects Against Rusting

The oil film protects steel parts from rusting. Air, moisture, and corrosive substances cannot reach the metal to oxidize or corrode the surface.

## FRICTION BEARINGS

There are three types of friction bearings used in a small gasoline engine: journal, guide, and thrust. The journal bearing is the most familiar. This bearing supports a revolving or oscillating shaft. The connecting rod around the crankshaft and the main bearings are examples. The guide bearing reduces the friction of surfaces sliding longitudinally against each other such as the piston in the cylinder. The thrust bearing supports or limits the longitudinal motion of a rotating shaft.

Bearing inserts are commonly used on larger engines or heavy-duty small engines, particularly on the connecting rod and cap and the main bearings. The inserts are precision-made of layers of various metals and alloys. Alloys such as babbit, copper-lead, bronze, aluminum, cadmium, and silver are commonly used. Crankshaft surfaces are, of course steel. Most small engines, however, do not have bearing inserts, using just the aluminum connecting rod around the steel journal of the crankshaft.

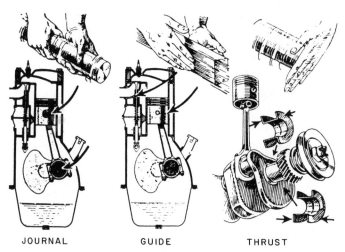

JOURNAL          GUIDE          THRUST

Fig. 5-2 Three Major Classifications of Friction Type Bearings.

## ANTI-FRICTION BEARINGS

Anti-friction bearings are also commonly used in engines. They substitute rolling friction for sliding friction. Ball bearings, roller bearings and needle bearings are of this type. On many small engines the main bearings are of the anti-friction type.

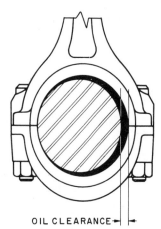

OIL CLEARANCE

Fig. 5-3 Oil Clearance between Journal and Bearing (Exaggerated).

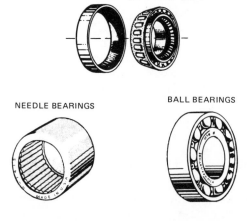

TAPERED ROLLER BEARINGS

NEEDLE BEARINGS          BALL BEARINGS

Fig. 5-4 Types of Anti-Friction Bearings.

## QUALITY DESIGNATION OF OIL AND SAE NUMBER

Selecting engine lubricating oils can be confusing: one must be aware of different viscosities, different qualities, different refining companies, different additives, and the meaning of a multitude of advertising phrases. It's a lot of information to sort out and to understand. Generally, lubricating oils used for various small gasoline engines are the same ones that are used for automobile engines. However, two-stroke cycle engines almost always use special two-cycle oil.

### Quality Designation by the American Petroleum Institute

The API classifications are usually found on the top of the oil can and refer to its quality.

● Oils for Service SE (Service Extreme)

SE oils are suitable for the most severe type of operation beginning with 1972 models and some 1971 automobiles. Extreme conditions of start-stop driving; short trip, cold weather driving; and high speed, long distance, hot weather driving can be handled by this oil. The oil meets the requirements of automobiles that are equipped with emission control devices and engines operating under manufacturers' warranties.

● Oils for SD (Service Deluxe)

Most small engine manufacturers approve the use of SD (formerly MS) oil in their engines. These oils provide protection against high and low temperature engine deposits, rust, corrosion, and wear.

● Oils for Service SC

This oil was also formerly classified as being suitable for MS. It has much the same characteristics as SD but is not quite as effective as SD oil. SC oil was developed for auto engines of 1964-67, while SD oil was developed for engines of 1968-70 manufacture.

● Oils for Service SB (Formerly MM)

This oil is recommended for moderate operating conditions such as moderate speeds in warm weather; short distance, high speed driving; and alternate long and short trips in cool weather. It is satisfactory for certain older autos but not for new autos under warranty. It is seldom recommended for small engine use.

● Oils for Service SA (Formerly ML)

No performance requirements are set for this oil. It is straight mineral oil and may be suitable for some light service requirements. SA oil is not recommended by small engine manufacturers.

The new classifications for oils suitable for diesel service are CA, CB, CC, and CD; these replace the old classifications of DG, AM (Supp-1), DM (MIL-L2104B), and DS respectively.

It is wise to buy the best quality oil for your engine. Skimping on quality for a few cents savings may be more expensive in the long run due to engine wear.

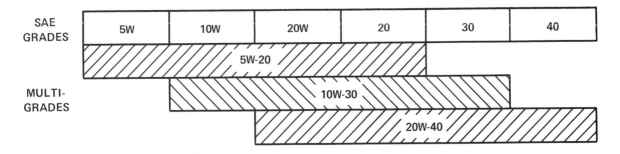

Fig. 5-5 Multigrade Motor Oils Span Several SAE (single) Grades.

Viscosity Classification by the Society
of Automotive Engineers

The SAE (Society of Automotive Engineers) number of an oil indicates its viscosity, or thickness. Oils may be very thin (light), or they may be quite thick (heavy). The range is from SAE 5W to SAE 50; the higher the number, the thicker the oil. The owner should consult the engine manufacturer's instruction book for the correct oil. SAE 10W, SAE 20W, SAE 20, and SAE 30 are the most commonly used oil weights. Usually, manufacturers recommend SAE 30 for summer use and either SAE 10W or SAE 20W for cold, sub-freezing weather. Winter use demands a thinner oil since oil thickens in cold weather. The "W", as in 5W, 10W, and 20W, indicates that the oil is designed for service in sub-freezing weather.

● Multigrade Oils

Multigrade oils may also be used in small gasoline engines. These oils span several SAE classifications because they have a very high viscosity index. Typical classifications are SAE 5W-20 or 5W-10W-20; 5W-30 or 5W-10W-20W-30; SAE 10W-30 or 10W-20W-30; 10W-40, and 20W-40. The first number represents the low temperature viscosity of the oil; the last number represents its high temperature viscosity. For example, 10W-30 passes the viscosity test of SAE 10W at low temperatures and the viscosity test of SAE 30 at high temperatures. These oils are also referred to as all-season, all-weather oils, multi-viscosity, or multiviscosity grade oils.

Motor Oil Additives

The best oil could not do its job properly in a modern engine if additives were not blended into the base oil.

● Pour-Point Depressants

Pour - Point depressants keep the oil liquid even at very low temperatures when the wax in oil would otherwise congeal into a buttery consistency to render the oil ineffective.

● Oxidation and Bearing Corrosion Inhibitors

These additives prevent the rapid oxidation of the oil by excessive heat. Without these inhibitors viscous, gummy materials are formed. Some of these oxidation products attack metals such as lead, cadmium, and silver which are often used in bearings. The inhibiting compounds are gradually used up and, thus, regular oil changes are needed.

● Rust and Corrosion Inhibitors

These inhibitors protect against the damage that might be caused by acids and water which are by-products of combustion. Basically, acids are neutralized by alkaline materials, much the same as vinegar can be neutralized with baking soda. Special chemicals surround or capture molecules of water, preventing their contact with the metal, while other chemicals with an extreme affinity for metal form an unbroken film on the metal parts. These inhibitors are also used up in time.

● Detergent/Dispersant Additives

This type of additive prevents the formation of sludge and varnish. Detergents work much the same as household detergents in that they have the ability to disperse and suspend combustion contaminants in the oil but do not affect the lubricating quality of the oil. When the oil is changed, all the contaminants are discarded with the oil so that the engine is kept clean. Larger particles of foreign matter in the oil either settle out in the engine base or are trapped in the oil filter if one is used.

● Foam Inhibitors

Foam inhibitors are present in all high quality motor oils to prevent the oil from being whipped into a froth or foam. The action in the crankcase tends to bring air into the oil, and foaming oil is not an effective lubricant. Foam inhibitors called silicones have the ability to break down the tiny air bubbles and cause the foam to collapse.

## LUBRICATION OF FOUR-CYCLE ENGINES

Since all moving parts of the engine must be lubricated to avoid engine failure, a constant supply of oil must be provided. Each engine, therefore, carries its own reservoir of oil in its crankcase where the main engine parts are located.

Basically the oil is either <u>pumped</u> to or <u>splashed</u> on the parts and bearing surfaces that need lubrication. There are several lubrication systems used on small engines and the systems discussed below are among the most common.

1. Simple Splash
2. Constant Level Splash
3. Ejection Pump
4. Barrel-Type Pump
5. Full Pressure Lubrication

The <u>Splash System</u> is perhaps the simplest system for lubrication. It consists of a splasher or dipper that is fastened to the connecting rod cap. Each time the piston nears the bottom on its stroke the dipper splashes into the oil reservoir in the crankcase, splashing oil onto all parts inside the crankcase. Since the engine is operating at 2000 to 3000 r.p.m.'s, the parts are literally drenched by millions of oil droplets. Some engines use an oil slinger that is driven by the camshaft. The slinger performs a similar function to the dipper.

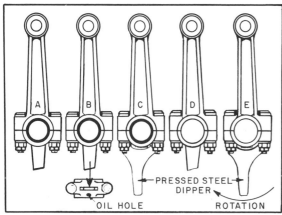

Fig. 5-6 Dippers used on Different Connecting Rods.

The <u>Constant Level Splash System</u> has three refinements over the simple splash system: (1) a pump, (2) a splash trough, and (3) a strainer. With this system a cam-operated pump brings oil from the bottom of the crank-

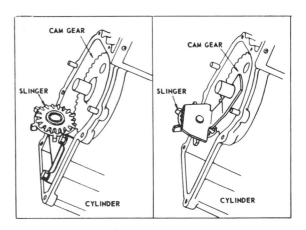

Fig. 5-7 Oil Slinger.

case into a splash trough. Again the splasher on the connecting rod dips into the oil, splashing it on all parts inside the crankcase. The strainer prevents any large pieces of foreign matter from recirculating through the system. The pump maintains a constant oil supply in the trough regardless of the oil level in the crankcase.

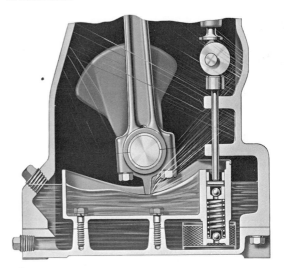

Fig. 5-8 Constant Level Splash System used on Some Models of Wisconsin Engines.

<u>Ejection Pumps</u> of various types are found on many small engines. With this method, a cam-operated pump draws oil from the bottom of the crankcase and sprays or squirts it onto the connecting rod. Some of the oil enters the connecting rod bearing through small holes, while the remainder is deflected onto the other parts within the crankcase.

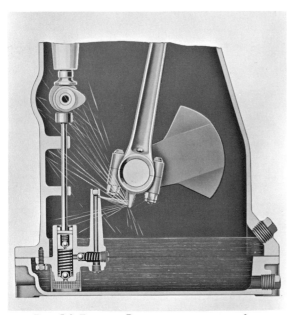

Fig. 5-9 Ejection Pump as it is used on Some Wisconsin Engines.

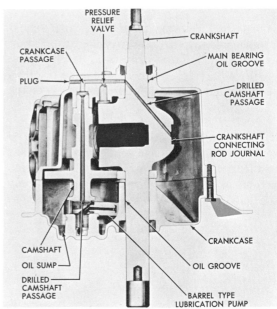

Fig. 5-11 Lubrication Oil Flow of Barrel Type Lubrication System used on Some Lauson Engines.

The Barrel-Type Pump is also driven by an eccentric on the camshaft. The camshaft is hollow and extends to the pump of the vertical crankshaft engine. As the pump plunger is pulled out on intake, an intake port in the camshaft lines up, allowing the pump body to fill. When the plunger is forced into the pump body on discharge, the discharge ports in the camshaft line up, allowing the oil to be forced to the main bearing and to the crankshaft connecting rod journal. Small drilled passages are used to channel the oil. Oil is also splashed onto other crankcase parts.

Full Pressure Lubrication is found on many engines, especially the larger of the small engines and on automobile engines. Lubricating oil is pumped to all main, connecting, and camshaft bearings through small passages drilled in these engine parts. Oil is also delivered to tappets, timing gears, etc. under pressure. The pump used is usually a positive displacement gear type. It is also common to use a splash system in conjunction with full pressure systems.

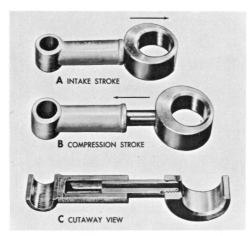

Fig. 5-10 Barrel Type Lubrication Pump used on Some Lauson Engines.

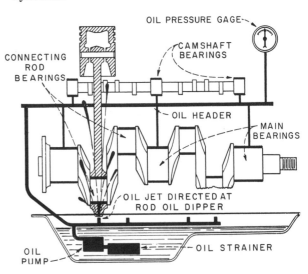

Fig. 5-12 Full Pressure Lubrication

## LUBRICATING CYLINDER WALLS

Oil is splashed or sprayed onto cylinder walls and the piston rings spread the oil evenly for proper lubrication. Piston rings must function properly to avoid excessive oil consumption. The rings must exert an even pressure on the cylinder walls and provide a good seal. If piston ring grooves are too large, the piston rings will begin a pumping action as the piston moves up and down, and excess oil will be brought into the combustion chamber.

Worn cylinder walls, worn pistons, and worn rings can all contribute to high oil consumption as well as loss of compression and the resulting loss of power.

## BLOW-BY

Blow-by, the escape of combustion gases from the combustion chamber to the crankcase, occurs when piston rings are worn or too loose in their grooves. Carbon and soot from burned fuel are forced into the crankcase by the rings. Much of the carbon is deposited around the rings, hindering their operation further.

Another damaging result of worn rings can be crankcase dilution. If raw, unburned gasoline is in the combustion chamber it can leak by the piston rings and into the crankcase, diluting the crankcase oil and, thereby, reducing the oil's lubricating properties.

## CRANKCASE BREATHERS

Four-stroke cycle engines do not have completely airtight, oiltight crankcases. Engine crankcases must breathe. Without the ability to breathe, pressures build up in the crankcase and may rupture oil seals or allow contaminants to remain in the crankcase. Pressure buildup may be caused by the expansion of the air as the engine heats up, by the action of the piston coming down the cylinder and by the blow-by of combustion gases along cylinder walls.

Most single-cylinder engines use breathers that allow air to leave but not reenter a reed-type check valve or a ball-type check valve. These breathers place the crankcase under a slight vacuum and are called closed breathers.

Open breathers allow the engine to breathe freely in and out and are usually equipped with air filters. They are located where the splashing of oil is not a problem. Open breathers are frequently incorporated with the valve access cover. If an engine with this type of breather is tipped on its side, oil may run out through it. Some breathers are vented to the atmosphere while others are vented back through the carburetor.

## LUBRICATION OF TWO-CYCLE ENGINES

Lubrication of the two-cycle engine is quite different from the four-cycle engine. Since the fuel mixture must travel through the crankcase, a reservoir of oil cannot be stored there. The lubricating oil is mixed with the gasoline and then put into the gas tank. The lubricating oil for all crankcase parts enters the crankcase as a part of the fuel mixture. Millions of tiny oil droplets suspended in the mixture of gasoline and air settle onto the moving parts in the crankcase, providing lubrication. Oil droplets, being relatively large and heavy, quickly drop out of suspension. Of course, much oil is carried on into the combustion chamber where it is burned along with the gasoline and air.

On a two-cycle engine, oil must be mixed with the gasoline. The engine is not operated on straight gasoline. If it were, the heat of friction would burn up the engine in a short time. It should be pointed out that some two-cycle engine manufacturers are developing and marketing engines with oil metering devices that eliminate the need of premixing the oil and gasoline. Mixing is done automatically in the correct proportions.

In preparing the mixture of gasoline and oil for most two-cycle engines, observe the following rules:

1. Mix a good grade of regular gasoline and oil in a separate container. Do not mix in the gas tank unless it is a remote tank such as is found on many outboards.

2.  Pour the oil into the gasoline to in-
    sure good mixing and shake the con-
    tainer vigorously. If poorly mixed,
    the oil will settle to the bottom of the
    tank, causing hard starting.

3.  Strain fuel with a fine mesh strainer
    as you pour it into the tank to prevent
    any moisture from entering the tank.

4.  Use the oil that is specified for your
    particular two-cycle engine. Most
    manufacturers specify their own pri-
    vate brand. In an emergency, other
    oils may be used, usually SAE 30SB
    (formerly MM) or SAE 30 SD (form-
    erly MS) nondetergent oil. The man-
    ufacturer's brand, however, provides
    the best lubrication with a minimum
    of deposit formation.

5.  Mix gasoline and oil in the propor-
    tions recommended by the engine
    manufacturer. One common propor-

tion is three-fourths pint of oil to one
gallon of gasoline when breaking in a
new engine, and one-half pint of oil to
one gallon of gasoline for normal use.

ADDITIONAL LUBRICATION POINTS

Whether the engine has two-cycle or
four-cycle lubrication it should be remembered
that there may well be other lubrication to consider besides the crankcase area. On an outboard engine do not neglect the lower unit which
needs a special gear lubricant at several points.
If an engine is powering an implement or other
machinery there may be transmissions, gear
boxes, chains, axles, wheels, shafts, linkages,
etc. that need periodic lubrication. Lubricate
these additional parts with the oil or lubricant
recommended by the manufacturer.

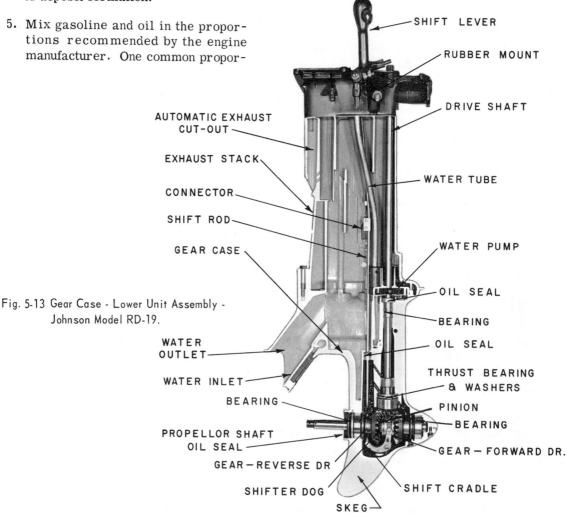

Fig. 5-13 Gear Case - Lower Unit Assembly -
Johnson Model RD-19.

## GENERAL STUDY QUESTIONS

1. What is the main job of a lubricant?

2. Explain how the lubricating oil also:

   a. Seals power
   b. Helps to dissipate heat
   c. Keeps the engine clean
   d. Cushions bearing loads
   e. Protects against rusting

3. What are the three types of friction bearings?

4. What is an anti-friction bearing?

5. What does an oil's SAE number refer to?

6. What is a multi-grade oil?

7. Explain how a detergent oil works.

8. What are the quality designations of oil?

9. List five common four-cycle engine lubrication systems.

10. How are cylinder walls lubricated?

11. Explain blow-by.

12. Briefly explain how two-cycle lubrication is accomplished.

13. What is one common proportion of oil to gasoline?

14. What kind of oil should be used for two-cycle engines?

## CLASS DISCUSSION TOPICS

● Discuss how friction causes heat and wear.

● Discuss the jobs a lubricant performs.

● Discuss the types of bearings used on a " demonstration" engine.

● Discuss the good features of the various lubrication systems; also discuss the system's weak points, if any.

## CLASS DEMONSTRATION TOPICS

◗ Illustrate the theory of lubrication using round pencils and a book.

◗ Demonstrate oil viscosity by showing and pouring several different weights of oil.

◗ Remove and inspect oil control rings.

◗ Remove an ejection pump from an engine and demonstrate the pump's operation.

◗ Remove and inspect the dipper on a splash lubrication system.

# LABORATORY EXPERIENCES

Laboratory Experience 10

## DRAIN OIL AND REFILL CRANKCASE

### OBJECTIVE

▶ To learn how to correctly drain and refill the crankcase with oil.

### REFERENCE

● Review Pages 61-68

### INTRODUCTION

The crankcase oil should be changed periodically. The exact number of engine operating hours between oil changes varies from manufacturer to manufacturer. It may be as short a time as every 20 hours or as long a time as every 100 hours. (Every 25 hours is most common.) True, the manufacturer's suggested oil change interval can be stretched, but to insure minimum engine wear and maximum engine life, follow the manufacturer's lubrication suggestions.

Manufacturers generally recommend SD (formerly MS) quality engine oil; however, some manufacturers permit the use of SB (formerly MM) oil. Avoid the use of light duty oil. The viscosity recommended is often SAE 30 for summer and SAE 20W for winter.

It is a good idea to drain the oil when the engine is hot since more dirt and slightly more oil can be removed. Remember, dirty oil should be replaced because it will not give proper, high quality lubrication.

### STUDENT ASSIGNMENT

You are to drain the crankcase oil and then refill the crankcase with the correct type oil. Take care to prevent a mess; a good workman is not sloppy. It is essential that you record your work in the work record box on the next page as you complete each step of the procedure.

#### Procedure

Your instructor may supplement or revise specific steps of the procedure which follows since there are many makes of engines. The following procedure is your general guide:

1. Remove the add-oil plug.

2. Loosen and carefully remove the drain plug. Do not drop the plug when it comes out of the engine. Be sure to have a container right under the drain hole.

3. Allow oil to drain, then tip the engine slightly to get the last bit of oil from the engine.

4. Replace the drain plug.

5. Refill the crankcase with clean oil of the correct quality and viscosity.

6. Check the oil level with the dip stick if the engine has one.  On engines not having a dip stick, fill the crankcase until oil can be seen at the hole or in the fill pipe.

7. Replace add-oil plug.

## WORK RECORD BOX

| Part | Disassembly (nuts, bolts, etc.) | Operation performed | Tool used |
|---|---|---|---|
|  |  |  |  |
|  |  |  |  |
|  |  |  |  |
|  |  |  |  |
|  |  |  |  |
|  |  |  |  |
|  |  |  |  |
|  |  |  |  |
|  |  |  |  |
|  |  |  |  |
|  |  |  |  |
|  |  |  |  |
|  |  |  |  |
|  |  |  |  |
|  |  |  |  |

## GENERAL STUDY QUESTIONS

Complete the work above, then answer the following questions.

1. On most engines, how often should lubricating oil be changed?

2. What quality oil is generally used?

3. What viscosity (SAE No.) oil is often used in the summer?    Winter?

4. Why is it a good idea to drain the oil just after the engine has been operated and it is hot?

Laboratory Experience 11

EJECTION OIL PUMP

## OBJECTIVES

◗ To learn how an ejection pump operates.

◗ To learn the basic construction of the pump.

◗ To observe the operation of the ejection oil pump.

## REFERENCE

● Review Pages 61-68

## INTRODUCTION

The oil pump must provide oil for all bearing surfaces within the crankcase; at any point in the engine where one part is moving against another, oil is needed to reduce friction and wear. Generally, the ejection pump sprays or squirts oil onto all parts in the crankcase. A similar pump action can be seen in the constant level splash system where oil is pumped into the splash trough.

The parts of the pump are the base, screen, check valve, spring and plunger. The spring tends to push the plunger up but the plunger is driven down every revolution by a cam (usually on the camshaft). A check valve will allow the chamber to be filled with oil when the plunger goes up but when the cam pushes the plunger down, the check valve closes, and the trapped oil is squirted or sprayed from the pump.

NOTE: Any engine with a camshaft driven pump that sprays or squirts oil onto the parts or pumps oil into the splash trough is suitable for this laboratory experience.

## STUDENT ASSIGNMENT

You are to disassemble the engine, exposing the pump, then remove the pump from the engine. Study the construction of the pump and then observe its operation, working it slowly by hand. It is essential that you record your work in the work record box on the following page as you complete each step of the disassembly procedure.

Disassembly Procedure (Ejection Pump)

Your instructor may supplement or revise specific steps of the procedure which follows since there are many makes of engines. The following procedure is your general guide.

1. Remove air shrouding if necessary.

2. Drain fuel system and oil bath air cleaner.

3. Drain oil from crankcase.

4. Remove the crankcase from the base or sump. Note: there will be a gasket between these sections.

5. Looking up into the bottom of the crankcase, locate the crankshaft, camshaft, and oil pump.

6. Remove the oil pump from the engine.

7. Disassemble the pump and study its main parts.

8. Reassemble pump.

9. Study pump operation by:

    a. pouring oil into the engine base.

    b. placing oil pump base in the oil supply.

    c. using your finger on the top of the plunger as a substitute for cam action, working the pump.

CAUTION: Have a shield to stop oil if it comes out of the pump with too much force.

## WORK RECORD BOX

| Part | Disassembly (nuts, bolts, etc.) | Operation performed | Tool used |
|------|---------------------------------|---------------------|-----------|
|      |                                 |                     |           |
|      |                                 |                     |           |
|      |                                 |                     |           |
|      |                                 |                     |           |
|      |                                 |                     |           |
|      |                                 |                     |           |
|      |                                 |                     |           |
|      |                                 |                     |           |
|      |                                 |                     |           |
|      |                                 |                     |           |
|      |                                 |                     |           |
|      |                                 |                     |           |
|      |                                 |                     |           |
|      |                                 |                     |           |
|      |                                 |                     |           |
|      |                                 |                     |           |
|      |                                 |                     |           |
|      |                                 |                     |           |

Reassembly Procedure

Reverse the disassembly procedure.  A new gasket may be needed between the base and crankcase.

GENERAL STUDY QUESTIONS

Study the ejection oil pump and its operation and then answer the following questions.

1.  What are the main parts of the pump?

2.  Is the oil discharge directed at any particular part within the crankcase or just the crankcase in general?

3.  Why is a gasket necessary between the base and crankcase?

4.  If the engine is operating at 3600 r.p.m., how many pump strokes would there be each minute?

5.  Would a drop in crankcase oil level affect the pump's output?  Explain.

Laboratory Experience 12

SIMPLE SPLASH OIL SYSTEM (Horizontal Crankshaft)

## OBJECTIVE

▶   To study simple splash oil system.

## REFERENCE

●   Review Pages 61-68

## INTRODUCTION

The simple splash oil system is an uncomplicated but very effective lubrication system. It consists of a dipper that is fastened to the connecting rod cap. Every revolution the dipper comes sweeping down and through the oil reservoir in the crankcase. Oil is splashed onto all parts that are within the crankcase. There is a drenching "rain" of oil in the crankcase when the engine is operating.

The dipper may be of several different sizes and shapes. The dipper may be bolted on with the connecting rod cap or the dipper may be cast as a part of the connecting rod cap.

## STUDENT ASSIGNMENT

You are to disassemble the engine, exposing the oil dipper. Slowly revolve the crankshaft and study the path of the dipper. Remove the dipper and study its construction. It is essential that you record your work in the work record box on the following page as you complete each step of the disassembly procedure.

## Disassembly Procedure

Your instructor may supplement or revise specific steps of the procedure which follows since there are many makes of engines. The following procedure is your general guide:

1.  Remove air shrouding if necessary.

2.  Drain fuel system and oil bath air cleaner.

3.  Drain oil from crankcase.

4.  Remove crankcase from base or sump (on some engines remove the cover assembly from crankcase). Note: there will be a gasket between these sections.

5.  Locate the oil dipper, slowly revolve the crankshaft and observe the path of the dipper.

6.  Remove the connecting rod cap and dipper assembly. Study the part.

## WORK RECORD BOX

| Part | Disassembly (nuts, bolts, etc.) | Operation performed | Tool used |
|------|-------------------------------|---------------------|-----------|
|      |                               |                     |           |
|      |                               |                     |           |
|      |                               |                     |           |
|      |                               |                     |           |
|      |                               |                     |           |
|      |                               |                     |           |
|      |                               |                     |           |
|      |                               |                     |           |
|      |                               |                     |           |
|      |                               |                     |           |
|      |                               |                     |           |

Reassembly Procedure

Reverse the disassembly procedure. Use care to replace the dipper and connecting rod cap exactly as they came off. A new gasket may be needed between the base and crankcase.

GENERAL STUDY QUESTIONS

Study the splash oil system and then answer the following questions.

1. Is the dipper on "your" engine case as a part of the connecting rod cap or is it a separate part?

2. If an engine is operating at 4000 r.p.m., how many times a minute will the dipper splash into the oil reservoir?

3. Would a drop in crankcase oil level affect the lubrication within the crankcase? Explain.

## Unit 6

### COOLING SYSTEMS

In internal combustion engines, the temperature of combustion often reaches over 4000° F., a temperature well beyond the melting point of the engine parts. This intense heat cannot be allowed to build up. A carefully engineered cooling system is, therefore, a part of every engine. A cooling system must maintain a good engine operating temperature without allowing destructive heat to build up and cause engine part failure.

The cooling system does not, of course, have to dispose of all the heat produced by combustion. A good portion of the heat energy is converted into mechanical energy by the engine; the more, the better for engine efficiency. Some heat is lost in the form of hot exhaust gases. The cooling system, however, must dissipate about one-third of the heat energy caused by combustion.

Engines are either air-cooled or water-cooled; both systems are in common use. Generally, air-cooled engines are used to power portable machinery, lawnmowers, garden tractors, chain saws, etc. As a rule, the air-cooled system is lighter in weight and simpler; hence, its popularity for portable equipment.

The water-cooled engine is often used for permanent installation or stationary power plants. Most automobile engines are water-cooled, as are all outboard motors.

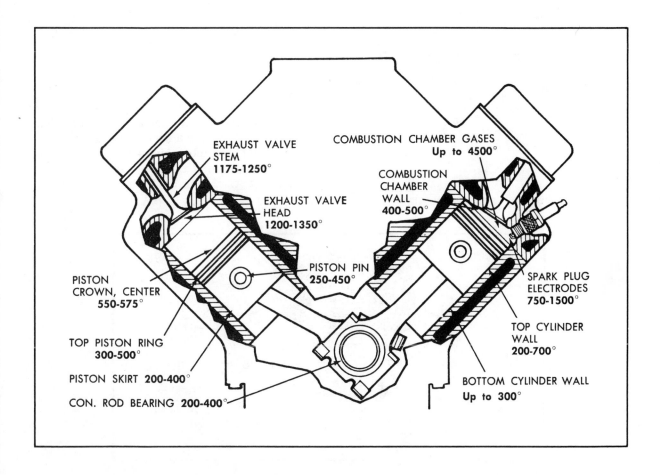

Fig. 6-1 Approximate Engine Operating Temperatures.

## AIR COOLING SYSTEM

The air-cooling system consists of (1) heat radiating fins, (2) flywheel blower, and (3) shrouds for channeling the air.

Heat radiating fins are located on the cylinder head and cylinder because the greatest concentration of heat is in this area. The fins increase the heat radiating surface of these parts allowing the heat to be carried away more quickly.

The flywheel blower consists of air vanes cast as a part of the flywheel. As the flywheel revolves, these vanes blow cool air across the fins, carrying away the heated air and replacing it with cool air.

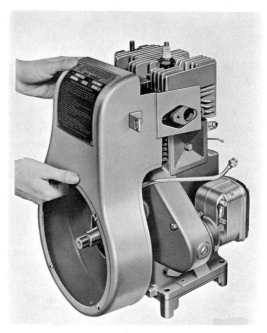

Fig. 6-3 The Air Shroud is an Important Part of the Air-cooled Engine.

Fig. 6-2 Typical Air-cooled Engine.

The shrouds direct the path of the cool air to the areas that demand cooling. The shroud may look like a decorative cover serving no real purpose but this is not true. Shrouds must be in place if the cooling system is to operate at its maximum efficiency.

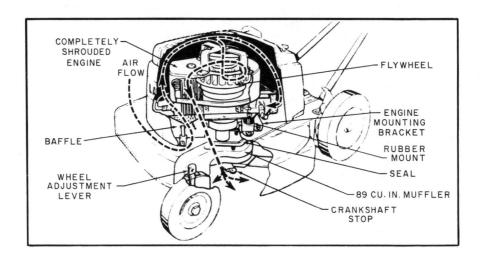

Fig. 6-4 The Path of Air Flow on Certain Lawn-Boy Engines.

## CARE OF THE AIR-COOLING SYSTEM

The air-cooling system is almost foolproof, but not infallible. Several points should be considered. Heat radiating fins are thin and often fragile, especially on aluminum engines. If, through carelessness, they are broken off, a part of the cooling system is gone. Besides losing some cooling capacity, hot spots may develop, warping the damaged area. Also, it is easy for grass, and oil to accumulate between the fins. As an accumulation builds up, the cooling system's efficiency goes down. Keep the radiating fins clean.

The flywheel vanes should not be chipped or broken. Besides reducing the cooling capacity of the engine, such damage may destroy the balance of the flywheel. An unbalanced flywheel will cause vibration and more than the normal amount of wear on engine parts.

## WATER COOLING SYSTEM

Many small engines are water-cooled as are most larger engines. Such engines have an enclosed water jacket around the cylinder walls and cylinder head. Cool water is circulated through this jacket, picking up the heat and carrying it away.

Fig. 6-5 Cross-section Showing Water Passages in Head and Block.

The basic parts of a water-cooling system such as is commonly found on stationary small gas engines or an automobile engine are: radiator, fan, thermostat, water pump, hoses, and water jacket.

The water pump circulates the water throughout the entire cooling system. The hot water from the combustion area is carried from the engine proper to the radiator. In the radiator, many small tubes and radiating fins dissipate the heat into the atmosphere. A fan blows cooling air over the radiating fins. From the bottom of the radiator the cool water is returned to the engine.

Engines are designed to operate with a water temperature of between 160° to 180° F. To maintain the correct water temperature a thermostat is used in the cooling system. When the temperature is below the thermostat setting, the thermostat remains closed and the cooling water circulates only through the engine. However, as the heat builds up to the thermostat setting, the thermostat opens and the cooling water moves throughout the entire system.

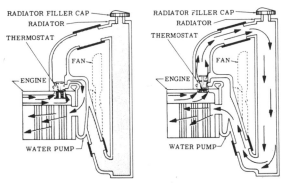

Fig. 6-6 Thermostat Closed: Water Recirculated through Engine Only. Thermostat Open: Water Circulated through Both Engine and Radiator.

## WATER COOLING THE OUTBOARD ENGINE

Cooling the outboard engine with water is a simpler process because there is an inexhaustible supply of cool water present where the engine operates. Outboards pump water from the source through the engine's water jacket and then discharge the water back into the source.

The water pump on outboards is located in the lower unit. It is driven by the main driveshaft or the propeller shaft. The cool water is pumped up copper tube passages to the water jacket. After the cooling water picks up heat, it is discharged into the exhaust area of the lower unit and out of the engine.

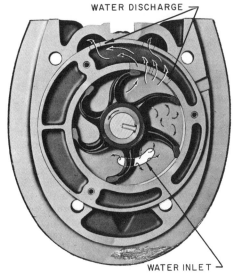

Fig. 6-7 An Impeller Water Pump with the Cover Removed to Show the Impeller.

Several types of water pumps are used on outboard motors: Plunger Type Pumps, Eccentric Rotor Pumps, Impeller Pumps, and others.

Many outboard motors, especially the recent, large horsepower models, are equipped with a thermostatically controlled cooling

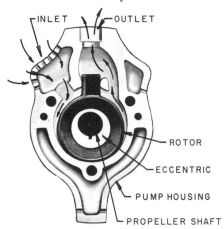

Fig. 6-8 An Eccentric Rotor Water Pump with the Cover Removed to Show the Eccentric and Rotor.

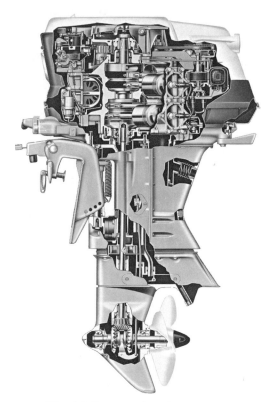

Fig. 6-9 Cutaway of an Outboard Motor.

system. The temperature of the water circulating through the water jacket is maintained at about 150° F.

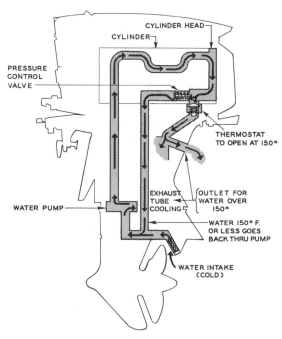

Fig. 6-10 Thermostat Controlled Cooling System used on Outboard Engines.

## GENERAL STUDY QUESTIONS

1. How high can the temperature of combustion reach?

2. Look up the melting points of aluminum and iron.

3. Does the cooling system remove all the heat of combustion? Explain.

4. Why are air-cooling systems often used for "portable" equipment?

5. What are the main parts of the air-cooling system?

6. Why are cylinders and cylinder heads equipped with fins instead of being cast with a smooth surface?

7. What are the main parts of the water-cooling system?

8. What is the function of the thermostat?

9. What are several types of water pumps used on outboard motors?

## CLASS DISCUSSION TOPICS

● Discuss how heat can damage engine parts.

● Discuss the path of heat flow from the inside of the engine to the outside.

● Discuss the advantage of the air-cooled engine.

● Discuss the advantages of the water-cooled engine.

● Discuss why it is best for the engine to operate at a constant temperature.

## CLASS DEMONSTRATION TOPICS

▶ Trace the air flow through an air-cooled engine.

▶ Trace the water flow through an outboard engine.

▶ Disassemble various types of water pumps; show their operation and construction.

▶ Show how the air-cooling system can be damaged.

Laboratory Experience 13

WATER JACKET OF OUTBOARD MOTOR

OBJECTIVES

◗ To study the construction of the water jacket.

◗ To trace the path of cooling water through the engine.

REFERENCE

● Review Pages 77-80

INTRODUCTION

The water jacket is constructed around the upper cylinder and head, the area of greatest heat concentration. Cooling water is pumped through the system, picking up heat, as it passes along. Water jackets are relatively trouble free; however, damaging deposits can build up over a period of time. Salt corrosion, scale, lime, silt, etc. can restrict the flow of water and heat transfer. Water jackets are found on all outboard motors and on the vast majority of automobile engines.

STUDENT ASSIGNMENT

You are to disassemble and inspect the water jacket of an outboard engine. Determine the path of the cooling water within the jacket. Use a small horsepower outboard engine if possible. It is essential that you record your work in the work record box on the following page as you complete each step of the disassembly procedure.

Disassembly Procedure

Your instructor may supplement or revise specific steps of the procedure which follows since there are many makes of outboards. The following procedure is your general guide:

1. Remove shrouds.

2. Remove spark plugs.

3. Remove the machine screws in the top of the water jacket.

4. Remove the top of the water jacket. (Note: the gasket between the engine block and the top of the water jacket is usually glued on and may be difficult to remove.)

5. Examine the construction of the water jacket. Note how deep it is and trace the path of the water flow.

## WORK RECORD BOX

| Part | Disassembly (nuts, bolts, etc.) | Operation performed | Tool used |
|------|--------------------------------|---------------------|-----------|
|      |                                |                     |           |
|      |                                |                     |           |
|      |                                |                     |           |
|      |                                |                     |           |
|      |                                |                     |           |
|      |                                |                     |           |
|      |                                |                     |           |
|      |                                |                     |           |
|      |                                |                     |           |
|      |                                |                     |           |

Reassembly Procedure

Reverse the disassembly procedure. A new gasket has to be installed if the engine is to be operated. All metal gasket surfaces must be absolutely clean before a new gasket is installed.

GENERAL STUDY QUESTIONS

Study the water jacket and then answer the following questions.

1. What can harm or damage the water jacket?

2. What would happen if an outboard engine were operated out of water?

3. What are the basic parts of the water-cooled engine?

Laboratory Experience 14
## WATER PUMP OF OUTBOARD MOTORS

## OBJECTIVES

- To study the construction of the water pump.
- To understand the water pump's operation.
- To trace the path of water through the pump.

## REFERENCE

- Review Pages 77-80

## INTRODUCTION

There are several different types of water pumps used on outboard motors. Among the more common are (1) eccentric rotor type, (2) impeller type, and (3) plunger type. The location of water pumps varies a great deal from manufacturer to manufacturer and in fact from model to model. However, the pump is always in the lower unit area. It is driven by the propeller shaft or the main drive shaft. The water intake may also be in a number of places on the underwater area of the lower unit. The water pump operates continually, providing a supply of cool water for the engine.

## STUDENT ASSIGNMENT

You are to disassemble and inspect the water pump of an outboard engine. There is such a wide variance in the location and disassembly procedure that it is not practical to include a general disassembly procedure in this assignment. Therefore, your instructor will give you instructions on just what parts to remove and how to do the work. It is essential that you record your work in the work record box on the following page as you complete each step of your disassembly.

## GENERAL STUDY QUESTIONS

Study the water pump and answer the following questions.

1. What type of water pump does "your" engine have?

2. What drives the water pump?

3. Describe the location of the water intake.

4. Is "your" engine's cooling system thermostatically controlled?

5. Why is it important to check to be sure the engine is pumping water after you start it?

WORK RECORD BOX

| Part | Disassembly (nuts, bolts, etc.) | Operation performed | Tool used |
|------|--------------------------------|---------------------|-----------|
|      |                                |                     |           |
|      |                                |                     |           |
|      |                                |                     |           |
|      |                                |                     |           |
|      |                                |                     |           |
|      |                                |                     |           |
|      |                                |                     |           |
|      |                                |                     |           |
|      |                                |                     |           |
|      |                                |                     |           |
|      |                                |                     |           |

Laboratory Experience 15

AIR COOLING SYSTEM

## OBJECTIVES

> To study the basic parts of the air cooling system.

> To trace the path of cooling air through the engine.

## REFERENCE

● Review Pages 77-80

## INTRODUCTION

The air cooling system is simpler in construction and maintenance than the water cooling system. No supply of water is necessary, just the air around the engine. The basic parts are:

1. the heat radiating fins

2. the flywheel vanes

3. the air shroud

The heat radiating fins around the upper cylinder provide a large radiating surface to liberate heat. The vanes on the flywheel provide a blast of cooling air. The air shroud channels the air from the flywheel to and across the radiating fins.

The main consideration is to keep the system parts clean, particularly the heat radiating fins. Dust, dirt, oil, grass clippings, etc. can build up in a short time. Any buildup of foreign matter reduces the engine's cooling capacity. Actual damage or breakage of parts is possible through neglect or careless attempts at engine repair.

## STUDENT ASSIGNMENT

You are to disassemble and inspect the basic parts of the air cooling system. Inspect the parts for damage and cleanliness. It is essential that you record your work in the work record box on the following page as you complete each step of the disassembly procedure.

If you have proper ventilation and facilities for running the engine, you can demonstrate the air flow through the system before the disassembly and inspection portion of this assignment. Attach a thin, 5-inch strip of tissue (one that responds to light movement of air currents) to the end of a pencil. Start the engine and run it at normal operating speed. Bring the paper strip close to the various areas of the heat radiating fins and note its behavior. Then bring it close to the flywheel blower and note the movement of the strip. A flow of air currents should be clearly demonstrated. Be careful not to get too close to moving parts of the engine or to foul the system with bits of tissue.

## Disassembly Procedure

1. Remove the air shroud, grass screen, recoil starter, etc.

2. Examine the air shroud for cleanliness and any possible damage.

3. Examine the flywheel air vanes for cleanliness and any possible damage.

4. Examine the heat radiating fins for cleanliness and any possible damage.

### WORK RECORD BOX

| Part | Disassembly (nuts, bolts, etc.) | Operation performed | Tool used |
|------|------|------|------|
|  |  |  |  |
|  |  |  |  |
|  |  |  |  |
|  |  |  |  |
|  |  |  |  |
|  |  |  |  |
|  |  |  |  |
|  |  |  |  |

## Reassembly Procedure

Reverse the disassembly procedure.

## GENERAL STUDY QUESTIONS

Study the air cooling system and answer the following questions.

1. Trace the air flow through the engine. Make a small sketch.

2. Explain the function of each of the three main parts of the air cooling system.

3. Explain how you would clean heat radiating fins.

4. How often should the system be cleaned?

5. How can the system be damaged?

## IGNITION SYSTEMS

Small gasoline engines normally use a magneto for supplying the ignition spark. A magneto is a self-contained unit that produces the spark for ignition; no outside source of electricity is necessary. It is a simple and very reliable ignition system. Since most small gas engines do not have electric starters, lighting systems, radios and other electrical accessories, a storage battery is not necessary. The magneto is, therefore, ideally suited for the small gasoline engine.

The basic parts of the magneto ignition system are: (1) permanent magnets, (2) high tension coil (primary and secondary), (3) laminated iron core, (4) breaker points, (5) breaker cam, (6) condenser, (7) spark plug cable, and (8) spark plug. Before trying to understand how these parts work together, it will be well to review some essentials of electricity and magnetism and also to study the construction and function of each individual part.

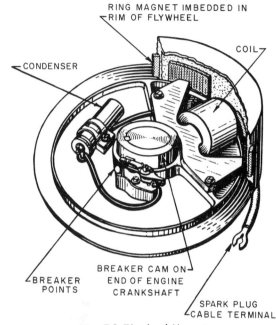

Fig. 7-1 Flywheel Magneto.

## ELECTRON THEORY

All matter is composed of atoms and, of course, these atoms are infinitesimally small. The atom, itself, is composed of electrons, protons, and neutrons. The number and arrangement of these particles determines the type of atom: hydrogen, oxygen, carbon, iron, lead, copper, or any other element. Weight, color, density, and all other characteristics of an element are determined by the structure of the atom. Electrons from an atom of copper would be the same as electrons from any other element.

The electron is a very light particle that spins around the center of the atom. Electrons move in an orbit. The number of electrons orbiting around the center or nucleus of the atom varies from element to element. The electron has a negative (-) electrical charge.

The proton is a very large and heavy particle in relationship to the electron. One or more protons will form the center or nucleus

of the atom. The proton has a positive (+) electrical charge.

The neutron consists of an electron and proton bound tightly together. Neutrons are located near the center of the atom. The neutron is electrically neutral; it has no electrical charge.

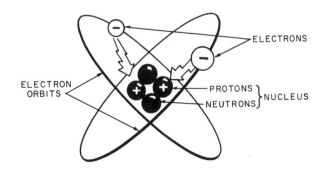

Fig. 7-2 Atomic Structure: Electron, Protron, and Neutron.

Atoms are normally electrically neutral, that is, the number of electrons and protons are the same, cancelling out each other's electrical force. Atoms "stay together" because <u>unlike</u> <u>electrical</u> <u>charges</u> <u>attract</u> <u>each</u> <u>other</u>. The electrical force of the protons holds the electrons in their orbits. <u>Like</u> <u>electrical</u> <u>charges</u> <u>repel</u> <u>each</u> <u>other</u> so negatively charged electrons will not collide with each other.

In most materials it is very difficult, if not impossible, for electrons to leave their orbit around the atom. Materials of this type are called nonconductors of electricity, or insulators. Some typical insulating materials are glass, mica, rubber, paper, etc. Electricity will not flow through these materials.

In order to have electric current, electrons must move from atom to atom. Insulators will not allow this electron movement.

However, there are quite a few substances in which it is relatively easy for an electron to jump out of its orbit and begin to orbit in an adjoining or nearby atom. Substances which permit this movement of electrons are called conductors of electricity. Everyone is familiar with such typical examples as copper, aluminum and silver.

Electron flow in a conductor takes place when there is a difference in electrical potential and there is a complete circuit or path for electron flow. Another way of stating this is that the source of electricity is short of electrons; it is positively charged and since unlike charges attract each other, electrons, being negatively charged, will move toward the positive source.

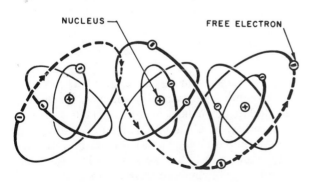

Fig. 7–3 Current: Flow of Electrons Within a Conductor.

A source of electricity can be produced or seen in three basic forms: (1) mechanical, (2) chemical, (3) static. Electricity is produced mechanically in the electrical generator which is commonly lashed to water power or steam turbines. The electricity we use in our homes and factories is produced mechanically. In the magneto, mechanical energy is used to rotate the permanent magnet. Electricity produced by chemical action is seen in the storage battery and dry cell. Static electricity can be seen in nature when lightning strikes. The lightning occurs when the air insulation breaks down and electrons are in a positive area. The lightning may be between clouds, from cloud to earth, or from earth to cloud.

## UNITS OF ELECTRICAL MEASUREMENT

There are three basic units of electrical measurement:

1. Rate of electron flow - amperes.

2. Force or pressure causing electron flow - volts.

3. Resistance to electron flow - ohms.

The <u>ampere</u> is the measurement of electrical current, the number of electrons flowing past a given point in a given length of time. If you could stand at a point on a wire and count the electrons passing by in one second and you counted 6,250,000,000,000,000,000 you would have counted one ampere of current. To help visualize amperage, think of water flowing in a pipe. A small pipe might deliver two gallons of water a minute. A larger pipe might deliver five gallons of water a minute. Electric wires are generally the same; larger wires can handle more amperage or electron flow than smaller wires.

The <u>volt</u> is the measurement of electrical pressure or the difference in electrical potential that causes electron flow in an electrical circuit. The energy source is short of electrons and the electrons in the circuit want to go to the source. The pressure to satisfy the source is called voltage. Voltage might be compared to the pressure that water in a high tank places on the pipe located at the street level. The higher the water pressure, the faster the water flow from a pipe below. Likewise, a higher voltage tends to cause greater flow of electrons.

The <u>ohm</u> is the unit of electrical resistance. Every substance puts up some resistance to the movement of electrons. Insulators such as porcelain, oils, mica, glass, etc. put up a tremendous resistance to electron flow. Conductors such as copper, aluminum, and silver put up very little resistance to electron flow. Even though conductors readily permit the flow of electric current they do tend to put up some resistance. In the water pipe example, this resistance might be seen as the surface drag by the sides of the pipe, or scale and rust in the pipe. Using a larger pipe, or, electrically, a larger wire, is one way of reducing resistance.

## OHM'S LAW

In every example of electricity flowing in an electrical circuit, amperes, volts, and ohms each play their part; they are related to each other. This relationship is stated in Ohm's Law.

$$\text{Amperes (rate)} = \frac{\text{volts (potential)}}{\text{ohms (resistance)}}$$

The formula is usually abbreviated to:

$$I = \frac{E}{R}$$

For example, if the voltage were 6, and the resistance 12 ohms, calculate the current.

$$I = \frac{E}{R} \quad I = \frac{6}{12} \quad I = .5 \text{ amperes}$$

Of course, the formula can be written to find the resistance or the voltage.

$$R = \frac{E}{I} \quad E = IR$$

## MAGNETISM

No doubt everyone has played with a magnet at sometime, watched it pick up steel objects and watched it attract or repel another magnet. These effects are curious and still not entirely explained, but scientists generally agree on the molecular theory of magnetism. Molecules are the smallest divisions of substance that are still recognizable as that substance. Several different atoms may make up one molecule. For example, a molecule of iron oxide will contain atoms of iron and oxygen. In many substances the atoms in the molecules are

more positive at one spot and more negative at another spot. This is termed a north pole and a south pole. Usually the poles of adjoining molecules are arranged in a random pattern and there is no magnetic force since their effects cancel one another. However, in some substances, such as iron, nickle, and cobalt, the molecules are able to align themselves so that all north poles point in one direction and all south poles point in the opposite direction. The small magnetic forces of many tiny molecules combine to make a noticeable magnetic force. In magnets, like poles repel each other, unlike poles attract each other, just as like and unlike electrical charges react. Electricity and magnetism are very closely tied together.

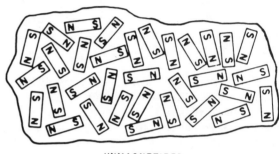

**UNMAGNETIZED**

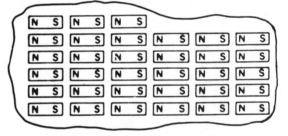

**MAGNETIZED**

Fig. 7-4 In an Unmagnetized Bar the Molecules Are in a Random Pattern. In a Magnetized Bar the Molecules Align Their Atomic Poles.

Some substances can retain their molecular alignment permanently and are, therefore, classed as permanent magnets. Hard steel has this ability. A piece of soft iron such as a nail can attain the molecular alignment of a magnet only when it is in a magnetic field. As soon as soft iron is removed from the magnetic field, its molecules disarrange themselves and the magnetism is lost.

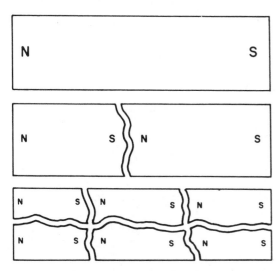

Fig. 7-5 A Magnetic Field Surrounds Every Magnet. Like Poles Repel Each Other; Unlike Poles Attract Each Other.

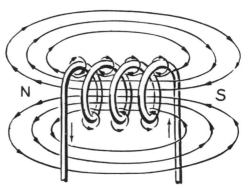

Fig. 7-7 When Electricity Flows Through a Coil of Wire, a Magnetic Field is Set Up around the Coil.

More than 100 years ago Michael Faraday discovered that magnetism could produce electricity. Magnetos used on gasoline engines use this discovery: magnetism producing electricity. Faraday found that if a magnet is moved past a wire, electrical current will start through the wire. If the magnet is stopped near the wire, the current will stop. Electricity will flow only when the magnetic field or magnetic lines of force are being cut by the wire.

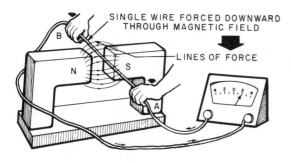

Fig. 7-6 Current Flows in the Wire As It Moves Down Through the Magnetic Field.

Another principle that the magneto uses is that when electrons flow through a coil of wire, a magnetic field is set up around the coil. The coil itself becomes a magnet. Therefore, when electrons flow through the coils in a magneto, a magnetic field is set up.

The principle of the transformer and induced voltage is also used in the magneto. In a transformer there is a primary coil and a secondary coil wound on top of the primary; the two are insulated from each other. These coils are wound on a soft iron core. When alternating current passes through the primary coil there is an alternating magnetic field set up in the iron core. The magnetic lines of force cut the secondary coil and induce an alternating voltage within the coil. The voltage produced depends on the ratio of windings in the primary coil and secondary coil. If there are more windings in the secondary than the primary, the secondary voltage will be higher, a step-up transformer. If there are more windings in the primary than the secondary, the secondary voltage will be smaller, a step-down transformer. Although the magneto does not operate on alternating current, it does use the principle of the step-up transformer.

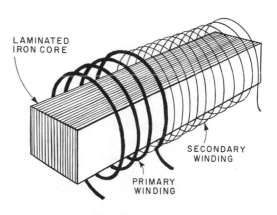

Fig. 7-8 A Simple Transformer.

In a small gasoline engine magneto, there is a magnetic field which induces current in the primary coil, thus setting up a magnetic field around both the primary and secondary coils. At the point of maximum current, the circuit is broken in the primary. Electrons can no longer flow; therefore, the magnetic field collapses. This rapidly collapsing magnetic field induces a very high voltage, igniting the fuel mixture.

## BASIC MAGNETO PARTS

Before studying in detail how the magneto operates, it would be well to examine the basic parts.

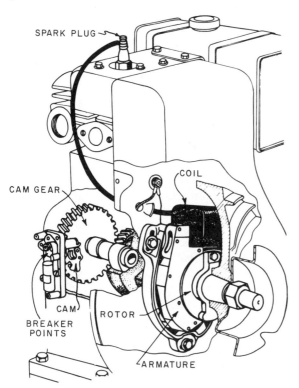

Fig. 7-9 The Basic Parts of a Briggs-Stratton Magneto Ignition System.

### PERMANENT MAGNETS

Permanent magnets are usually made of an alloy called Alnico, a combination of aluminum, nickle and cobalt. This magnet is quite strong and will retain its magnetism for a very long time. On a flywheel magneto the magnet is cast into the flywheel and cannot be removed. The other magneto parts often are mounted on a fixed plate underneath the flywheel. The magnet, therefore, revolves around the other parts of the magneto. Sometimes the other magneto parts are mounted near the outside rim of the flywheel and the permanent magnets pass by each revolution.

Rotor type permanent magnets are also in use. With this type of construction the permanent magnet rotor may be mounted on the end of the crankshaft or the rotor may be geared to the crankshaft. The rotor lies "within" the other magneto parts. Care should be taken not to drop or pound the magnet as this will cause it to lose some of its magnetism.

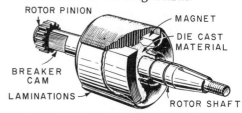

Fig. 7-10 Rotor Type Permanent Magneto.

### HIGH TENSION COIL
### (PRIMARY AND SECONDARY WINDINGS)

The primary winding of wire consists of about 200 turns of a heavy wire (about 18 gage) wrapped around a laminated iron core. The primary coil is in the electrical circuit containing the breaker points and condenser. When a magnet is brought near this coil and iron core, magnetic lines of force cut the coil and electrical current is produced. Normally this current flows from the coil, through the closed breaker points and into ground, a complete circuit.

The secondary winding of wire consists of about 20,000 turns of a very fine wire wrapped around the primary coil. The secondary coil is in the electrical circuit containing the spark plug. When current flows in the primary, a magnetic field gradually expands around both coils, but voltages produced in the secondary are quite small. However, when the breaker points open, the circuit is broken, electricity stops flowing and the magnetic field suddenly collapses. The suddenly collapsing magnetic field induces very high voltage in the secondary coil, enough to jump the spark gap in the spark plug.

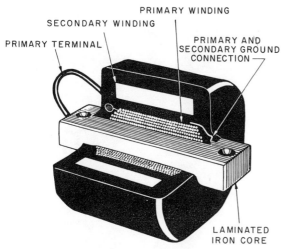

Fig. 7-11 Construction of A High Tension Magneto Ignition System.

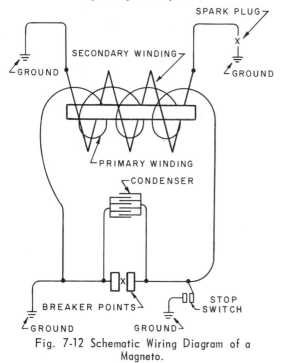

Fig. 7-12 Schematic Wiring Diagram of a Magneto.

## LAMINATED IRON CORE

The laminated iron core is made of many strips of soft iron fastened tightly together. The soft iron core helps to strengthen the magnetic field around the primary and secondary coils, but the core will not retain the magnetism and become permanently magnetized. The purpose of using many strips instead of a solid core is to reduce eddy currents which create heat in the core. The general shape of the laminated core may vary from magneto to magneto but its function remains the same.

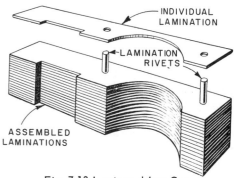

Fig. 7-13 Laminated Iron Core.

## BREAKER POINTS

The breaker points are made of tungsten and mounted on brackets. The two points are normally closed or touching each other, providing a path for electron flow. However, just before the spark is desired, the breaker points are opened, breaking the electrical circuit. Breaker points open and close anywhere from 800 times per minute to 4500 or more times per minute, depending on the engine speed.

When the breaker points are open they are usually separated by .020 of an inch; the exact opening varies from magneto to magneto. This separation is critical to the function of the magneto; therefore, the breaker point gap must be adjusted correctly.

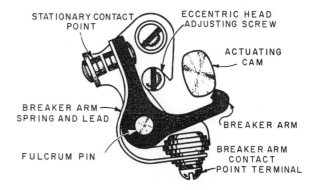

Fig. 7-14 Breaker Point Assembly.

## BREAKER CAM

The breaker cam actuates the breaker points. One bracket of the breaker assembly rides on this cam. As the cam rotates, it opens and closes the breaker points.

On most two-cycle engines this cam is mounted on the crankshaft and opens the normally closed breaker points once each revolution. On most four-cycle engines, it is mounted to operate from the camshaft which is turning at one-half crankshaft speed. By mounting the breaker points here, they open once every two revolutions of the crankshaft, thereby providing a spark for the power stroke but none for the exhaust stroke.

The shape of the cam depends on the number of cylinders and the design of the magneto.

Fig. 7-15 Common Breaker Cam Shapes.

## CONDENSER

The condenser acts as an electrical storage tank in the primary circuit. When the breaker points open quickly, the electrons tend to keep flowing and, if no condenser were present, a spark might actually jump across the breaker points. If this happened, the breaker points would soon burn up, not to mention weakening effect on the voltage produced by the magneto secondary coil. The condenser provides an electrical storage tank for this last surge

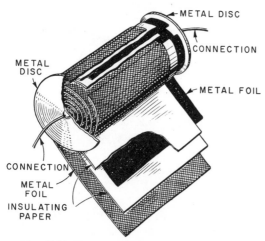

Fig. 7-16 Cutaway Showing the Construction of a Condenser.

Fig. 7-17 Typical Condensers.

of electron flow. The condenser can be easily located because it usually looks like a miniature tin can.

## SPARK PLUG CABLE

The spark plug cable connects the secondary coil and the spark plug, providing a path for the high-tension voltage. This part is often referred to as the high-tension lead.

## SPARK PLUG

The spark plug is a vital part of the ignition system. In this part the resulting work of the magneto parts is seen. Basically, the spark plug consists of a shell, ceramic insulator, center electrode and ground electrode. The two electrodes are separated by a gap of about .030 of an inch. The path of electricity is down the center electrode, across the air gap, to the ground electrode. Of course, the voltage must jump the air gap. When a high-tension voltage of about 20,000 volts is reached, a spark will jump between the electrodes. This spark ignites the fuel mixture within the combustion chamber.

## THE COMPLETE MAGNETO CYCLE

Now let us "walk through" one revolution of the crankshaft and observe the flywheel magneto operation. When the permanent magnet is far away from the high-tension coil, it has no effect on the coil. But as the permanent magnet comes closer and closer, the primary coil "feels" the increasing magnetic field; the coil is being cut by magnetic lines of force, and, therefore, electrons flow in the primary coil. This current passes through the breaker points and into the ground. When the permanent magnet is just about opposite the high-tension coil the magnetic field around both coils is reaching its peak. Also, the piston is reaching the top of its stroke, compressing the fuel mixture.

The position of the permanent magnet is now causing the polarity of the laminated iron core and the coils to reverse direction. The reversing of direction is momentarily choked or held back by the coil. Then the breaker points open, interrupting the current flow and allowing the reversal and subsequent rapid collapse of the intense magnetic field that had been built up around the primary and secondary coils. Magnetic lines of force are cutting coils very rapidly, and high voltages are induced in the coils. In the secondary coil the voltage may reach 18,000 to 20,000 volts, enough to jump across the spark gap in the spark plug. This spark ignites the fuel mixture and the piston is forced down the cylinder.

## SPARK ADVANCE

When fuel burns in the combustion chamber, it does not explode and exert all of its power instantaneously. A very short period of time is required for the fuel to ignite and reach its full power. True, this time is very short but in an engine operating at high speeds this small time lag is important.

For example, if we waited until the piston reached dead center before igniting the mixture, the piston would already be started back down the cylinder before the full force of the burning fuel is reached. This results in loss of power.

Therefore, it is necessary to ignite the fuel slightly before the piston reaches the top of its stroke to realize the full force of combustion. Causing the spark to occur earlier in the engine cycle is called spark advance.

The spark is advanced more and more as the engine speed increases, because there is less time for combustion to take place. For example, in a four-cycle engine operating at 2,000 r.p.m., each power stroke takes about 1/64 of a second, but if the speed is increased to 4,000 r.p.m., each power stroke will take only 1/128 of a second. If the speed is doubled, there is only one-half as much time for combustion to take place. Also, high speeds give the engine higher compression and more explosive mixture. At high speeds the spark jumps the spark gap before the piston reaches the top of its stroke.

At slow speeds the spark is retarded and occurs later in the cycle, slightly before the piston reaches top dead center or sometimes at top dead center. At slow speeds there is more time for combustion to take place. Also, compression is lower and not as much explosive mixture is drawn into the combustion chamber.

Regulating spark advance is done by controlling the time that the breaker points open. Advancing the spark can be done automatically or manually; both methods are commonly used on small gasoline engines.

## MANUAL SPARK ADVANCE

Manual spark advance is usually accomplished by loosening the breaker point assembly and rotating it slightly to an advanced position. It is then locked in its new position.

Many outboard motors have a type of manual spark advance although it is generally referred to by manufacturers as a "spark-gas" synchronization system. The magneto plate, on which the breaker points are mounted, is located underneath the flywheel. This plate can be rotated through about 25°. The breaker cam is securely mounted on the crankshaft; its relative position cannot be changed. Spark advance is obtained by moving the magneto plate so the breaker points will be opened earlier in the cycle. The throttle and magneto plates are linked together so that opening the throttle also advances the spark. At full throttle the spark is fully advanced. At idling speeds the throttle is closed and the magneto plate is positioned for minimum spark advance.

## AUTOMATIC SPARK ADVANCE

Automatic spark advance is usually accomplished by a centrifugal mechanism which is capable of changing the relative position of the breaker cam and the breaker points. Here the breaker cam can be rotated through a small distance on its shaft, about 25°. A spring holds the cam in the retarded position at idling and slow speeds but as the engine speed increases, centrifugal force throws the mechanism's hinged weights outward. This outward motion overcomes the spring's tension and this motion is used to rotate the cam to a more advanced position. At full speed the cam has been rotated its full limit for maximum spark advance.

Some engines, especially larger types, also have a vacuum advance mechanism working with a centrifugal mechanism to provide more accurate spark advance, especially at slow speeds. Automatic spark advance can also be used to move the breaker point assembly to secure the proper advance.

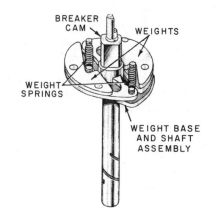

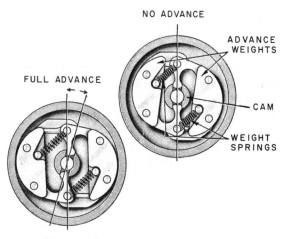

Fig. 7-19 Automatic Spark Advance Mechanism Changes the Breaker Cam's Position in Relation to the Points.

## IMPULSE COUPLING

When an engine is started by hand, it is turned over slowly. Since the voltages produced by the magneto depend upon the speed that magnetic lines of force cut the primary coil, the voltages produced for starting can be quite low, resulting in a weak spark.

Some engines are equipped with an impulse coupling device to supply higher voltages and a hotter spark for slow starting speeds. Using a tight spring and retractable pawls, the rotation of the magneto's magnetic rotor can be stopped for all but the last few degrees of its revolution. During the last few degrees of the revolution the pawl retracts, allowing the spring to snap the magnetic rotor past the firing position at a very high speed. A high voltage can be produced because magnetic lines of force are cutting the primary coil rapidly.

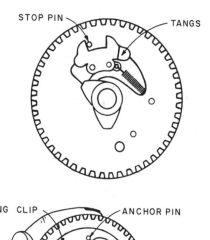

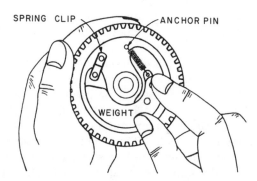

Fig. 7-18 Spark Advance Mechanism with Breaker Cam and Weight Mounted on the Camshaft Gear.

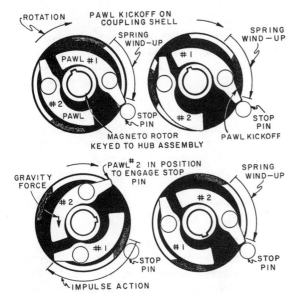

Fig. 7-20 Sequence of Operation for Impulse Coupling for 180° Spark Magneto.

## MAGNETO IGNITION FOR MULTI-CYLINDER ENGINES

Magnetos are often used for multi-cylinder engines. However, having more than one cylinder to supply with a spark does present a problem. Two solutions to this problem are in common use today.

Two-, three- and four-cylinder engines can have magneto ignition by simply installing a separate magneto for each cylinder. This method is commonly used with outboard engines using a flywheel magneto. Instead of mounting just one magneto on the armature plate under the flywheel, a magneto is installed for each cylinder. The breaker points of each magneto

ride on the common cam. In two-cylinder engines the magnetos would be 180° apart, three-cylinder engines 120° apart, and four-cylinder engines 90° apart. Each magneto functions separately to supply its cylinder with a spark.

Another solution is to use a distributor and two-pole or four-pole magnetic rotor. Only one complete magneto is used even though the engine may have two or four cylinders. In the case of a two-pole rotor used on a two-cylinder engine, the magneto can produce two sparks every revolution of the magnetic rotor, one every 180° rotation. A two-lobed cam is used to open the breaker points twice each rotor revolution. The distributor rotor channels the high-tension voltage to the correct spark plug.

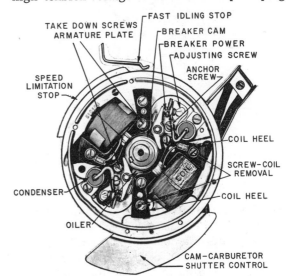

Fig. 7-21 Two Complete Magnetos are Installed on this Armature Plate.

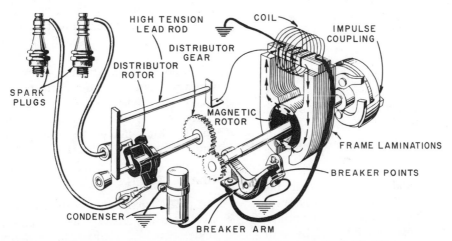

Fig. 7-22 Diagram of Rotating Magnet Magneto with Jump-Spark Distributor.

## ENGINE TIMING

The spark must jump the spark gap at exactly the right time, just before the piston reaches top dead center. In many engines, the breaker cam is driven by the camshaft, therefore, the gear on the crankshaft and the camshaft gear must be assembled correctly. These two gears are marked in some manner, usually punch marks, so the repairman can easily make the correct assembly. Incorrect alignment of the gears may cause poor operation or the engine may not operate at all.

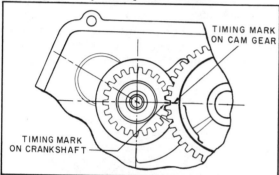

Fig. 7-23 Timing Marks on Crankshaft Gear and Cam Gear Must Be Aligned Correctly.

## SOLID STATE IGNITION

Solid state ignition refers to the fact that solid state electronic parts, namely transistors, replace the breaker points. The breaker points in a conventional ignition system can be a source of trouble. Sometimes the systems are called Capacitor Discharge Systems, Breakerless Ignition, or Transistorized Ignition. These systems may be used with just a conventional flywheel magnet as the source of the magnetic force. They may be used with a generator or an alternator battery system.

The main components of the solid state ignition system are a generator or alternator coil, trigger module, ignition coil assembly, and special flywheel with trigger projection. The system has a conventional spark plug and lead.

The trigger module contains transistor diodes which rectify the alternating current, changing it into direct current. Transistors control the flow of electric current by acting somewhat like a valve. Their resistance to

flow can be changed by a small current to the transistors. In addition to the diode rectifiers, the trigger module contains a resistor, a sensing coil and magnet, and a silicon-controlled rectifier (SCR). The SCR acts as a switch.

The ignition coil contains primary and secondary windings similar to those of a conventional magneto coil plus a condenser or capacitor. Electrically speaking, capacitors and condensers are basically the same.

The operation of the solid state ignition system follows this cycle:

1. The rotating magnet on the flywheel sets up an alternating current in the alternator or generator coil. This alternating current is rectified into direct current and stored in the capacitor. The diode rectifiers permit flow in one direction only so the capacitor cannot discharge back through the diodes.

2. The magnet group passes the trigger coil, setting up a small current which triggers or gates the SCR. This gating makes the SCR conductive so that the stored voltage of the capacitor surges from capacitor through the SCR and is applied across the primary winding of the ignition coil and to the negative side of the capacitor. This instantaneous surge of energy sets up a magnetic field in the primary winding of the ignition coil. The magnetic field is also induced around the secondary coil, and voltages sufficient to jump the spark gap at the spark plug are reached.

Solid state ignition offers several advantages, such as automatic retarding of the spark at starting speeds, longer spark plug life, faster voltage rise, and a high energy spark which makes the condition of the plug and its gap less critical.

## SPARK PLUG

The spark plug is the part of the ignition system that ignites the fuel mixture. It operates under severe and varying temperature conditions and is a critical part in engine operation.

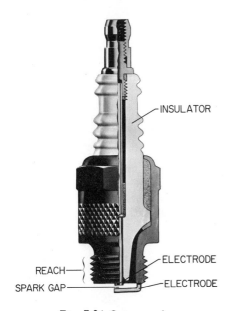

Fig. 7-24 Cutaway of a
Spark Plug.

will quickly burn up. The heat range for spark plugs depends on how fast the heat can be carried away from the electrodes. The path of heat transfer is from the electrodes to the ceramic insulator through the shell and into the cylinder head. The length of the ceramic insulator exposed to the combustion chamber determines the heat range of a spark plug. The longer this insulator, the longer the heat path, and the "hotter" the spark plug's operating temperature. Likewise, the shorter this insulator, the shorter the heat path, and the "colder" the spark plug's operating temperature.

The spark gap or distance between the electrodes must be correctly set. It is within this small space that the spark jumps and combustion begins. The gap must be large enough for sufficient fuel mixture to "get between" the electrodes but not so large as to prevent the spark from jumping across. The spark gap for various plugs ranges from about .020″ to .040″.

All spark plugs are basically the same but they do differ in these respects: (1) thread size, (2) reach, (3) heat range, (4) spark gap. There are hundreds of different types of spark plugs, each designed for the special requirements of a certain engine.

The shell of the spark plug is threaded so that it can easily be installed or removed from the cylinder head. Various spark plugs have different thread sizes. Some of the more common standard thread sizes are 7/8″, 10 mm., 14 mm., and 18 mm.

The reach of the spark plug is the distance between the gasket seat and the bottom of the spark plug shell, or roughly the length of the cut threads. The reach ranges from about 1/4″ to 3/4″. Each engine must be equipped with a spark plug of the correct reach since reach determines how far the electrodes protrude into the combustion chamber. If the reach is too small, the electrodes will find it difficult to ignite the fuel when the spark jumps. If the reach is too great, the top of the piston may strike the electrodes on its upward stroke.

The heat range of a spark plug is the range of temperature within which the spark plug is designed to operate. If a spark plug operates at too low a temperature, it will quickly foul with oil and carbon. If the spark plug operates at too high a temperature, the electrodes

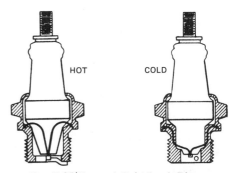

Fig. 7-25 Hot and Cold Spark Plugs.

If the spark plug is removed for cleaning, the gap should be checked and reset according to the manufacturer's specifications. A wire gage should be used.

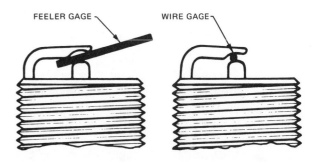

Fig. 7-26 A Plain, Flat Feeler Gage Cannot Accurately Measure the True Width of a Spark Gap.

## GENERAL STUDY QUESTIONS

1. What three particles make up the atom?

2. Explain how electrons can move in a conductor.

3. What are the three ways that electricity can be produced or seen?

4. Explain the electrical measurements: (1) amperes, (2) volts, and (3) ohms.

5. State Ohm's Law.

6. Explain how permanent and temporary magnets differ.

7. What happens when a wire is cut by magnetic lines of force?

8. What happens to a coil of wire when electric current flows through it?

9. Explain how a transformer works.

10. In a magneto, what is the source of the magnetic field?

11. What are the two parts of the high-tension coil?

12. What purpose does the laminated iron core serve?

13. What is the function of the breaker points? How are they opened?

14. What is the function of (1) the condenser? (2) the spark plug?

15. What are the two electrical circuits in the magneto?

16. Why must the spark be advanced at high speeds?

17. What is the advantage of impulse coupling?

18. Can magneto ignition be used for multicylinder engines?

19. In what four ways do spark plugs differ?

## CLASS DISCUSSION TOPICS

● Discuss atomic structure.

● Discuss how conductors and insulators differ.

● Discuss the molecular theory of magnetism.

● Discuss the advantages of magneto ignition.

● Discuss the complete magneto cycle.

## CLASS DEMONSTRATION TOPICS

▶ Demonstrate a magnetic field around a magnet using a permanent magnet, iron filings, and paper.

▶ Demonstrate current flow caused by a varying magnetic field using a galvanometer, coil of wire, and permanent magnet.

▶ Demonstrate a magnetic field around a coil of wire using a d-c source, coil of wire, iron filings, and paper.

▶ Disassemble a magneto showing the basic parts.

▶ Demonstrate how the breaker points are opened and show their separation at maximum opening (feeler gage).

Laboratory Experience 16

BASIC FLYWHEEL MAGNETO PARTS

## OBJECTIVES

▶ To study the basic parts of the magneto.

▶ To study how the parts are constructed.

▶ To study how the parts are mounted on the engine.

## REFERENCE

● Review Pages 88-99

## INTRODUCTION

The magneto ignition system is a very reliable and trouble-free system. Of course, one big advantage of the magneto is that it does not require a storage battery for a power source. The magneto provides the spark for ignition: voltages of a few hundred volts are stepped up to about 20,000 volts, enough to jump the spark gap in the spark plug.

There are seven basic parts which work together to produce the ignition spark:

1. high tension coil

2. laminated iron core

3. condenser

4. breaker points

5. permanent magnets (on flywheel)

6. spark plug lead

7. spark plug

A brief review of the complete magneto cycle might be helpful in the study of the parts. When the permanent magnet is far away from the high-tension coil it has no effect on the coil. But as the permanent magnet comes closer and closer, the primary coil "feels" the increasing magnetic field; the coil is being cut by magnetic lines of force, and, therefore, there is current in the primary coil. This current travels through the breaker points and into ground. When the permanent magnet is just about opposite the high-tension coil the magnetic field around both coils is reaching its peak. Also, the piston is reaching the top of its stroke, compressing the fuel mixture.

The position of the permanent magnet is now causing the polarity of the laminated iron core and the coils to reverse direction. The reversing of direction is momentarily choked or held back by the coil. Then the breaker points open, interrupting the current flow and allowing the reversal and subsequent rapid collapse of the intense magnetic field that had been built up around the primary and secondary coils. Magnetic lines of force are cutting coils very rapidly and high voltages are induced in the coils. In the secondary coil the voltage may reach 18,000 to 20,000 volts, enough to jump across the spark gap in the spark plug. This spark ignites the fuel mixture and the piston is forced down the cylinder.

STUDENT ASSIGNMENT

You are to disassemble the engine to expose flywheel magneto parts. Study the arrangement of the parts. Turn the engine over and observe how the breaker points are opened and closed. Remove the basic parts of the ignition system for closer inspection. It is essential that you record your work in the work record box on the following page as you complete each step of the disassembly procedure.

Disassembly Procedure

Your instructor may supplement or revise specific steps of the procedure which follows since there are many makes of engines. The following procedure is your general guide:

1. Remove spark plug lead from spark plug.

2. Remove any air shrouding, grass screens, recoil starters, etc. from the flywheel area.

3. Remove the flywheel and flywheel nut. Use a flywheel puller if one is available. If a flywheel puller is not at hand, deliver a sharp blow to the end of the crankshaft with a plastic or soft hammer.

4. Remove breaker point cover (on some engines).

5. Turn the crankshaft over and observe the opening and closing of the breaker points.

6. Remove the high-tension coil and laminated iron core.

7. Remove the condenser.

8. Remove the breaker point assembly.

9. Remove the breaker cam (on some engines).

## WORK RECORD BOX

| Part | Disassembly (nuts, bolts, etc.) | Operation performed | Tool used |
|---|---|---|---|
|  |  |  |  |
|  |  |  |  |
|  |  |  |  |
|  |  |  |  |
|  |  |  |  |
|  |  |  |  |
|  |  |  |  |
|  |  |  |  |
|  |  |  |  |
|  |  |  |  |
|  |  |  |  |

<u>Reassembly Procedure</u>

Reverse the disassembly procedure. If the engine is to be operated upon reassembly several points are very important.

1. Reinstall the breaker cam in the same way as it came off.

2. Use care with the key and the keyways, don't force.

3. Breaker points will need to be reset to manufacturer's specifications.

4. Laminated iron core must be positioned for the proper air gap between it and the flywheel magneto.

5. All connections should be checked for tightness.

## GENERAL STUDY QUESTIONS

Study the flywheel magneto system and then answer the following questions.

1. List the magneto parts in the primary circuit.

2. List the magneto parts in the secondary circuit.

3. Explain how the spark is triggered.

4. On which engine stroke is the spark provided?

5. What opens and closes the breaker points?

6. What happens to the electrical circuit when the breaker points open?

7. What happens to the magnetic field when the breaker points open?

8. What is the purpose of using a laminated iron core instead of a solid core?

9. What is the function of the condenser?

10. Discuss briefly what happens in the magneto cycle with one revolution of the crankshaft.

## ROUTINE CARE AND MAINTENANCE - AND WINTER STORAGE

A gasoline engine represents an investment in money, perhaps only fifty dollars, but possibly several hundred dollars. To safeguard this investment the engine operator must perform certain routine steps in care and maintenance. Routine care and maintenance will insure the longest life possible for engine parts and may save costly repair bills.

Certainly there are persons who provide little or no special care for their engines. For example, they may operate an engine all summer with no regard for its needs, other than gasoline. When fall comes, the engine is simply parked in the corner of the garage until the next spring.

Such engine owners are gamblers; they may get away with their neglect for one year, two years, or three years, but, on the other hand, they may soon have a depreciated, worn out engine that is still quite young. The correct care of the engine will insure many years of useful life with a minimum of repair bills.

The best source of information on engine care is the "Owner's Manual" or "Operator's Instruction Book". These books, supplied with every new engine, are prepared by the engine manufacturer in order to acquaint the engine owner or operator with that particular engine's requirements.

## ROUTINE CARE AND MAINTENANCE

Routine care and maintenance is given to an engine during the engine's normal use. It is provided to keep the engine operating at its peak efficiency and to prevent undue wear of engine parts. There are four basic points to consider: (1) oil supply, (2) cooling system, (3) spark plug, and (4) air cleaner.

### OIL SUPPLY

On a four-cycle engine, the oil supply in the crankcase should be checked daily or each time the engine is used. If the oil level has dropped below the add mark, fill the crankcase to the proper level.

Most manufacturers recommend that the oil be changed after a short period of time when breaking in a new engine. Depending on the manufacturer, this first oil change should be accomplished from 2 to 20 hours.

After the engine has had its oil changed once, it can go for a longer period of time between oil changes. Lauson engines specify changing the oil every 10 hours of operation; Briggs & Stratton, Whizzer, Kohler, and Clinton engines every 20 hours; Gravely and Wisconsin engines every 50 hours; Onan engines after 100 hours. Each manufacturer's instruction book will give the length of time between oil changes.

Remember, on two-cycle engines, oil changes are not necessary since all lubricating oil is mixed with the gasoline.

### COOLING SYSTEM

The most important consideration regarding the cooling system is to keep it clean. On air-cooled engines, clean the radiating fins, flywheel vanes, and shrouds whenever they begin to accumulate grass, dirt, etc. Do not allow deposits to build up, reducing the engine's cooling capacity. How often the cooling system is cleaned depends on the dust conditions under which the engine operates.

Use length of stiff wire to dislodge accumulated dirt around cylinder fins.
Avoid damage to fins.

Fig. 8-1 Keep Heat Radiating Fins Clean.

On a water-cooled engine, check the water level in the radiator before operating the engine. If it is low, fill it to the correct level.

In the case of an outboard motor, there is little routine care required for the cooling system. However, each time the engine is started the operator should check to see that the engine is "pumping water". This can be detected on most engines by a small amount of water coming from the "telltale holes". If the engine is not pumping water it should be stopped immediately and the source of the trouble corrected. Do not put your hand by the underwater discharge to determine if the engine is pumping water; you may be dangerously close to the propeller. If your engine's cooling system is thermostatically controlled it may take a few moments for the thermostat to open, allowing a flow of water from the engine.

## SPARK PLUGS

Spark plugs need to be cleaned and re-gapped periodically. Spark plugs are usually cleaned after 100 hours of operation, but some manufacturers recommend cleaning after as little as 50 hours. Since spark plugs operate under severe conditions, they become fouled easily. Knowing the signs of fouling can often tell about the engine's overall condition. Common problems that develop with spark plugs are carbon fouling, oil fouling, gas fouling, lead fouling, burned electrodes, chipped insulator, and splash fouling.

Normal spark plugs have light tan or gray deposits but show no more than .005″ increase in the original spark gap. These can be cleaned and reinstalled in the engine.

Worn out plugs have tan or gray colored deposits and show electrode wear of .008″ to .010″ greater than the original gap. Throw such plugs away and install new ones.

Oil fouling is indicated by wet, oily deposits. This condition is caused when oil is pumped (by the piston rings) to the combustion chamber. A hotter spark plug may help but the condition may have to be remedied by engine overhaul.

Gas fouling or fuel fouling is indicated by a sooty, black deposit on the insulator tips,

the electrodes and shell surfaces. The cause may be excessively rich fuel mixture, light loads, or long periods at idle speed.

Carbon fouling is indicated if the plug has dry, fluffy, black deposits. This condition may be caused by excessively rich fuel mixture; improper carburetor adjustment, choke partly closed, clogged air cleaner. Also, slow speeds, light loads, long periods of idling and the resulting "cool" operating temperature may cause deposits not to be burned away. A hotter spark plug may correct carbon fouling.

Lead fouling is indicated by a soft, tan, powdery deposit on the plug. These deposits of lead salts build up during low speeds and light loads. They cause no problem at low speed but at high speeds, when the plug heats up, the fouling will often cause the plug to misfire, thus limiting the engine's top performance.

Burned electrodes are indicated by thinned out, worn away electrodes. This condition is caused by the spark plug overheating. This overheating can be caused by lean fuel mixture, low octane fuel, cooling system failure, or long periods of high speed heavy load. A colder plug may correct this trouble.

Splash fouling may occur if accumulated cylinder deposits are thrown against the spark plugs. This material can be cleaned from the plug and the plug reinstalled. If spark gap tools and or pliers are not properly used, the electrode can be misshaped into a curve.

## CLEANING SPARK PLUGS

If inspection indicates that the spark plug needs cleaning it can be cleaned within a few minutes. First, wire brush the shell and threads, not the insulator and electrodes. Then wipe the plug with a rag that has been saturated with solvent. This will remove any oil film on the plug. Next, file the sparking surfaces of the electrodes with a point file. Finally, regap the electrodes, setting according to specifications. Check the gap with a wire spark gap gage. Most service stations have an abrasive blast machine that is good for cleaning around the electrodes and insulator. Do not allow any foreign material to fall into the cylinder while the spark plug is out. And

NORMAL SPARK PLUG

WORN OUT SPARK PLUG

CARBON-FOULED SPARK PLUG

CHIPPED INSULATOR ON SPARK PLUG

OVERHEATED SPARK PLUG

OIL-FOULED SPARK PLUG

SPLASH-FOULED SPARK PLUG

BENT SIDE ELECTRODE

Fig. 8-2  Normal and Damaged Spark Plugs.

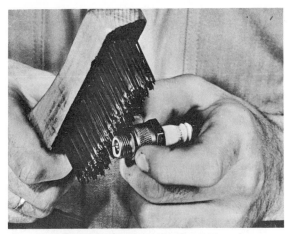

Fig. 8-3 Wire Brush the Shell and Threads.

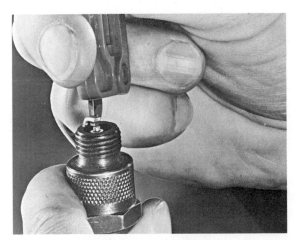

Fig. 8-5A Regap the Plug.

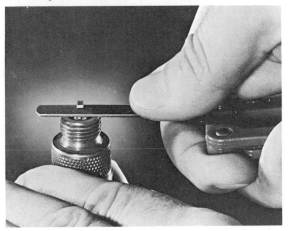

Fig. 8-4 File Electrodes.

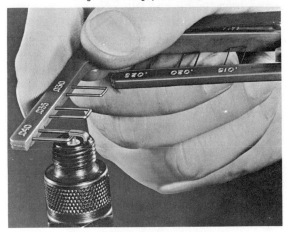

Fig. 8-5B Check the Spark Gap.

also, do not forget the spark plug gasket when you reinstall the spark plug. This copper ring provides a perfect seal.

Of course, cleaning cannot repair a broken, cracked, or otherwise severely damaged spark plug. Cleaning is designed to maintain good operation and prolong spark plug life. It is not uncommon for small engine manufacturers to recommend the installation of a new spark plug at the beginning of each season. On a single-cylinder engine, the spark plug is relatively more critical than on a six- or eight-cylinder engine.

## AIR CLEANER

The air cleaner serves the important function of cleaning the air before it is drawn through the carburetor and into the engine. Small abrasive particles of dust and dirt are trapped in the air cleaner. The air cleaner

should be periodically cleaned: just how often depends mainly on the atmosphere in which the engine is operating. In a dusty atmosphere, a garden tractor used in a dry garden for example, the air cleaner should be cleaned every few hours. Under normal conditions, the air cleaner should be cleaned every twenty-five hours or sooner.

Fig. 8-6 About This Much Abrasive Material Would Enter a Six-cylinder Engine Every Hour if the Air Cleaner Were Not Used.

Air cleaners can be classified as (A) oil-type, which includes (1) oil bath air cleaner, and (2) oil-wetted polyurethane (foam) filter element, and (B) dry-type, which includes (1) foil, moss or hair element, (2) felt or fibre hollow element, and (3) metal cartridge air cleaner.

### OIL BATH AIR CLEANER

The oil bath air cleaner carries a small amount of oil in its bowl. The level of this oil should be checked before each use of the engine. If the oil level is low, fill it to the mark, not above. Use the same type of oil as is used in the crankcase. As this cleaner works, both the oil and filter element will become dirty. To clean an oil bath air cleaner, disassemble the unit and then pour out the dirty oil. Wash the bowl, cover, and filter element in solvent; dry all parts; refill the bowl to the correct level and then reassemble the unit.

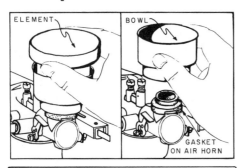

Fig. 8-7 Oil Bath Air Cleaner.

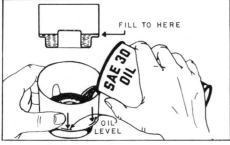

Fig. 8-8 Clean, Fill, Reassemble Air Cleaner (Foam).

### OIL-WETTED POLYURETHANE FILTER ELEMENT AIR CLEANER

This type of air cleaner is perhaps the most common. Clean it by washing the element in kerosene, liquid detergent and water, or approved solvent. Dry the element by squeezing it in a cloth or towel. Apply considerable oil to the foam and work it throughout the element. Squeeze out any excess oil and then reassemble the air cleaner.

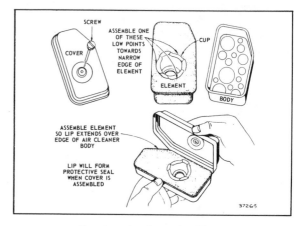

Fig. 8-9 Oil Foam Air Cleaner.

### FOIL, MOSS, OR HAIR ELEMENT AIR CLEANERS

This type of element is also washed in solvent. After washing, allow the element to dry, then return it to the air cleaner body.

### FELT OR FIBRE CYLINDER ELEMENT AIR CLEANER

These air cleaners should be cleaned by blowing compressed air through them in the opposite direction from normal flow. Dirt and dust particles will be blown out of the element.

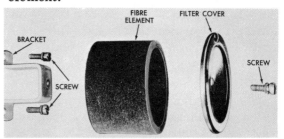

Fig. 8-10 Fibre Element Type Air Cleaner.

## METAL CARTRIDGE AIR CLEANER

These air cleaners are cleaned by tapping or shaking to dislodge dirt accumulations.

Air cleaner elements are replaceable parts. If they wear out or become excessively clogged, they should be thrown away and replaced with a new filter element. As a simple test to determine if the air cleaner is badly clogged: (1) run the engine with the air cleaner removed; (2) with engine still running, replace the air cleaner; (3) notice if the engine speed remained constant or dropped down. Any noticeable drop in speed would probably indicate that the filter element is clogged.

Periodically inspect the engine for loose parts and do not neglect lubricating the engine's associated linkages, gear reduction units, chains, shafts, wheels, or the machinery the engine powers. These requirements vary greatly from engine to engine. On an outboard engine remember that the lower unit requires special lubrication.

Fig. 8-11 Metal Cartridge
Type Air Cleaner.

## WINTER STORAGE AND CARE

Putting up an engine at the end of the season should be done carefully. Here are several items that should be accomplished:

1. Drain the fuel system.

2. Inject oil into the cylinder (upper cylinder).

3. Drain the crankcase (four cycle).

4. Clean the engine.

5. Wrap the engine in a canvas or blanket and store in a dry place.

The entire fuel system should be drained; tank, fuel lines, sediment bowl, and carburetor. Gasoline that is stored over a long period of time has a tendency to form gummy deposits. These deposits could impare and block the fuel system if gasoline stands in the system for a long time. Do not plan to hold over gasoline from season to season. Purchase a new supply when you return the engine to use.

Many manufacturers recommend that a small amount of oil be poured into the cylinder prior to storage. Remove the spark plug and pour in the oil (about a tablespoon in most cases), then turn the engine over by hand a few times to spread the oil evenly over the cylinder walls. Finally, replace the spark plug.

Some manufacturers suggest that the oil be introduced into the cylinder while the engine is running at a slow speed and just before the engine is stopped. To do this, the air cleaner is removed and a small amount of oil is poured in. The oil goes through the carburetor and on into the combustion chamber. When dark blue exhaust is produced the engine can be stopped.

The crankcase should be drained while the engine is warm so the oil will drain more readily. In some cases the crankcase is then refilled but on most engines it need not be refilled until the engine is returned to service.

Any unpainted surfaces that might rust should be lightly coated with oil before storage. Linkages should be oiled. The radiating fins and the engine in general should be cleaned. Do not put too much oil on the engine as it will collect dirt and be difficult to remove.

Finally, wrap the engine in a canvas or dry blanket and store the engine in a dry place. A garage, dry shed, or dry basement is good. Do not allow the engine to be left outside, exposed to the elements.

## RETURNING THE ENGINE TO SERVICE

Upon returning the engine to service, refill the gas tank with new gasoline. Before filling the gas tank check to see if any water has condensed in the tank. If so, drain the water completely.

Check for condensation in the crankcase and refill the crankcase with new oil of the correct type. Also, clean the air cleaner and refill the bowl with oil if it is an oil bath type.

Check the spark plug; clean and regap it. Many manufacturers of small engines recommend that a new plug be installed at the beginning of each season to insure peak performance throughout the season.

## CHECK OUT - BEFORE STARTING ENGINE

1. Gas tank full.

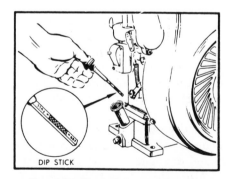

Fig. 8-12 Fill Gas Tank.

2. Oil in crankcase at correct level.

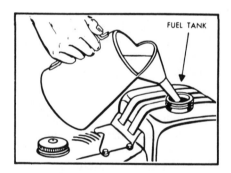

Fig. 8-13 Check Oil in Crankcase.

3. Fuel shutoff valve open.

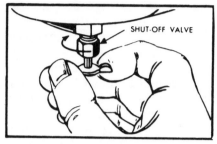

Fig. 8-14 Fuel Shut-off Valve Open.

4. Choke closed.

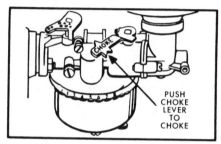

Fig. 8-15 Choke Closed.

5. Spark plug shorting bar off spark plug.

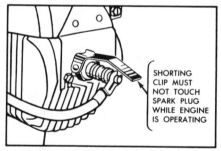

Fig. 8-16 Spark Plug Shorting Bar Off Spark Plug.

6. Air cleaner clean.

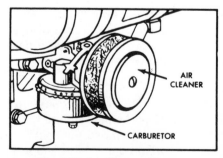

Fig. 8-17 Air Cleaner Clean.

## SAFETY WITH GASOLINE ENGINES

Gasoline engines are made to be man's friend; in work and in play. Through carelessness and disregard for simple safety rules a gasoline engine can be a dangerous killer. A list of persons injured or maimed through carelessness is a long one. Follow the safety rules listed below; a few minutes of time saved on a dangerous shortcut is never worth the price of an accident.

### SAFETY RULES

1. <u>Do not operate a gasoline engine in a closed building.</u> The exhaust of an engine contains carbon monoxide, a deadly poison that is colorless and odorless.

2. <u>Do not fill gas tank when the engine is running or hot.</u> If gasoline is spilled on a hot engine, a fire or explosion can result. If you have not accomplished your job and the engine needs more gas, stop the engine and let it and yourself cool off before refilling the tank. It is a good idea to start each job with a full gas tank.

3. <u>Do not make any adjustments to machinery being driven by an engine without first stopping the engine and removing the high-tension lead from the spark plug.</u> It is possible to accidentally turn the engine over and start it while working on machinery, especially if the engine is warm. With the spark plug cable removed the engine cannot start.

4. <u>Keep gasoline in a red gasoline can, in the garage or a tool shed, away from fire or open flame.</u> Gasoline fumes are explosive; if you are working around open gasoline, be sure that no one is smoking.

Any piece of machinery demands the use of common sense precautions. In the case of the rotary power mower and other cutting machines, keep children out of the way. Do not point the grass discharge chute toward anyone. It is possible for the blade to throw a stick, stone, or other object with great force. Naturally, keep your hands and feet away from a rotating blade.

---

## SPECIAL CONSIDERATIONS FOR OUTBOARD MOTORS

### WINTER STORAGE

Generally, winter storage for outboard motors is similar to that for other engines. One notable difference is the cooling system. Being water cooled, all water must be removed from the cooling system. If a water filled cooling system on an idle engine is exposed to freezing weather, cracked water jackets and other major damage can result.

To remove the water from the system, remove the engine from the water, set the speed control on "stop" (to prevent accidental starting), and turn the engine over several times by hand. This will allow the water to drain from the water jackets and passages.

### SALT WATER OPERATION

Although most engines are treated with anti-corrosives, not all engines are corrosive proof. If an engine normally used in salt water is not to be used for a while, its cooling system should be flushed with fresh water to prevent any possible corrosion.

### USE IN FREEZING TEMPERATURES

If the engine is being used during freezing temperatures, care must be taken not to allow the cooling water to freeze in the engine or lower unit during an idle period. Of course while the engine is operating there is no danger of freezing.

## GENERAL STUDY QUESTIONS

1. Explain what routine care and maintenance is and why it is important.

2. Where can routine care and maintenance information be found?

3. What are the four basic points to be considered in routine care and maintenance?

4. How often should the oil in the crankcase be checked?

5. How often should the oil in the crankcase be changed (Briggs-Stratton for example)?

6. What are the two types of cooling systems?

7. How often should the air-cooling system be cleaned?

8. How is an air-cooling system cleaned?

9. How do you care for a water-cooling system?

10. How often should spark plugs be cleaned?

11. What is the purpose of cleaning a spark plug?

12. List several types of spark plug fouling.

13. What are the steps in cleaning a spark plug?

14. What is the purpose of the air cleaner?

15. How often should air cleaners be cleaned?

16. What are the two basic types of air cleaners?

17. Discuss the cleaning of the several types of air cleaners.

18. List the general steps in winter storage of engines.

19. List the general steps in returning the engine to service.

20. List four safety rules for gasoline engines.

21. What special considerations must be made for outboard motors?

## CLASS DISCUSSION TOPICS

● Discuss the importance of routine care and maintenance.

● Discuss the importance of care in winter storage.

● Discuss the types of cooling systems and their maintenance.

● Discuss the types of spark plug fouling.

● Discuss the importance and function of the air cleaner.

● Discuss the various types of air cleaners and how each might be used.

● Discuss the importance of safety with gasoline and gasoline engines.

● Discuss your state laws in regard to gasoline storage.

## CLASS DEMONSTRATION TOPICS

- Demonstrate cleaning and care of cooling systems.
- Demonstrate cleaning spark plugs.
- Demonstrate cleaning air cleaners.
- Demonstrate putting an engine into winter storage.
- Demonstrate returning an engine to service after winter storage.
- Demonstrate the check-out of an engine prior to starting.
- Demonstrate routine care and maintenance on an outboard engine.
- Demonstrate routine care and maintenance on a four-stroke cycle engine.

# LABORATORY EXPERIENCES

## Laboratory Experience 17
## CLEAN AND REGAP SPARK PLUGS

**OBJECTIVE**

▶ To learn how to clean and adjust spark plugs

**REFERENCE**

● Review Pages 104-111

**INTRODUCTION**

Spark plug performance can often be improved by periodic cleaning. Also spark plug life can be lengthened. Most manufacturers of engines recommend that spark plugs be cleaned every 100 hours of engine operation. Of course, if a plug is damaged, insulator cracked, electrodes worn away, etc., cleaning cannot repair the damage.

Since spark plugs operate under severe conditions they become fouled easily. And, knowing the signs of fouling can often tell about the engine's overall condition. Common problems that develop with spark plugs are: carbon fouling, oil fouling, gas fouling, lead fouling, burned electrodes, chipped insulator, and splash fouling.

Normal spark plugs have light tan or gray deposits but show no more than .005″ increase in the original spark gap. These can be cleaned and reinstalled in the engine.

Worn out plugs have tan or gray colored deposits and show electrode wear of .008″ to .010 greater than the original gap. Throw this plug away and install a new plug.

Oil fouling is indicated by wet, oily deposits. This condition is caused when oil is pumped (by the piston rings) to the combustion chamber. A hotter spark plug may help but the condition may have to be remedied by engine overhaul.

Gas fouling or fuel fouling is indicated by a sooty, black deposit on the insulator tips, the electrodes and shell surfaces. The cause may be excessively rich fuel mixture, light loads, or long periods at idle speed.

Carbon fouling is indicated if the plug has dry, fluffy, black deposits. This condition may be caused by excessively rich fuel mixture; improper carburetor adjustment, choke partly closed, clogged air cleaner. Also slow speeds, light loads, long periods of idling and the resulting "cool" operating temperature may cause deposits not to be burned away. A hotter spark plug may correct carbon fouling.

Lead fouling is indicated by a soft, tan, powdery deposit on the plug. These deposits of lead salts build up during low speeds and light loads. They cause no problem at low speed but at high speeds, when the plug heats up, the fouling will often cause the plug to misfire, thus limiting the engine's top performance.

Burned electrodes are indicated by thinned out, worn away electrodes. This condition is caused by the spark plug overheating. This overheating can be caused by lean fuel mixture, low octane fuel, cooling system faulure, or long periods of high-speed heavy load. A colder plug may correct this trouble.

Splash fouling may occur if accumulated cylinder deposits are thrown against the spark plugs. This material can be cleaned from the plug and the plug reinstalled.

If spark gap tools and/or pliers are not properly used the electrode can be misshaped into a curve.

Correct spark plug type and correct spark plug gap setting are found in the engine operator's manual.

STUDENT ASSIGNMENT

You are to remove the engine spark plug, examine it for damage and fouling, clean the plug and regap it. It is essential that you record your work in the work record box on this page as you complete each step of the procedure.

Procedure

1. Remove the spark plug - Examine condition of plug.

2. Check spark gap prior to cleaning and resetting.

3. Wire brush shell and threads.

4. Clean insulator with a rag soaked in solvent.

5. Clean electrodes and sparking surfaces.

6. Regap the plug to the correct setting.

7. Reinstall plug (don't forget the spark plug gasket).

## WORK RECORD BOX

| Part | Disassembly (nuts, bolts, etc.) | Operation performed | Tool used |
|---|---|---|---|
|  |  |  |  |
|  |  |  |  |
|  |  |  |  |
|  |  |  |  |
|  |  |  |  |
|  |  |  |  |
|  |  |  |  |
|  |  |  |  |
|  |  |  |  |
|  |  |  |  |
|  |  |  |  |
|  |  |  |  |
|  |  |  |  |
|  |  |  |  |

GENERAL STUDY QUESTIONS

Upon completion of the above work answer the following questions.

1. What was "your" spark plug type (commercial designation)?

2. What was the spark gap prior to cleaning?

3. Does the manufacturer suggest any equivalent spark plug types?  List.

4. What is the correct spark gap for "your" plug?

5. Describe the condition of the plug prior to cleaning.

6. Explain the purpose of cleaning spark plugs.

Laboratory Experience 18
WINTER STORAGE OF ENGINES

OBJECTIVES

◗ To learn the important steps in winter storage.

◗ To learn how to correctly perform winter storage.

REFERENCE

● Review Pages 104-111

INTRODUCTION

Winter storage is an important but often neglected aspect of engine care.  A few minutes of time spent at laying up the engine may save hours of engine trouble when the engine is returned to service.  Fuel system, lubrication system, and cooling system need attention during winter storage.

STUDENT ASSIGNMENT

You are to prepare an engine for winter storage (either 2- or 4-cycle).  It is essential that you record your work in the work record box on the following page as you complete each step of the procedure.

Winter Storage Procedure

Your instructor may supplement or revise specific steps of the procedure which follows since there are many makes of engines.  The following procedure is your general guide:

1.  Remove spark plug lead.

2.  Drain the fuel system:  tank, fuel lines, sediment bowl, and carburetor.  Clean the air cleaner.

3.  Inject oil into the cylinder (upper cylinder).  Remove the spark plug and pour in about 1 ounce of oil.  Turn the engine over several times to spread the oil.

4.  Drain the crankcase (four-cycle).

5.  Clean the engine.  Pay special attention to the cooling system.

6.  Wrap the engine in a canvas or blanket and store in a dry place.

## WORK RECORD BOX

| Part | Disassembly (nuts, bolts, etc.) | Operation performed | Tool used |
|------|--------------------------------|---------------------|-----------|
|      |                                |                     |           |
|      |                                |                     |           |
|      |                                |                     |           |
|      |                                |                     |           |
|      |                                |                     |           |
|      |                                |                     |           |
|      |                                |                     |           |
|      |                                |                     |           |
|      |                                |                     |           |
|      |                                |                     |           |
|      |                                |                     |           |
|      |                                |                     |           |

GENERAL STUDY QUESTIONS

Answer the following questions.

1. Explain why winter storage is important.

2. Should gasoline be kept over for the next season?  If not, why not?

3. Is winter storage a job that can be done by the average engine owner?

4. Why should the air cleaner be cleaned now instead of when the engine is returned to service.

5. List several good places to store an engine.

Laboratory Experience 19

INSTRUCTION BOOK USAGE

## OBJECTIVES

◆ To learn the value of the engine manufacturer's instruction book.

◆ To learn the type of information that can be found in the engine manufacturer's instruction book.

## REFERENCE

● Review Pages 104-111

## INTRODUCTION

The manufacturer's instruction book is included with every new engine. The book contains the information that the manufacturer considers necessary for the owner to know. The information included will enable the owner to obtain top performance and long engine life. Some typical topics that are discussed are: lubrication procedures, carburetor adjustment, ignition system data, air cleaner cleaning instructions, winter storage, and care of the machine that the engine is used on. The information in the book is important; a person with a new engine should read and thoroughly understand the instruction book before he touches the engine. All too often the inexperienced person will adopt the poor attitude, "if all else fails, read the instruction book". The book is valuable, read it, understand it, place it in a safe place for future reference.

Also, it might be pointed out that some manufacturers issue very small instruction books, leaflets. Other manufacturers issue instruction books that are very inclusive, almost a repair manual. Regardless of the size of the book, it is an important piece of literature for the engine owner.

## STUDENT ASSIGNMENT

You are to read an instruction book (one of your own or one the instructor gives you) and then answer the questions below. Don't be disturbed if you are not able to answer all of the questions. Every manufacturer has a slightly different idea on just how much information the engine owner should have to operate the engine.

## QUESTIONS

Engine Manufacturer's Name

Engine Model Number

2- or 4-cycle Engine

Rated Horsepower _____ at _____ r.p.m.

Bore _____ Stroke _____ Displacement

Lubrication System:

     Summer Oil Type _____

     Winter Oil Type _____

     Oil Checked - How Often _____

     Oil Changed - How Often _____

Ignition System:

     Spark Plug Type _____

     Spark Plug Gap _____

     Spark Plug Cleaned - How Often _____

     Breaker Points Checked - How Often _____

     Breaker Points Set To _____

Air Cleaner:

     Dry Type or Oil Bath (Underline which one used)

     Cleaned - How Often _____

     Air Cleaner Cleaned With _____

Cooling System:

     Air-Cooled or Water-Cooled (Underline which one used)

     Cleaned - How Often (Air-Cooled) _____

     Water Level Checked (Water-Cooled) - How Often _____

NOTE: Most questions are answered in terms of hours between cleaning, changing, setting, checking, etc.

Laboratory Experience 20

CLEANING THE AIR CLEANER

## OBJECTIVE

◗  To learn how to clean an air cleaner.

## REFERENCE

●  Review Pages 104-111

## INTRODUCTION

Care of the engine's air cleaner is important since all air that enters the engine goes through this part. A clogged air cleaner restricts air flow. A damaged air cleaner may allow dirt to enter the engine. The frequency of cleaning really depends on the atmosphere in which the engine is operated. Dusty conditions require frequent cleaning of the air cleaner. Clean atmospheric conditions enable the air cleaner to go for a longer time between cleaning.

## STUDENT ASSIGNMENT

You are to disassemble, inspect, clean, and reassemble the air cleaner. After completing the work, record it in the work record box on the following page.

### Cleaning Procedure

The engine instruction book is the final word on the correct cleaning of the air cleaner. If you do not have an instruction book available, the following procedure is your general guide. Be careful not to allow any dirt to fall into the carburetor when the air cleaner is removed.

1.  Oil Bath Air Cleaner

    a.  Loosen and carefully remove air cleaner from carburetor.

    b.  Wash out the filter element in solvent.

    c.  Pour old oil out of the bowl, wipe bowl clean.

    d.  Refill bowl to correct level (use same type oil as is in crankcase).

    e.  Reassemble air cleaner.

2.  Oil-Wetted Polyurethane (foam) Filter Element

    a.  Loosen and carefully remove air cleaner from carburetor.

    b.  Wash out the filter element in solvent.

c. Squeeze out excess solvent.

d. Work about 1 teaspoon of oil into the filter.

e. Reassemble air cleaner.

3. Foil, Moss, or Hair Elements; Dry Type

a. Loosen and carefully remove air cleaner from carburetor.

b. Wash out the filter element in solvent.

c. Allow to dry.

d. Reassemble air cleaner.

4. Felt or Fiber Cylinder Element; Dry Type

a. Loosen and carefully remove air cleaner from carburetor.

b. Blow out element with compressed air, reverse direction of normal flow.

c. Reassemble air cleaner.

5. Metal Cartridge Air Cleaner; Dry Type

a. Loosen and carefully remove air cleaner from carburetor.

b. Tap or shake air cleaner to dislodge dirt and dust.

c. Reassemble air cleaner.

## WORK RECORD BOX

| Part | Disassembly (bolts, nuts, etc.) | Operation performed | Tool used |
|------|------|------|------|
|  |  |  |  |
|  |  |  |  |
|  |  |  |  |
|  |  |  |  |
|  |  |  |  |
|  |  |  |  |
|  |  |  |  |
|  |  |  |  |
|  |  |  |  |
|  |  |  |  |
|  |  |  |  |
|  |  |  |  |

GENERAL STUDY QUESTIONS

Upon completion of the work, answer the following questions.

1. Explain what would happen to the fuel mixture if the air cleaner gradually became clogged.

2. What harmful effect can "dirty" air have on an engine?

3. Classify the following atmospheric conditions: dusty, average, or clean:

    a. Engine operated in feed mill

    b. Engine on small snow plow

    c. Engine mulching dry leaves

    d. Outboard motor on lake

    e. Engine on garden tractor

## TROUBLESHOOTING - TUNE-UP - RECONDITIONING

Troubleshooting is the intelligent, step-by-step process of locating engine trouble. The troubleshooter examines and/or tests the engine to determine the cause of its "sickness". To engage in this process a person must thoroughly understand the "how" and "why" of engine operation. Really, troubleshooting is more of a mental activity than a physical one.

The troubleshooter first establishes the engine's symptoms. Then he checks the most common causes for these symptoms. If the solution is not found, he moves on and explores another possible cause for the engine's problem. The possible causes for engine failure must quickly be narrowed down, because there are hundreds of afflictions that can creep into an ailing engine.

An experienced mechanic will do his troubleshooting quickly and with little apparent effort. It would seem as if some sort of intuition guides him to the solution of the problem. Actually, it is his years of experience and his thorough understanding of engine operation that allows him to work with such competence.

The engine owner can do his own troubleshooting when he has an understanding of engine operating principles. Many "Owners Manuals" contain a troubleshooting chart that is a great assistance. With the aid of an engine troubleshooting chart, the engine owner or operator can locate and correct many engine difficulties without calling in a professional mechanic.

Even in the event your efforts at troubleshooting should fail and you find it necessary to consult an expert, you will derive a measure of satisfaction in being able to intelligently discuss your engine's troubles.

Troubleshooting is not a mysterious subject, but it does take a knowledge of engine operation and you must use common sense. For example, if the engine does not start there are two very logical reasons: either (1) fuel is not getting into the combustion chamber, or (2) fuel is being provided but it is not being ignited. Therefore, we look for the trouble in either the fuel system or the ignition system. Lubrication or cooling systems would have little bearing on the ability of the engine to start, so these systems are not inspected.

The troubleshooter starts with simple and most frequent causes of trouble. In inspecting the fuel system, the first step is to check for fuel in the tank. If this is not the cause of the trouble, then check the fuel shutoff valve, continuing logical steps until the trouble is found. It would be a mistake to completely disassemble the carburetor or magneto as the first step in troubleshooting.

Look at the Troubleshooting Charts in the Appendix, pages 182-187, and discover how many of the common engine troubles can be corrected by an owner who has the normal household tools at his disposal.

---

## ENGINE TUNE-UP

Engine tune-up does not involve major engine repair work. Rather, it is a process of cleaning and adjusting the engine so that it will give top performance. Tune-up can be done by an experienced engine owner or it can be done by a mechanic.

A typical tune-up procedure might include the following steps:

1. Inspect air cleaner; clean and reassemble air cleaner. Is the cleaner damaged in any way? Is the filter element too clogged for cleaning? If so, replace the cleaner and/or element. Clean the unit according to the manufacturer's instructions.

2. Clean the gas tank, fuel lines, and any fuel filters or screens.

3. Check compression. This can be done by slowly turning the engine over by hand; as the piston nears top dead center, considerable resistance should be felt. As top dead center is passed the piston should "snap" back down the cylinder. A more thorough test can be made with a compression gage. The manufacturer's repair manual should be consulted for normal and minimum acceptable compression pressure.

Fig. 9-1 Checking Compression with a Compression Gage.

4. Check spark plug; clean, regap or replace. Remove high-tension lead from plug and hold it about 1/8" from the plug base. Be sure to hold it on the insulation. Turn the engine over. If a good spark jumps to the plug, magneto is providing sufficient spark. Now replace the high-tension lead and lay the plug on a bare spot on the engine. Turn engine over. If a good spark jumps at the plug electrodes, the plug is good. This is not an absolute test but is a good indication. If the plug is questionable, replace it.

5. Check operation of the governor. Be certain governor linkages do not bind at any point.

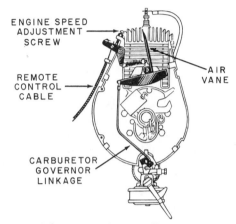

Fig. 9-2 Air Vane Governor Parts.

6. Check magneto. On most engines, the flywheel must be removed for access to the magneto parts. Use a flywheel or gear puller, if available. Otherwise, pop the flywheel loose by removing the flywheel nut and delivering a sharp hammer blow to a lead block held against the end of the crankshaft.

Fig. 9-3 Removing a Flywheel Using a Special Puller.

Fig. 9-4 Removing the Flywheel with a Soft Hammer.

Another method is to back off the flywheel nut until it is about 1/3 off the crankshaft, then strike it sharply. In no case should you hammer on the end of the crankshaft as this may damage the threads.

Adjust the breaker point gap and check the condenser and breaker point terminals for tightness. Breaker points will be set for .020″, in most cases, although the correct setting may vary according to the manufacturer. Turn the engine over until the breaker points reach their maximum opening, then check with a flat feeler gage. Adjust the points if the setting is incorrect. Points can be cleaned if necessary. If the points are pitted or do not line up, they should be replaced.

7. Fill crankcase with clean oil of the correct type. (four-stroke cycle engines)

8. Fill gasoline tank with regular gasoline. (four-stroke cycle engines)

 Fill gasoline tank with correct mixture of gasoline and oil. (two-stroke cycle engines)

9. Start engine.

10. Adjust the carburetor for peak performance.

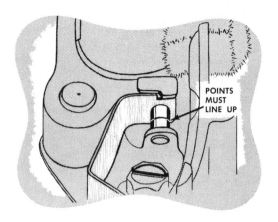

Fig. 9-6 Breaker Points Must Line Up.

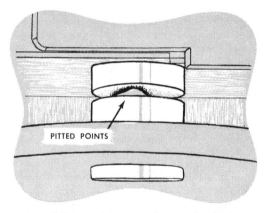

Fig. 9-7 Pitted Breaker Points Should Be Replace.

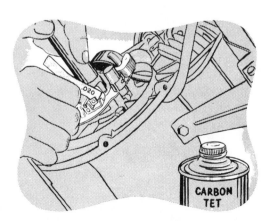

Fig. 9-5 Clean and Check
Breaker Points.

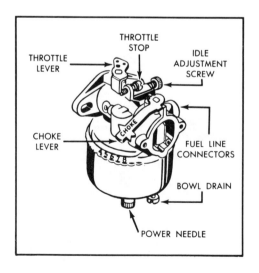

Fig. 9-8 Carburetor Parts.

## RECONDITIONING

Reconditioning or overhauling an engine is generally the job for the mechanic; one who has the tools and know-how to do the job correctly. However, much reconditioning and overhauling can be done by the amateur who has the essential tools and the mechanic's workmanlike approach. Care and precision are vitally important; slipshod workmanship is never tolerated in engine work. Every part must be in place correctly, none missing or left over.

These points are stressed because at times the novice mechanic with an engine is like the small boy taking a watch apart to see just what makes it tick. Rarely does the boy get the watch back together so it works. Engine parts are larger but there are hundreds of parts that make up any engine and they all must go back together correctly.

Before you begin disassembly of an engine, provide a spot to receive the parts as they are removed. One good method is to lay out a large sheet of paper and as the parts are placed on the paper, label them so they will not be lost. It is often difficult to remember just where a part came from when forty or fifty pieces are laid out, and it may be several days before you reassemble the engine.

A "Mechanic's Handbook" or "Service Manual" is essential for top quality overhaul work. These books can sometimes be obtained direct from the engine manufacturer or borrowed from a mechanic. In only a few instances is this type of book supplied with the new engine. The service manual goes into great detail, fully explaining each step of overhaul or reconditioning. Allowances, clearances, torque data, and other specifications are given as well. Without the use of the service manual there is too much guesswork left to the amateur mechanic. The amateur mechanic will want the service manual for his engine before any repair work is started.

### CLINTON ENGINES TORGUE DATA — INCH POUNDS
### "Red Horse"

| | | 1600<br>A1600<br>A1690 | 1800<br>1890 | 2500<br>A2500 | B2500<br>B2590<br>2790 |
|---|---|---|---|---|---|
| Bearing Plate P.T.O. | Min.<br>Max. | 160<br>180 | 160<br>180 | 160<br>180 | 160<br>180 |
| Back Plate to Block | Min.<br>Max. | 70<br>80 | 70<br>80 | 70<br>80 | 70<br>80 |

### CLINTON ENGINES SERVICE CLEARANCES
### "Red Horse"

| | | 1600 | A1600 | A1690 | 1800 | 1890 | 2500 | B2500 | B2590 | A2500 | 2790 |
|---|---|---|---|---|---|---|---|---|---|---|---|
| Piston Skirt Clearance | Min.<br>Max.<br>Rework | .007<br>.009<br>.010 | .007<br>.009<br>.010 | .007<br>.009<br>.010 | .007<br>.009<br>.010 | .007<br>.009<br>.010 | .0065<br>.0085<br>.010 | .0065<br>.0085<br>.010 | .0065<br>.0085<br>.010 | .005<br>.007<br>.0085 | .005<br>.007<br>.0085 |
| Ring End Gap | Min.<br>Max.<br>Rework | .007<br>.017<br>.025 | .007<br>.017<br>.025 | .007<br>.017<br>.025 | .007<br>.017<br>.025 | .007<br>.017<br>.025 | .010<br>.020<br>.028 | .010<br>.020<br>.028 | .010<br>.020<br>.028 | .010<br>.020<br>.028 | .010<br>.020<br>.028 |

### CLINTON ENGINES TOLERANCES AND SPECIFICATIONS
### "Red Horse"

| | 1600 | A1600 | A1690 | 1800 | 1890 | 2500 | B2500 | B2590 | A2500 | 2790 |
|---|---|---|---|---|---|---|---|---|---|---|
| Cylinder - Bore | 2.8125<br>2.8135 | 2.8125<br>2.8135 | 2.8125<br>2.8135 | 2.9995<br>3.0005 | 2.9995<br>3.0005 | 3.1245<br>3.1255 | 3.1245<br>3.1255 | 3.1245<br>3.1255 | 3.1245<br>3.1255 | 3.1245<br>3.1255 |
| Skirt - Diameter | 2.8045<br>2.8055 | 2.8045<br>2.8055 | 2.8045<br>2.8055 | 2.9915<br>2.9925 | 2.9915<br>2.9925 | 3.117<br>3.118 | 3.117<br>3.118 | 3.117<br>3.118 | 3.1185<br>3.1195 | 3.1185<br>3.1195 |

Fig. 9-9 Torque Data, Clearances, Tolerances, and Specifications as Excerpted from a Service Manual.

Unless the engine owner is a skilled mechanic and has an adequately equipped repair shop, he will not be able to perform all types of engine repair and overhaul. Most owners would not find it practical to purchase the equipment necessary to do all types of overhaul and repair. Professional repairmen may have anywhere from $500 to several thousand dollars invested in tools and equipment: magneto testers, valve seat resurfacers, air compressors, steam cleaners, special sharpeners, grinders, lapping stands, special factory tools, general repair tools, repair parts, etc.

However, a modest investment in tools will enable a person to perform many repair jobs. Most home workshops have a number of the basic tools that are necessary and with the addition of some specialized tools he will have a reasonably good set of tools. A tentative list of necessary tools includes:

1.  Screwdriver (various sizes)
2.  Combination wrenches (set)
3.  Adjustable wrench
4.  Socket set
5.  Torque wrench
6.  Deep well spark plug socket
7.  Needle nose pliers
8.  Feeler gage
9.  Spark gap gage
10. Piston ring compressor
11. Piston ring expander
12. Valve spring compressor

Additional tools:

1.  Flywheel puller
2.  Compression gage
3.  Tachometer
4.  Valve grinder - hand operated
5.  Arbor press

Reconditioning or overhaul of an engine involves four basic steps: (1) disassembly, (2) inspection of parts, (3) repair or replacement of worn or broken parts, and (4) reassembly. The following disassembly procedure is a general guide for a four-stroke cycle engine.

1.  Disconnect spark plug lead - remove spark plug.
2.  Drain fuel system - tank, lines, carburetor.
3.  Drain oil from crankcase.
4.  Remove air cleaner.
5.  Remove carburetor.
6.  Remove metal air shrouding, gas tank and recoil starter.
7.  Remove flywheel.
8.  Remove breaker assembly and push rod.
9.  Remove magneto plate assembly.
10. Remove breather plate assembly (valve spring cover).
11. Remove cylinder head.
12. Remove valves.
13. Remove base.
14. Remove piston assembly.
15. Remove crankshaft.
16. Remove camshaft and tappets.
17. Remove mechanical governor.

In the following discussion, disassembly, inspection, repair, and reassembly will be discussed for each engine part. The material is, of course, general, and the illustrations cover several different makes of engines. In actual practice a service manual would be followed for these steps. However, this information is an excellent source for the general procedure followed by most manufacturers.

(1) disconnect spark plug lead - remove spark plug, (2) drain fuel system - tank, lines, carburetor, (3) drain oil from crankcase, (4) remove air cleaner, (5) remove carburetor, and (6) remove metal air shrouding. Gas tank and recoil starter are steps that have been thoroughly covered in earlier units and not of sufficient difficulty to be discussed at greater length. Be certain to inspect any parts removed for damage and wear. Replacement or repair may be indicated.

Removal of the flywheel is necessary to gain access to the ignition system parts. If a flywheel puller is available, it is best; however, the flywheel can be removed by striking the end of the crankshaft with a plastic or soft hammer. Use care not to damage the end of the crankshaft. The key on the crankshaft should not be lost. Keep it on the crankshaft or in a safe place. When reassembling the flywheel onto the crankshaft, carefully fit the key into the keyway.

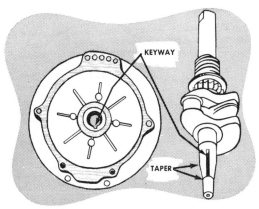

Fig. 9-10 Keyway on Tapered End of the Crankshaft and the Flywheel.

## MAGNETO PARTS

The magneto parts - high-tension coil, breaker points, condenser - may need to be removed for checking or replacement. The coil may be visually inspected for cracks and gouges in insulation, evidence of overheating, and the condition of the leads where they go into the coil. If an ignition coil tester is available, the coil can be checked for (1) firing check, (2) leakage check, (3) secondary continuity check, and (4) primary continuity check. This checking should be done using the procedure recommended by the manufacturers.

Breaker points can be visually inspected for pitting, alignment, and contact surface.

The condenser can be visually inspected for dents, terminal lead damage, and broken mounting clip. A condenser tester is used to check the condenser for capacity, leakage, and series resistance. Follow the test procedure suggested by the test equipment manufacturer.

Fig. 9-11 Checking a Condenser.

When the magneto is reassembled, the laminated iron core must be close to the flywheel magnet but not touching it. Generally, the closer the better, but not close enough to rub. This air gap is specified by the manufacturer. Too large an air gap can cause faulty magneto operation.

## ENGINE TIMING

Engine timing refers to the magneto timing to the piston: the position of the piston just as the breaker points start to open. Timing is set at the factory but it is possible for timing to cause engine trouble. If the breaker points open too late in the cycle, power is lost; if the breaker points open too early in the cycle, detonation may result. Improper engine timing could be caused by the crankshaft and camshaft gears being installed one tooth off, spark advance mechanism stuck, breaker points incorrectly set, magneto assembly plate loose or slipped, or rotor incorrectly positioned. These causes of trouble depend on the engine and type of magneto.

The position of the piston for timing a magneto varies from engine to engine. The piston may be at top dead center (TDC) or slightly before top dead center (BTDC). Check engine specifications for this information.

One common method of checking timing is to locate TDC. This is the point where the piston does not seem to move as the flywheel is rotated. A dial indicator can be used for greater accuracy. With TDC located, place a reference mark on the flywheel and the magneto assembly plate. Now remove the flywheel. Rotate the crankshaft until the breaker points just open (.001″). Carefully replace the flywheel and put another mark on the magneto plate, aligned with the flywheel reference mark. The difference between the marks on the magneto plate is the magneto timing to the piston. This can be figured in degrees by dividing the number of flywheel vanes into 360°. Twenty vanes; each vane 18°. The correct number of degrees of firing before top dead center is found in the engine specifications.

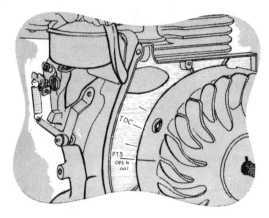

Fig. 9-12 Timing Marks.

If the engine has a magnetic rotor magneto, the rotor and armature must be timed to the piston. Timing is correctly set when the engine leaves the factory, but if the armature has been removed or the crankshaft or cam gear replaced, it is necessary to retime the rotor. Breaker points are first set correctly (.020″). Rotor is on the shaft correctly and tightened. Armature is mounted but mounting screws are not tight. Turn the crankshaft until the breaker points just start to open (place a piece of tissue paper between the points to detect when the points "let go"). Now turn the armature slightly until the timing marks on the rotor and the armature line up.

Two-cycle engine timing is quite similar. One common procedure is to remove the spark plug and, using a ruler and straightedge across the head, locate top dead center. With TDC located, back the piston down the cylinder the

correct distance (check manufacturer's specifications for the measurement before TDC). At this point, the breaker points should just begin to open. If timing is incorrect, loosen the stator plate setscrew and rotate the stator plate slightly until the points just begin to open. Retighten the stator plate setscrew.

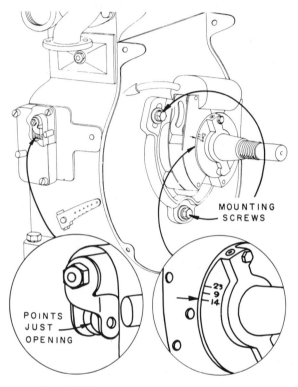

Fig. 9-13 Timing the Rotor and Armature to the Piston. The Numbers Represent Model Numbers.

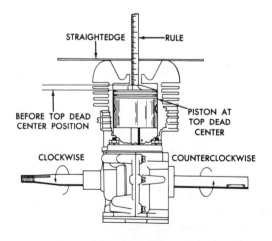

Fig. 9-14 Two-cycle Engine Timing.

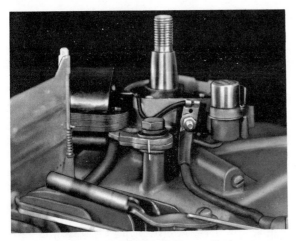

Fig. 9-15 Two-cycle Timing Marks.

Fig. 9-17 Tightening the Cylinder Head Bolts with a Torque Wrench.

Fig. 9-16 Two-cycle Timing Marks.

## CYLINDER HEAD

The cylinder head must be removed if work is to be done on the piston, piston rings, connecting rod, valves, or if the combustion chamber is to be cleaned. The head screws or nuts should be removed and set aside. After the head is removed, the head gasket should be removed and discarded. Before reassembly, carbon deposits should be scraped off and the head cleaned. A new head gasket should be installed and the cylinder head screws or nuts should be tightened in the correct sequence. To be certain of the correct degree of tightness a torque wrench should be used (generally 14 to 18 ft./lbs).

## VALVES

The valves can easily be inspected. Inspection may show that they are stuck, burned, cracked, or fouled with carbon. Also, valve stems and valve guides may be worn or the valves and valve seats may need to be reground. Further, tappet clearance may be wrong. The average engine owner may be able to do some valve work himself. However, extensive work or a complete renewal of the valve system might best be left to a mechanic with the tools and experience necessary.

A complete valve job might include:

1. Installing new valves

2. Installing new valve guides

3. Installing new valve seats

4. Installing new valve springs

5. Grinding valve seats

6. Lapping valves

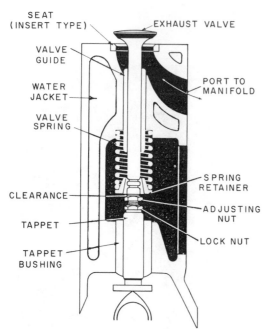

Fig. 9-18 Complete Valve Train.

To remove the valves, first compress the valve spring, then flip off or slip out the valve spring retainers, sometimes called keepers. Pull the valve out of the engine. Valve spring and associated parts will also come out.

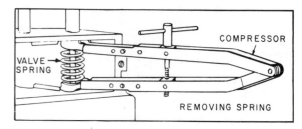

Fig. 9-20 Using a Valve Spring Compressor to Remove the Valve Spring.

With the valve out, the valve stem, face, and head can be closely inspected and cleaned. The valve guide and valve seat can also be inspected.

Many engines have replaceable valve guides. If these are worn or otherwise damaged, they must be pressed out using an arbor press or carefully driven out with a special punch. Also, the exhaust valve seat is removable on many engines; if the seat is beyond regrinding, remove it and reinstall a new valve seat. A special valve seat extracting tool is used for this job.

Fig. 9-19 Checking Tappet Clearance.

One of the first check points is the tappet clearance (space between tappet and end of valve). This clearance is checked with a feeler gage. On most small engines the clearance can be enlarged by grinding a small amount from the end of the valve. If the clearance is already too large the valve would have to be replaced. Some small engines do have adjustable tappet clearances.

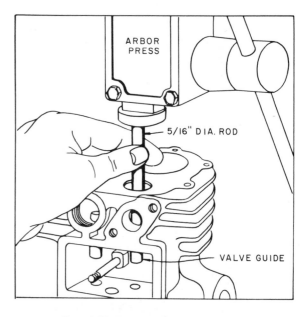

Fig. 9-21 Removing a Worn Valve Guide.

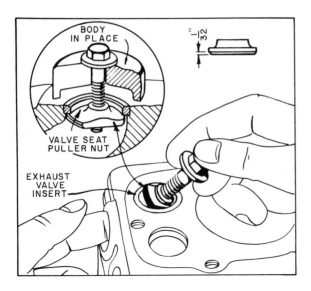

Fig. 9-22 Removing the Exhaust Valve Seat with a Special Puller.

Fig. 9-24 Power Drill Operated Valve Seat Grinder.

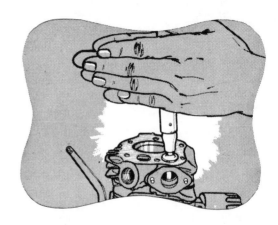

If the valves and/or valve seats need regrinding, this can be done with special valve grinding equipment. However, in some cases hand valve grinders can be used.

If either or both of these parts have been replaced or reground, the parts must be lapped to provide the perfect seal necessary for valve operation. When lapping, use a small amount of lapping compound. Rotate the valve against the seat a few times until the compound produces a dull finish on the valve face. Do not lap the valves too heavily.

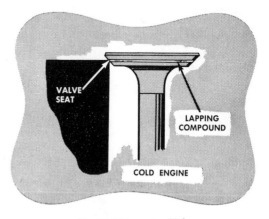

Fig. 9-25 Lapping Valves.

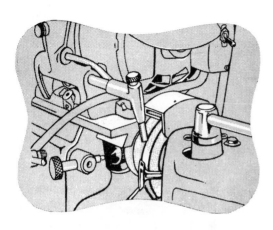

Fig. 9-23 Valve Grinder.

When the valves are replaced, oil the stems and be certain that the exhaust valve goes in the exhaust side, intake valve in intake side.

Remove the engine from the base or sump. This is done by loosening the bolts and breaking the seal. In most cases, a new gasket will have to be installed upon reassembly.

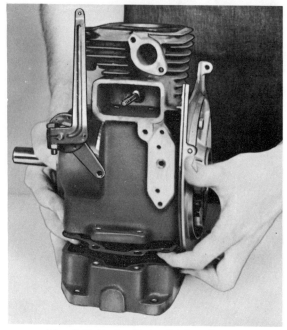

Fig. 9-26 Engine Base, Gasket, Engine.

To remove piston assembly, remove the connecting rod cap and push the piston assembly up out of the engine. Mark the piston so it can be reinstalled the same way it comes out. The cylinder should be checked for score marks. Scoring in the area of ring travel will cause excessive oil consumption and reduced engine power. Also the cylinder size should be checked with a cylinder gage. If the cylinder appears to be in good condition, it can be deglazed with a finish hone to prepare cylinder for new rings.

Fig. 9-27 Deglazing a Cylinder with a Finish Hone.

If the piston size and condition has checked out all right, the piston rings should be checked next. Check the edge gap with a feeler gage, rings still on the piston. The correct edge gap clearance is found in the engine overhaul specifications. Remove the piston rings from the piston with a piston ring expander. Carefully put the ring in the cylinder and check the end gap with a feeler gage. Too little end gap may cause the ring to freeze when it becomes hot and expands. Too much end gap may allow "blow-by" and the resulting loss of power. Piston ring grooves should be cleaned to remove any carbon accumulations. New piston rings are normally installed during engine overhaul.

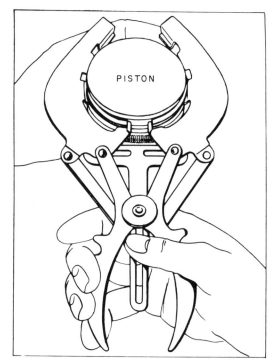

Fig. 9-28 Special Tool Used For Removing Piston Rings.

Fig. 9-29 Piston Ring Tool.

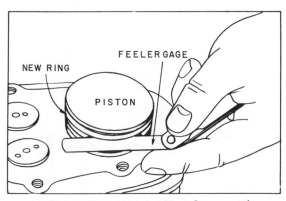

Fig. 9-30 Checking the Ring Groove with
a Feeler Gage.

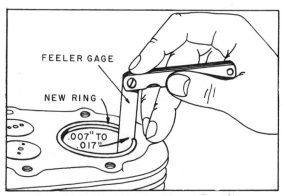

Fig. 9-31 Checking the Ring Gap with a
Feeler Gage. (End Gap)

Use a piston ring compressor to reinstall the piston assembly. Place the piston in the same way as it came out. Also, put the connecting rod cap on the same way as it came off — find the match marks. A torque wrench should be used to tighten the connecting rod cap. The crankshaft should be removed and checked for scoring and any metallic pickup.

The journal and crankpin should be checked with a micrometer for roundness. The gear and keyway should be checked for wear. In some cases the main ball bearings may come out with the crankshaft. Upon reinstallation, the bearings may have to be pressed into place; an arbor press is good for this job.

Fig. 9-32 Piston Ring Compressor.

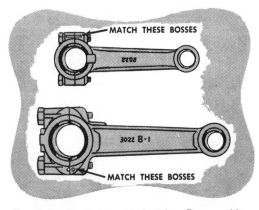

Fig. 9-34 Match Boss Marks When Reassembling
the Connecting Rod and Connecting Rod Cap.

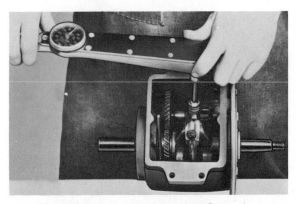

Fig. 9-33 Torque Wrench Used to Correctly
Tighten Connecting Rod Cap.

Fig. 9-35 Pressing in the Main Ball Bearing.

Fig. 9-36 Reinstalling the Crankshaft.

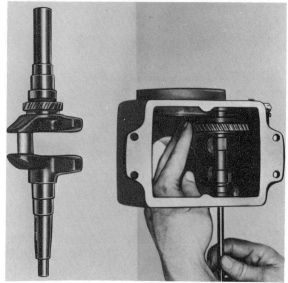

Fig. 9-37 Reinstalling the Camshaft.

The camshaft and valve tappets can also be removed for inspection and repair. The camshaft pin should be driven out with a drift punch from the power takeoff side of the engine. Upon reassembly of the camshaft and crankshaft, be certain to line up the timing marks.

## GENERAL STUDY QUESTIONS

1. Define troubleshooting.

2. Of what value is a troubleshooting chart?

3. Can troubleshooting be done by the average engine owner or operator?

4. Define engine tune-up.

5. Define engine reconditioning or overhaul.

6. Can any reconditioning or overhaul be accomplished by the amateur mechanic?

7. Why is the careful layout of parts important during disassembly?

8. Why is a Mechanic's Handbook or Service Manual essential for the reconditioning of an engine?

9. Explain engine timing.

10. What might a complete valve job include?

## CLASS DISCUSSION TOPICS

● Discuss the troubleshooting chart.

● Discuss the steps in engine tune-up.

● Discuss the importance of care, accuracy, etc. in engine reconditioning and overhaul work.

● Discuss the tools necessary for reconditioning work.

● Discuss the steps in engine reconditioning.

## CLASS DEMONSTRATION TOPICS

▶ Demonstrate troubleshooting by putting troubles into an engine and having students observe engine operation and then troubleshoot the engine. Simple examples: no fuel in tank, poor compression, shorting bar on plug, fuel shutoff valve closed, spark plug lead loose, bad spark plug, etc.

▶ Demonstrate how to tune up an engine.

▶ Demonstrate the correct use of the basic tools.

▶ Demonstrate checking the magneto for damage or wear.

▶ Demonstrate timing an engine.

▶ Demonstrate the tightening sequence and correct torque on a cylinder head.

▶ Demonstrate removing and inspecting valves for wear and damage.

▶ Demonstrate checking tappet clearance.

▶ Demonstrate lapping valves.

▶ Demonstrate removing and inspecting piston assembly for damage and wear.

▶ Demonstrate removal and inspection of the camshaft and tappets.

Laboratory Experience 21

CLEAN AND ADJUST THE BREAKER POINTS

OBJECTIVE

▶ To learn how to correctly clean and adjust the breaker points.

REFERENCE

● Review Pages 124-136

INTRODUCTION

The correct setting of the breaker points is essential to the operation of the magneto. The maximum opening of the points is most often .020″, however, some magnetos specify .018″, .023″ or other settings; check the manufacturer's recommendations.

The breaker points should fully line up with each other, and they should contact flat against each other. The breaker points have a chrome or silvery appearance when they are new and as they are used they become gray. If they have become pitted they should be replaced.

STUDENT ASSIGNMENT

You are to clean and reset the breaker points. It is essential that you record your work in the work record box on the following page as you complete each step of the procedure.

Procedure

Your instructor may supplement or revise specific steps of the procedure which follows since there are many makes of engines. The following procedure is your general guide:

1. Remove the spark plug lead.

2. Remove air shroud, grass screens, etc. in the area of the magneto.

3. Remove the flywheel. This is not necessary if the points are not located under the flywheel.

4. Remove breaker point cover.

5. Rotate the crankshaft until maximum point opening is attained.

6. Check the breaker point gap, using a flat feeler gage, prior to cleaning and resetting.

7. Clean the points with carbon tetrachloride on a lint-free cloth.

8. Loosen the breaker point assembly lock screw.

9. With points at maximum opening - turn the breaker point adjusting screw to attain the correct setting. Check the setting with a flat feeler gage.

10. Tighten breaker point assembly lock screw.

11. Rotate the crankshaft several times.

12. Recheck breaker point setting with a flat feeler gage.

## WORK RECORD BOX

| Part | Disassembly (nuts, bolts, etc.) | Operation performed | Tool used |
|---|---|---|---|
| | | | |
| | | | |
| | | | |
| | | | |
| | | | |
| | | | |
| | | | |
| | | | |
| | | | |
| | | | |
| | | | |
| | | | |
| | | | |
| | | | |
| | | | |
| | | | |
| | | | |

## GENERAL STUDY QUESTIONS

Reset the breaker points then answer the following questions.

1. What was the breaker point gap prior to adjustment?

2. What is the correct breaker point setting for "your" engine?

3. Were the breaker points under the flywheel? If so, could the breaker cam be seen?

4. Were the breaker points mounted outside the flywheel?

Laboratory Experience 22

## TEST SPARK PLUG AND MAGNETO OUTPUT

## OBJECTIVES

▶ To learn how to test the spark produced at the spark plug.

▶ To learn how to test the magneto output.

## REFERENCE

● Review Pages 124-136

## INTRODUCTION

Trouble in the ignition system may stem from the spark plug or from the magneto itself. It is often helpful in troubleshooting to determine (1) if the magneto is delivering high-tension voltage to the spark plug, and (2) if the spark plug is delivering a spark. Poor ignition can result in: engine missing, poor performance under heavy load, and hard starting. If trouble exists, these two simple checks can help to establish whether or not the ignition system is the source of difficulty.

## STUDENT ASSIGNMENT

You are to perform the tests listed below, testing (1) the magneto output and (2) the output at the spark plug. Record your work in the work record box on the following page.

### Procedure

Your instructor may supplement or revise specific steps of the procedure which follows since there are many makes of engines. The following procedure is your general guide:

1. Test strength of magneto output.

   a. Remove high-tension lead from spark plug.

   b. Hold high-tension lead about 1/8″ from spark plug base.

   c. Turn engine over as if it were being started.

   d. If a good spark jumps to the plug, the magneto output is satisfactory.

2. Test strength of spark at spark plug.

   a. Remove high-tension lead from spark plug.

   b. Remove spark plug from engine and replace high-tension lead.

   c. Lay spark plug on engine so the plug base touches bare metal.

d. Turn engine over as if it were being started.

e. If a good spark jumps at the electrodes, the spark plug is good. Note: this is not an absolute test, since it is more difficult for a spark plug to fire under compression. If the plug is questionable, do not hesitate to install a new one.

## WORK RECORD BOX

| Part | Disassembly (nuts, bolts, etc.) | Operation performed | Tool used |
|------|-------------------------------|---------------------|-----------|
|      |                               |                     |           |
|      |                               |                     |           |
|      |                               |                     |           |
|      |                               |                     |           |
|      |                               |                     |           |
|      |                               |                     |           |
|      |                               |                     |           |
|      |                               |                     |           |
|      |                               |                     |           |
|      |                               |                     |           |
|      |                               |                     |           |
|      |                               |                     |           |
|      |                               |                     |           |

## GENERAL STUDY QUESTIONS

Upon completion of the two tests, answer the following questions.

1. Is it possible for the magneto to be good and the spark plug to be bad?

2. Is it possible to get the correct spark at the plug if the magneto is bad?

3. Why is it important to tighten the spark plug securely upon reassembly?

4. How would you describe the sparks that you saw? Circle one:

   "Fat Blue",                "Thin Blue",                "Yellowish Blue"

5. If the spark plug fires correctly when it is out of the cylinder, will it necessarily fire correctly when it is under compression?

Laboratory Experience 23

ADJUST ENGINE TIMING

## OBJECTIVES

▶ To learn how to correctly adjust engine timing.

▶ To gain an understanding of the importance of correct engine timing.

## REFERENCE

● <u>Manufacturer's Engine Repair Manual</u>

## INTRODUCTION

Engine timing refers to the magneto timing to the piston: the position of the piston just as the breaker points start to open. Timing is set at the factory but it is possible for timing to cause engine trouble. If the breaker points open too late in the cycle, power is lost; if the breaker points open too early in the cycle, detonation may result. Improper engine timing could be caused by the crankshaft and camshaft gears being installed one tooth off, spark advance mechanism stuck, breaker points incorrectly set, magneto assembly plate loose or slipped, or rotor incorrectly positioned. These causes of trouble depend on the engine and type of magneto.

The position of the piston for timing a magneto varies from engine to engine. The piston may be at top-dead-center (TDC) or slightly before-top-dead-center (BTDC). Check engine specifications for this information.

NOTE: It is recommended that the adjustment of engine timing be attempted only when the engine repair manual is available for reference. Specific instructions and procedures should be followed. It should be impressed on the student that the work cannot be done in an "off hand" manner without specific engine data.

## STUDENT ASSIGNMENT

You are to correctly adjust the engine timing on your assigned engine. Your instructor will provide a manufacturer's book which has specific instructions and procedures to follow. Record your work in the work record box on the next page.

## GENERAL STUDY QUESTIONS

Upon completion of the assigned work, answer the following questions.

1. Explain how you can locate top-dead-center (TDC)

2. Why are the breaker points timed to open at TDC or before TDC? Why not after TDC?

3.  List the steps you followed in adjusting engine timing.

4.  What problems can incorrect engine timing cause?

### WORK RECORD BOX

| Part | Disassembly (nuts, bolts, etc.) | Operation performed | Tool used |
|------|--------------------------------|---------------------|-----------|
|      |                                |                     |           |
|      |                                |                     |           |
|      |                                |                     |           |
|      |                                |                     |           |
|      |                                |                     |           |
|      |                                |                     |           |
|      |                                |                     |           |
|      |                                |                     |           |
|      |                                |                     |           |
|      |                                |                     |           |
|      |                                |                     |           |

Laboratory Experience 24

REPLACE PISTON RINGS

## OBJECTIVE

▶ To learn how to correctly replace piston rings.

## REFERENCE

● Review Pages 124-136

## INTRODUCTION

The piston rings fit into the slotted grooves around the piston and they provide the seal between the moving piston and the cylinder wall. The rings actually exert a pressure on the cylinder wall; an oil film between the rings and the cylinder wall prevents excessive friction and provides a power seal. The two types of piston rings are (1) compression rings, and (2) oil control rings.

The piston rings are exposed to extremely hard usage and over a long period of time it is quite possible that replacement with new rings may be needed. Worn piston rings can result in loss of power, excessive oil consumption, crankcase dilution, hard starting, to list a few of the problems. The replacement of piston rings is a common repair job and is generally done when the engine is overhauled. It might be noted that the condition of the cylinder wall also has a bearing on piston ring efficiency. Worn or warped cylinder walls cannot be corrected with new rings; honing or reboring of the cylinder would be necessary.

## STUDENT ASSIGNMENT

You are to remove the piston assembly from the engine, remove the piston rings, inspect the condition of the piston, install new rings, and reassemble the piston assembly in the engine. If you are actually installing new rings you should have access to the piston ring clearance specifications for your engine. These clearances are checked with a feeler gage to determine whether or not they are within the tolerance limits. It is essential that you record your work in the work record box on the following page as you complete each step of the disassembly procedure.

## Disassembly Procedure

Your instructor may supplement or revise specific steps of the procedure which follows since there are many makes of engines. The following procedure is your general guide for four-stroke cycle engines:

1. Remove the necessary parts to expose the crankshaft.

2. Remove the cylinder head.

3. Remove the connecting rod cap (note markings on the cap so it can be reassembled in the same manner).

4. Push the piston assembly up and out of the engine (mark the piston so that it can be reinstalled the same way it came out).

5. Inspect the condition of the piston.

6. Check the edge gap with a feeler gage (rings are still on the piston).

7. Remove the piston rings with a piston ring expander.

8. Carefully put the ring in the cylinder and check the end gap with a feeler gage.

9. Clean the piston ring grooves, removing any carbon accumulations.

10. Install new rings or reinstall old rings using a piston ring expander.

11. Push the piston assembly back into the cylinder with the aid of a piston ring compressor.

12. Reassemble piston assembly to crankshaft.

## WORK RECORD BOX

| Part | Disassembly (nuts, bolts, etc.) | Operation performed | Tool used |
|---|---|---|---|
| | | | |
| | | | |
| | | | |
| | | | |
| | | | |
| | | | |
| | | | |
| | | | |
| | | | |
| | | | |
| | | | |
| | | | |
| | | | |
| | | | |
| | | | |
| | | | |

GENERAL STUDY QUESTIONS

Upon completion of the assigned work, answer the following questions.

1. What are the two types of piston rings and what is the main function of each?

2. Describe the condition of the piston itself.

3. What were the edge gaps?  Were they within tolerances?

4. What were the end gaps?  Were they within tolerances?

5. Describe the markings or indications on the connecting rod and connecting rod cap that indicate correct reassembly.

6. What are some common troubles that are caused by bad piston rings?

Laboratory Experience 25

## LAP VALVES

## OBJECTIVE

▶ To learn how to correctly lap valves.

## REFERENCE

● Review Pages 124-136

## INTRODUCTION

The valves must seat perfectly, forming a seal for both the compression and power stroke. Valves operate under very adverse conditions. The exhaust valve, in particular, is subjected to intense heat, as well as rapid motion. If the valves or valve seats become worn, cracked, or warped, sluggish engine operation as well as other problems will result. Upon overhauling an engine, the valve and valve seat condition are checked. Sometimes either or both the valve seats and valves are reground. If valves or valve seats have been reground or replaced they should be lapped. Lapping forms the necessary perfect seal between the seat and the valve.

## STUDENT ASSIGNMENT

You are to remove the valves from the engine, inspect the valves and valve seats, replace necessary parts, lap the valves, and reinstall the valves. Note: if you are working on an instructional engine the teacher may want you to assume that new parts have been installed even though they have not, lapping the valves for practice and experience. It is essential that you record your work in the work record box on the following page as you complete each step of the disassembly procedure.

### Disassembly Procedure

Your instructor may supplement or revise specific steps of the procedure which follows since there are many kinds of engines. The following procedure is your general guide:

1. Remove the valve spring cover exposing the valve springs.

2. Remove the cylinder head.

3. Compress the valve spring with a valve spring compressor.

4. Remove the valve spring retainers by slipping or flipping them out.

5. Remove the valve spring, still compressed.

6. Pull the valve out of the engine.

7. Inspect the valve and valve seat.

8. Replace the valve and valve seat or regrind the valve and valve seat only on instructions from the instructor.

9. Lap the valves. Place a small amount of lapping compound on the valve face and rotate the valve against its seat a few times. Lap the valves until there is a thin, dull ring around the entire valve face. The ring indicates that the valve will seat well. Do not lap the valves excessively.

10. Clean the valve and oil the valve stem.

## WORK RECORD BOX

| Part | Disassembly (nuts, bolts, etc.) | Operation performed | Tool used |
|------|-------------------------------|---------------------|-----------|
|      |                               |                     |           |
|      |                               |                     |           |
|      |                               |                     |           |
|      |                               |                     |           |
|      |                               |                     |           |
|      |                               |                     |           |
|      |                               |                     |           |
|      |                               |                     |           |
|      |                               |                     |           |
|      |                               |                     |           |
|      |                               |                     |           |
|      |                               |                     |           |
|      |                               |                     |           |
|      |                               |                     |           |
|      |                               |                     |           |
|      |                               |                     |           |
|      |                               |                     |           |
|      |                               |                     |           |

## Reassembly Procedure

Reverse the disassembly procedure. Remember to put the exhaust valve in the exhaust side and the intake valve in the intake side. On some engines a magnetic valve retainer inserter is a great help. The retainers often come out easily but are difficult to reinstall.

GENERAL STUDY QUESTIONS

Upon completion of the assigned work, answer the following questions.

1.  Describe the condition of the valves.

2.  Describe the condition of the valve seats.

3.  What is the purpose of lapping valves?

4.  What type of trouble can bad valves cause?

5.  How can you tell the exhaust valve from the intake valve? Are there any special markings?

6.  Can the exhaust valve seat on "your" engine be replaced?

7.  Can the intake valve seat on "your" engine be replaced?

Laboratory Experience 26
## CHECK ENGINE COMPRESSION

### OBJECTIVE

◗  To learn how to check the compression of an engine.

### REFERENCE

●  Review Pages 124-136

### INTRODUCTION

Good compression is essential for optimum engine performance.  Fuel mixture must be tightly compressed to insure proper ignition and maximum power.  Poor compression can be caused by worn piston rings, bad valves, worn or warped cylinders, leakage through the head gasket, or leakage around the spark plug.  Poor compression is a common trouble, especially with older engines that are in need of an overhauling.

If an engine starts with difficulty or lacks power and is sluggish, a troubleshooter might suspect poor compression as the possible cause for these troubles.  Checking the engine's compression is a part of most tune-up procedures.  Generally, each engine manufacturer specifies his own recommended method for checking engine compression.

### STUDENT ASSIGNMENT

You are to perform a compression check on an engine.  It is essential that you record your work in the work record box on the following page as you complete each step of the procedure.

#### Procedure

Your instructor may supplement or revise specific steps of the procedures which follow since there are many makes of engines.  The following procedure is your general guide:

1. Checking compression <u>without</u> a compression gage.

   a. Remove the spark plug high-tension lead from the spark plug.

   b. Turn the engine over slowly by hand.  As the piston reaches top-dead-center, considerable resistance should be felt.  As top-dead-center is passed, the piston should "snap" back down the cylinder, indicating good compression.

2. Checking compression <u>with</u> a compression gage.

   a. Remove the spark plug lead from the spark plug.

   b. Remove the spark plug.

   c. Carefully clean any dirt or foreign matter from around the spark plug hole.

d. Hold the compression gage tightly against the spark plug hole. (Some gages screw into the hole.)

e. Turn the engine over as if you were starting it.

f. Read the compression gage. Readings of 60 to 80 pounds per square inch (p.s.i.) generally indicate good compression, however, some engines may have a compression range of 110 to 120 p.s.i. The exact data for the engine you are working on should be at hand.

## WORK RECORD BOX

| Part | Disassembly (nuts, bolts, etc.) | Operation performed | Tool used |
|---|---|---|---|
|  |  |  |  |
|  |  |  |  |
|  |  |  |  |
|  |  |  |  |
|  |  |  |  |
|  |  |  |  |
|  |  |  |  |
|  |  |  |  |
|  |  |  |  |
|  |  |  |  |
|  |  |  |  |
|  |  |  |  |
|  |  |  |  |

## GENERAL STUDY QUESTIONS

Upon completion of the compression check, answer the following questions.

1. Name some of the engine parts whose failure can cause poor compression.

2. What are the common troubles that are caused by poor compression?

3. Does correcting a condition of poor compression always require a major repair job or overhaul of the engine? Explain.

4. Name the manufacturer of the engine you used. What type of compression check did the manufacturer recommend?

5. If you used a compression gage, record the compression.              p.s.i. Was this pressure within the manufacturer's "acceptable" range?

Laboratory Experience 27

TOLERANCES AND ENGINE MEASUREMENTS

OBJECTIVES

▶ To gain an appreciation of the importance of the close tolerances between engine parts.

▶ To gain experience in using the feeler gage and torque wrench.

REFERENCE

● Manufacturer's Engine Repair Manual

INTRODUCTION

The average engine owner often does not fully appreciate the precision workmanship that is involved in machining and assembling engine parts. The very nature of an engine, many fast moving parts under heavy load, make precision a necessity. Tolerances are very close, always within a few thousandths of an inch. Mechanics who repair and overhaul engines must duplicate the factory precision if their work is to be satisfactory. The poorly equipped mechanic or the mechanic with little regard for precision can do you and your engine a great disservice.

NOTE: The following measurements are simple, only a feeler gage is necessary. For tightening machine bolts and nuts a torque wrench is necessary. Of course, if instruments such as inside and outside micrometers and dial indicators are available, the unit can easily be expanded.

STUDENT ASSIGNMENT

You are to disassemble the engine in order to measure certain clearances. Do not disassemble the engine any more than you have to. Upon reassembly of the engine you will tighten certain nuts and machine bolts to the proper degree with a torque wrench.

If possible, obtain a repair manual for "your" engine and check the clearances against the tolerances. Also, use the torque data for "your" engine if it is available. It is essential that you record your work in the work record box on the following page as you complete each step of the disassembly procedure.

General Procedure

Your instructor may supplement or revise specific steps of the procedure which follows since there are many makes of engines. The following procedure is your general guide. Read the entire procedure carefully before you begin work.

Disassembly Procedure

Disassemble the engine. Your instructor will give you the necessary steps in the engine disassembly procedure.

Checking Procedure

Using a feeler gage:

1. Check the camshaft end clearance.     _____

2. Check the crankshaft end clearance.     _____

3. Check the connecting rod - large end side clearance.    _____

4. Check the valve clearance for both intake and exhaust valves (measured between tappet and valve stem)    _____    and    _____

5. Check the piston skirt clearance at thrust face.    _____

6. Check the ring end gap clearance.    _____

7. Check the ring edge gap clearance.    _____

8. Check the breaker points at maximum opening.    _____

## WORK RECORD BOX

| Part | Disassembly (nuts, bolts, etc.) | Operation performed | Tool used |
|------|--------------------------------|---------------------|-----------|
|      |                                |                     |           |
|      |                                |                     |           |
|      |                                |                     |           |
|      |                                |                     |           |
|      |                                |                     |           |
|      |                                |                     |           |
|      |                                |                     |           |
|      |                                |                     |           |
|      |                                |                     |           |

Reassembly Procedure

Using a torque wrench

1. Tighten the spark plug to 27 ft./lbs.

2. Tighten the connecting rod cap screws to 140 in./lbs.

3. Tighten the cylinder head cap screw to 200 in./lbs.

4. Tighten the flywheel nut to 45 ft./lbs.

NOTE: Use the torque data for your particular engine if it is available.

GENERAL STUDY QUESTIONS

1. Why is precision workmanship necessary in servicing an engine?

2. Briefly define engine tolerance.

3. Briefly explain the use of the feeler gage.

4. How does a torque wrench differ from other wrenches used by the mechanic?

5. Why is a torque wrench used instead of a regular wrench in tightening the various parts?

6. Explain the term ft./lb; in./lb.

Laboratory Experience 28

TUNE-UP FOR SMALL ENGINES

## OBJECTIVE

◗ To learn the general procedure that is followed for engine tune-up.

## REFERENCE

● Review Pages 124-136

## INTRODUCTION

Engine tune-up does not involve major engine repair work, rather, it is a process of cleaning and adjusting the engine so that it will give top performance. Tune-up can be done by an experienced engine owner or it can be done by a mechanic. Tune-up is typically done by the mechanic when an owner brings a lawnmower in for a spring checkup prior to summer use.

## STUDENT ASSIGNMENT

You are to perform the general steps in engine tune-up on your assigned engine. Work carefully, bring the engine up to its peak of cleanliness and operating efficiency. It is essential that you record your work in the work record box on the following page as you complete each step of the procedure.

Procedure

Your instructor may supplement or revise specific steps of the procedure which follows since there are many makes of engines. The following procedure is your general guide:

1. Inspect air cleaner, clean and reassemble air cleaner.

2. Clean the gas tank, fuel lines, and any fuel filters or screens.

3. Check compression.

4. Check spark plug: clean, regap or replace.

5. Check operation of the governor.

6. Check magneto.

7. Fill crankcase with clean oil of the correct type.

8. Fill gasoline tank with regular gasoline, be sure to mix oil with the gasoline if it is a two-stroke cycle engine.

9. Start engine.

10. Adjust carburetor for peak performance.

## WORK RECORD BOX

| Part | Disassembly (nuts, bolts, etc. | Operation performed | Tool used |
|------|------|------|------|
|  |  |  |  |
|  |  |  |  |
|  |  |  |  |
|  |  |  |  |
|  |  |  |  |
|  |  |  |  |
|  |  |  |  |
|  |  |  |  |
|  |  |  |  |
|  |  |  |  |
|  |  |  |  |
|  |  |  |  |
|  |  |  |  |
|  |  |  |  |
|  |  |  |  |
|  |  |  |  |
|  |  |  |  |
|  |  |  |  |
|  |  |  |  |
|  |  |  |  |

## GENERAL STUDY QUESTIONS

Upon completion of the assigned work, answer the following questions.

1. Explain the reason for engine tune-up.

2. Can engine tune-up be done by an engine owner at home?

3. If the engine fails to pass the compression check, what could be causing the trouble?

4. Explain the danger involved in operating a gasoline engine in a closed building.

5. Why is the spark plug on a single-cylinder engine of particular importance in engine tune-up?

6. List the tools that you used in tuning the engine.

# Unit 10

## HORSEPOWER - SPECIFICATIONS - BUYING CONSIDERATIONS

### HORSEPOWER

Horsepower is the yardstick of the engine's power, its capacity to do work. James Watt, the inventor of the steam engine, devised the unit. He assumed that the average horse could raise 33,000 pounds one foot in one minute. An engine that can lift 33,000 pounds one foot in one minute is a one-horsepower engine. Of course, the engine can lift 8,250 pounds four feet in one minute, and still be delivering 1 hp.

As discussed in Unit 2, the formula for horsepower is:

$$\text{hp.} = \frac{\text{Work}}{\text{Time (in minutes)} \times 33,000}$$

Remember that work is the energy required to move a weight through a distance. For example: lifting one pound, one foot, is one foot-pound of work. Lifting 50 pounds, two feet, is 100 foot-pounds of work. The element of time is not a factor.

In horsepower the element of time is added. For example, a heavily laden boat with an outboard motor might cross a river in ten minutes. An identical boat with a larger motor might make the crossing in five minutes. The same amount of work has been accomplished by each engine but the larger horsepower engine did the work faster.

Horsepower terms are varied and often misleading. Persons speak of Rated hp., Developed hp., Brake hp., Indicated hp., Maximum hp., Continuous hp., Corrected hp., Frictional hp., Observed hp., etc. Most of these terms will be discussed in the following paragraphs.

Brake Horsepower is usually used by manufacturers to advertise their engine's power. Brake horsepower is measured either with a prony brake or with a dynamometer. The prony brake consists basically of a flywheel pulley, adjustable brake band, lever, and scale measuring device. With the engine operating, the brake band is tightened on the flywheel and the pressure or torque is transmitted to the scale. The readings on the scale and other data are used to calculate the horsepower.

The dynamometer is a more recent device for measuring horsepower. The electric dynamometer contains a dynamo and as the engine drives the dynamo the current output can be carefully recorded. The more powerful the engine, the more current is produced.

Frictional Horsepower is the power that is used to overcome friction in the engine. The parts themselves absorb a certain amount of power. The pistons account for the greatest friction loss.

Indicated Horsepower is the power that is actually produced by the burning gases within the engine. It does not take into account the power that is absorbed by or used to move the engine parts. It would be the sum of the brake horsepower plus the power used to drive the engine (frictional horsepower).

SAE or Taxable Horsepower is the horsepower used to compute the license fee for automobiles in some states.

$$\text{SAE hp.} = \frac{D^2 \times \text{No. of Cylinder}}{2.5}$$

$D$ = Diameter of bore in inches

Example: $\dfrac{(3.5 \times 3.5) \times 6}{2.5} = 29.4$ hp.

### ESTIMATING HORSEPOWER

The following formula can be used to estimate the maximum horsepower of a four-stroke cycle engine.

$$\text{hp.} = \frac{D \times N \times S \times \text{r.p.m.}}{11,000}$$

D (Bore in Inches)
N (Number of Cylinders)
S (Stroke in Inches)
11,000 (Experimental Constant)

For a two-cycle engine, the formula can be used with 9000 as the experimental constant.

Engine Torque is a factor that relates to horsepower. Torque is the twisting force of the engine's crankshaft. Torque can be compared to the force a man uses to tighten a nut. At first a small amount of torque is used, but more and more torque is applied as the nut tightens; even when the nut stops turning, the man still may be applying torque. Motion is not necessary to have torque. Torque is measured in foot-pounds or inch-pounds. On an engine, the maximum torque is developed at speeds below the maximum engine speed. At top speeds, frictional horsepower is greater and volumetric efficiency is less.

Volumetric Efficiency relates to horsepower also. It refers to the engine's ability to breathe properly, that is, its ability to take in a full charge of fuel mixture in the short time allowed for intake. Engine design largely determines the volumetric efficiency of the engine. At high speeds the volumetric efficiency drops off. It can be increased with superchargers and turbochargers that force or blow air into the intake manifold. Also, volumetric efficiency can be increased by using multiple barrel carburetors (2 barrel and 4 barrel), the extra barrels opening up at high speed when the demand for air is greater.

Compression Ratio is another factor that affects horsepower. This is the relationship of the volume of the cylinder when the piston is at the bottom of its stroke compared to the volume of the cylinder (and combustion chamber) when the piston is at top dead center. For small gasoline engines it may be 6:1, for automobile engines, the compression ratio may be 8:1 or higher. The higher the compression ratio, the greater the horsepower delivered when the fuel mixture is ignited.

Piston Displacement is the volume of air the pistons displace from the bottom of their stroke to top dead center. Piston displacement also relates to horsepower. Generally, the greater the piston displacement the greater the horsepower. Most engines will deliver 1/2 to 7/8 horsepower per cubic inch displacement. High performance engines will develop about 1 horsepower per cubic inch displacement. Supercharged engines can deliver considerably more than 1 horsepower per cubic inch displacement.

Displacement equals Area of Bore × Stroke × Number of Cylinders, and is expressed in cubic inches.

## SPECIFICATIONS

Below are specifications for several models of some of the leading manufacturers of engines. In considering the best engine for a certain job, engineers (and prospective owners too) study such information.

CUSHMAN MOTORS, Lincoln, Nebraska — Principal Usage: Utility Vehicles*

| * Partial List of Models Model* | Rated hp. | R.p.m. | Bore | Stroke | Disp. cu. in. | Comp. Ratio | 2 or 4 Cycle | Weight |
|---|---|---|---|---|---|---|---|---|
| 100 | 9 | | 3.5 | 2.25 | 21.58 | 6.85/1 | 4 | |
| 200 | 18 | | 3.5 | 2.25 | 43.16 | 6.85/1 | 4 | |

KOHLER CO., Kohler, Wisconsin — Principal Usage: All engine powered equipment

| * Other models too numerous to mention Model* | Rated hp. | R.p.m. | Bore | Stroke | Disp. Cu. In. | Comp. Ratio | 2 or 4 Cycle | Weight |
|---|---|---|---|---|---|---|---|---|
| K91 | 4.1 | 4000 | 2 3/8 | 2 | 8.86 | 6.5/1 | 4 | 41 |
| K161 | 7.0 | 3600 | 2 7/8 | 2 1/2 | 16.22 | 6.25/1 | 4 | 65 |
| KV161 | 7.0 | 3600 | 2 7/8 | 2 1/2 | 16.22 | 6.25/1 | 4 | 65 |
| L160 | 6.5 | 3600 | 2 7/8 | 2 1/2 | 16.22 | 6.25/1 | 4 | 106 |
| K241 | 9.5 | 3600 | 3 1/4 | 2 7/8 | 23.9 | 6.00/1 | 4 | 105 |
| K331 | 12.5 | 3200 | 3 5/8 | 3 1/4 | 33.6 | 6.25/1 | 4 | 173 |
| K662 | 24.0 | 3200 | 3 5/8 | 3 1/4 | 67.2 | 6.00/1 | 4 | 250 |

## JACOBSEN MANUFACTURING CO., Racine, Wisconsin
### Principal Usage: Lawn Equipment

| Model | Rated hp. | R.p.m. | Bore | Stroke | Disp. Cu. In. | Comp. Ratio | 2 or 4 Cycle | Weight |
|---|---|---|---|---|---|---|---|---|
| J-125-H | 2.25 | | 2.0 | 1.5 | 4.71 | 5.5/1 | 2 | |
| J-100-H | 1.8 | | 2.0 | 1.5 | 4.71 | 5.5/1 | 2 | |
| J-125-V | 2.25 | | 2.0 | 1.5 | 4.71 | 5.5/1 | 2 | |
| J-175-H | 3.0 | | 2.12 | 1.75 | 6.2 | 5.5/1 | 2 | |
| J-175-V | | | | | | | | |
| J-225-V | 4.0 | | 2.25 | 2.0 | 7.95 | 5.3/1 | 2 | |
| J-321-V | 3.0 | | 2.12 | 1.75 | 6.2 | 5.0/1 | 2 | |
| J-321-H | | | | | | | | |

## BRIGGS AND STRATTON CORP., Milwaukee, Wisconsin 53201
### Principal Usage: General Power Use

* Other models too numerous to mention

| Model* | Rated hp. | R.p.m. | Bore | Stroke | Disp. Cu. In. | Comp. Ratio | 2 or 4 Cycle | Weight |
|---|---|---|---|---|---|---|---|---|
| 92500 | 3 | 3600 | 2 9/16 | 1 3/4 | 9.02 | | 4 | 19.5 |
| 100900 | 4 | 3600 | 2 1/2 | 2 1/8 | 10.43 | | 4 | 30.5 |
| 130900 | 5 | 3600 | 2 9/16 | 2 7/16 | 12.57 | | 4 | 30.75 |
| 60100 | 2 | 3600 | 2 3/8 | 1 1/2 | 6.65 | | 4 | 22.25 |
| 80100 | 2.5 | 3600 | 2 3/8 | 1 3/4 | 7.75 | | 4 | 22.25 |
| 80300 | 3 | 3600 | 2 3/8 | 1 3/4 | 7.75 | | 4 | 25.25 |
| 190400 | 8 | 3600 | 3 | 2 3/4 | 19.44 | | 4 | 45 |

## CLINTON ENGINES CORP., Maquoketa, Iowa
### Principal Usage: General Power Use

* Other models too numerous to mention

| Model* | Rated hp. | R.p.m. | Bore | Stroke | Disp. Cu. In. | Comp. Ratio | 2 or 4 Cycle | Weight |
|---|---|---|---|---|---|---|---|---|
| A2100 | 2.25 | 3600 | 2 3/8 | 1 5/8 | 7.2 | | 4 | 21 1/2 |
| 100 | 2.50 | 3600 | 2 3/8 | 1 5/8 | 7.2 | | 4 | 23 |
| 4100 | 2.75 | 3600 | 2 3/8 | 1 7/8 | 8.3 | | 4 | 21 1/2 |
| 3100 | 3.00 | 3600 | 2 3/8 | 1 7/8 | 8.3 | | 4 | 23 |
| V1000 | 3.25 | 3600 | 2 3/8 | 1 7/8 | 8.3 | | 4 | 36 |
| V1100 | 3.75 | 3600 | 2 3/8 | 2 1/8 | 9.5 | | 4 | 36 |
| B1290 | 4.00 | 3600 | 2 15/32 | 2 1/8 | 10.2 | | 4 | 45 |
| V1200 | 4.50 | 3600 | 2 15/32 | 2 1/8 | 10.2 | | 4 | 40 |
| A1600 | 6.30 | 3600 | 2 13/16 | 2 5/8 | 16.3 | | 4 | 87 |
| B2500 | 9.60 | 3600 | 3 1/8 | 3 1/4 | 25.0 | | 4 | 103 |
| 2790 | 10.30 | 3600 | 3 1/8 | 3 1/4 | 25.0 | | 4 | 103 |

## LAWN BOY, Galesburg, Illinois 61401
### Principal Usage: Lawn Mowers

* Other models too numerous to mention

| Model* | Rated hp. | R.p.m. | Bore | Stroke | Disp. Cu. In. | Comp. Ratio | 2 or 4 Cycle | Weight |
|---|---|---|---|---|---|---|---|---|
| C-10 | | 4000 | 1 15/16 | 1 1/2 | 4.43 | 6.5/1 | 2 | |
| C-12AA | | 4000 | 2 1/8 | 1 1/2 | 5.22 | 6.5/1 | 2 | |
| C-18 | | | 2 3/8 | 1 1/2 | 6.65 | | 2 | |
| D-400 | | | 2 3/8 | 1 1/2 | 6.65 | | 2 | |

### WISCONSIN MOTOR CORP., Milwaukee, Wisconsin
### Principal Usage:  Heavy Duty Industrial

| Model* | Rated hp. | R.p.m. | Bore | Stroke | Disp. Cu. In. | Comp. Ratio | 2 or 4 Cycle | Weight |
|--------|-----------|--------|------|--------|---------------|-------------|--------------|--------|
| *Other models too numerous to mention | | | | | | | | |
| ACN | 6 | 3600 | 2 5/8 | 2 3/4 | 14.88 | | 4 | 76 |
| BKN | 7 | 3600 | 2 7/8 | 2 3/4 | 17.8 | | 4 | 76 |
| AENL | 9.2 | 3600 | 3 | 3 1/4 | 23 | | 4 | 110 |
| AEH | 7.4 | 3200 | 3 | 3 1/4 | 23 | | 4 | 130 |
| AGND | 12.5 | 3200 | 3 1/2 | 4 | 38.5 | | 4 | 180 |
| THD | 18 | 3200 | 3 1/4 | 3 1/4 | 53.9 | | 4 | 220 |
| VE4 | 21.5 | 2400 | 3 | 3 1/4 | 91.9 | | 4 | 295 |
| V F4 | 25 | 2400 | 3 1/4 | 3 1/4 | 107.7 | | 4 | 295 |
| VH4 | 30 | 2800 | 3 1/4 | 3 1/4 | 107.7 | | 4 | 310 |
| VG4D | 37 | 2400 | 3 1/2 | 4 | 154 | | 4 | 410 |
| VR4D | 56.5 | 2200 | 4 1/4 | 4 1/2 | 255 | | 4 | 775 |

### GRAVELY TRACTORS, INC., Dunbar, West Virginia
### Principal Usage:  Gravely Tractors

| Model | Rated hp. | R.p.m. | Bore | Stroke | Disp. Cu. In. | Comp. Ratio | 2 or 4 Cycle | Weight |
|-------|-----------|--------|------|--------|---------------|-------------|--------------|--------|
| L | 6.6 | 2600 | 3 1/4 | 3 1/2 | 29.0 | 5/1 | 4 | 296 |

### O & R ENGINES, Los Angeles, California 90023
### Principal Usage:  General Power

| Model | Rated hp. | R.p.m. | Bore | Stroke | D isp. Cu. In. | C omp. Ratio | 2 or 4 Cycle | Weight |
|-------|-----------|--------|------|--------|----------------|--------------|--------------|--------|
| 13B | 1.0 | 6200 | 1.25 | 1.096 | 1.34 | 9/1 | 2 | 3.9 |
| 13A | 1.0 | 6600 | 1.25 | 1.096 | 1.34 | 9/1 | 2 | 3.9 |
| 20A | 1.6 | 7200 | 1.437 | 1.250 | 2 | | 2 | 4.9 |

### CHRYSLER OUTBOARD CORP. (Formerly West Bend) Hartford, Wisconsin
### Principal Usage:  Chain Saws, Scooters, Carts

| Model | Rated hp. | R.p.m. | Bore | Stroke | Disp. Cu. In. | Comp. Ratio | 2 or 4 Cycle | Weight |
|-------|-----------|--------|------|--------|---------------|-------------|--------------|--------|
| 27824 | 3 | 4500 | 2 | 1 5/8 | 5.1 | 5.5/1 | 2 | 13 1/2 |
| 27825 | 3 | 4500 | 2 | 1 5/8 | 5.1 | 5.5/1 | 2 | 13 1/2 |
| 27852 | 3 | 4500 | 2 | 1 5/8 | 5.1 | 5.5/1 | 2 | 13 1/2 |
| 27854 | 3 | 4500 | 2 | 1 5/8 | 5.1 | 5.5/1 | 2 | 13 1/2 |
| 27612 | 5 | 5500 | 2 1/4 | 1 3/4 | 7.0 | 5.7/1 | 2 | 13 1/2 |
| 2760 | 5 | 5500 | 2 1/4 | 1 3/4 | 7.0 | 5.7/1 | 2 | 13 1/2 |

### D. W. ONAN AND SONS, INC., Minneapolis, Minnesota
### Principal Usage: Compressors, Truck Ref. Mowers, Go-Carts, Scooters, etc.
### (Onan Generator units not listed)

| Model | Rated hp. | R.p.m. | Bore | Stroke | Disp. Cu. In. | Comp. Ratio | 2 or 4 Cycle | Weight |
|-------|-----------|--------|------|--------|---------------|-------------|--------------|--------|
| AS | 5.5 | 3600 | 2 3/4 | 2 1/2 | 14.9 | 6.25/1 | 4 | 85 |
| CCK | 12.9 | 2700 | 3 1/4 | 3 | 50.0 | 5.50/1 | 4 | 148 |

## TECUMSEH PRODUCTS CO., Grafton, Wisconsin
### Principal Usage: General Power Use

| Model* | Rated hp. | R.p.m. | Bore | Stroke | Disp. Cu. In. | Comp. Ratio | 2 or 4 Cycle | Weight |
|--------|-----------|--------|------|--------|---------------|-------------|--------------|--------|
| AH47 | 3.2 | 4800 | 2 | 1 1/2 | 4.7 | | 2 | 13 3/4 |
| AH81 | 5.5 | 5000 | 2 1/2 | 1 5/8 | 7.98 | | 2 | 13 3/4 |
| AV47 | 2.2 | 3800 | 2 | 1 1/2 | 4.7 | | 2 | 14 1/2 |
| V55 | 5.5 | 3600 | 2 5/8 | 2 1/4 | 13.53 | | 4 | 36 1/2 |
| HR30 | 3.0 | 3600 | 2 5/16 | 1 13/16 | 7.61 | | 4 | 28 1/4 |
| HB30 | 3.0 | 3600 | 2 5/16 | 1 13/16 | 7.61 | | 4 | 24 |

* Other models too numerous to mention

## McCULLOCH CORPORATION, Los Angeles, California
### Principal Usage: Chain Saws

| Model* | Rated hp. | R.p.m. | Bore | Stroke | Disp. Cu. In. | Comp. Ratio | 2 or 4 Cycle | Weight |
|--------|-----------|--------|------|--------|---------------|-------------|--------------|--------|
| 1-40 | | 6000 | 2 1/8 | 1 3/8 | 4.9 | 5.5/1 | 2 | 18 |
| 1-50 | | 6000 | 2 1/8 | 1 3/8 | 4.9 | 5.5/1 | 2 | 18 |
| 1-70 | | 7000 | 2 1/4 | 1 1/2 | 5.3 | 7.0/1 | 2 | 21 |
| 1-80 | | 7000 | 2 1/8 | 1 1/2 | 5.3 | 7.5/1 | 2 | 25 |

* Other models too numerous to mention

## BUYING CONSIDERATIONS

The person who is shopping for a gasoline engine will have no trouble in finding an engine for the job. There are many manufacturers of small gasoline engines and they produce engines in a variety of horsepower that are designed and engineered to satisfy every need. It is not uncommon to find a manufacturer's basic model with many variations to adapt the engine for a multitude of different jobs. Let us consider several points in buying an engine.

Cost: Don't be lead astray by bargain prices; true, a good bargain can be found now and then but the general rule, "You get what you pay for", is a good one. This is not to say that the most expensive engine is the best buy for you. Possibly the use the engine is to be put to does not require the added expense of special features, heavy-duty parts or more refined and embellished engine components. Your requirements might well be just an economical, dependable "workhorse" for cutting the grass once a week. However, if your engine will be exposed to continuous heavy usage it would be wise to buy a "heavy-duty" engine, one manufactured to take punishment for a long period of time without failure. The additional cost would be worthwhile in this case.

Reputation of the Manufacturer: Be certain the manufacturer's past record in the field justifies a faith in his new engines. Talk with engine dealers and individual owners of engines. Their opinions and experience may aid you with your selection.

Repair Parts: If you have an engine breakdown that requires a new part, will it be readily available? Can you "run down" to the local dealer and get the part or will you have to send to a factory that may be a thousand miles away? Delays caused by breakdowns can be costly as well as annoying. The availability of service and repair parts is an important consideration.

Power Requirements: Be certain the engine is big enough for the job. Constant overloading or constant operating at full throttle will shorten engine life. Talk with your dealer. He will help you select the correct power plant for the job.

Manufacturers today produce engines that operate on the four-cycle principle and engines that operate on the two-cycle principle; both have their place and both are entirely successful. Some engines are water cooled, some are air cooled, some have simple splash lubrication, some have pump lubrication, some have fuel pumps, some do not. In fact, no two engines look exactly alike or operate exactly alike.

Engine Warranties: Most engine manufacturers will give the purchaser of a new engine a warranty. A common type is good for ninety days. If, during the ninety days after purchase, any parts fail due to defective material or workmanship, the manufacturer will repair or replace the defective part.

In most cases the part or engine must be returned to the factory or to an authorized distributor. Most manufacturers require the owner to pay shipping charges to the factory. And, in some cases, the owner must also pay any labor costs involved in the repair.

If the engine has been damaged through misuse, negligence, or accident, most warranties are void. A few manufacturers require that you register your engine shortly after purchase; if you do not, the warranty is not valid. Generally, engine components such as magnetos, carburetors, starters, etc. are only covered by the terms of their individual manufacturer.

## GENERAL STUDY QUESTIONS

1. If an engine can lift 150,000 pounds in three minutes, what is its horsepower?

2. Generally speaking, can larger horsepower engines do work faster than smaller horsepower engines?

3. What type of horsepower rating do most manufacturers use in advertising their engines?

4. What is a dynamometer?

5. In what way is SAE horsepower used?

6. Estimate the horsepower of a two-stroke cycle having a bore of 2″, one cylinder, a stroke of 1 1/2″, and operating at 3600 revolutions per minute.

7. What is engine torque?

8. What is volumetric efficiency?

9. What is the relationship between compression ratio and horsepower?

10. What is the relationship between piston displacement and horsepower?

11. List four important considerations for a person contemplating the purchase of an engine.

## CLASS DISCUSSION TOPICS

● Discuss how horsepower increases as r.p.m. increases, remembering that engines deliver much less than their rated horsepower at slow speeds.

● Discuss and estimate the horsepower of a "live" engine in class. How does estimated horsepower compare with rated horsepower?

● Discuss how engine torque, volumetric efficiency, compression ratio, and piston displacement are functions of engine design.

● Discuss why there is a limit to the compression ratio that can practically be built into engines.

● Discuss the buying considerations for engines.

## ROTATING COMBUSTION ENGINES

A new power-producing device, or prime mover, has become a member of the internal combustion engine family: the rotating combustion (RC) engine, also referred to as the Wankel engine. The key word is rotating versus reciprocating. In an RC engine, heat energy rotates a three-lobe rotor (piston) within a chamber (cylinder) that has the shape of a fat figure 8. The motion of the rotor is in one direction only, figure 11-1, not back and forth as in a reciprocating engine.

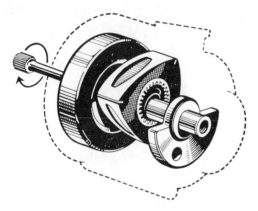

Fig. 11-1 The NSU-Wankel Combustion Engine Utilizes Rotary, Rather than Reciprocating Motion.

For years, engineers have recognized the advantages of smooth rotary motion over reciprocating motion. In a reciprocating internal combustion engine, much power is lost in overcoming the inertia of the piston at both the top and the bottom of its stroke when the motion must be stopped and the direction reversed. This power loss has resulted in the design of lightweight pistons and connecting rods in modern engines. Although a properly-tuned reciprocating engine may seem smooth, there is a great deal of vibration inherent in its design.

Considering these facts, it may appear ironic that reciprocating engines are in wide use and rotating combustion engines are just emerging. Scientists and engineers have thoroughly investigated both the rotating and reciprocating principles. However, since the reciprocating engine presented fewer manufacturing problems and a design that was easily understood, it caught on, and for some eighty years, work toward its perfection has been intensely continued throughout the industrialized nations of the world. The reciprocating principle was applied in many power devices: reciprocating steam engines, diesel engines, and reciprocating gasoline engines.

The development of steam turbines (and diesels) all but eliminated the reciprocating steam engine from the list of modern prime movers. In the commercial aircraft industry and in military aviation, the gas turbine or jet engine largely replaced the piston aircraft engine. Gas turbines are also being used in some applications for stationary and vehicular power plants. Rotating shaft turbines have made notable progress and today are firmly established as a major prime mover.

However, rotating combustion engines are not turbines that employ hot gases directed against the vanes of a spinning wheel. Rotating combustion engines operate on the basic cycle of intake, compression, power, and exhaust, occurring in a repetitive pattern.

## DEVELOPMENT AND APPLICATION OF ROTATING COMBUSTION ENGINES

Many people have experimented with and tested variations of RC engines.

1799   Mr. Murdock used a Pappeneim gear pump as a single rotating engine.

1846   Galloway invented and built a rotary combustion engine.

1860   Oldham/Franchot invented an internal axis rotary piston compressor.

1882   Parsons designed and built a secondary rotating piston steam engine.

1900   Cooley invented and produced an internal axis single rotation engine with epitrochoidal rotor.

1943   Millary patented an internal axis single planetary rotation machine in which the inner rotor had hypotrochoidal contours.

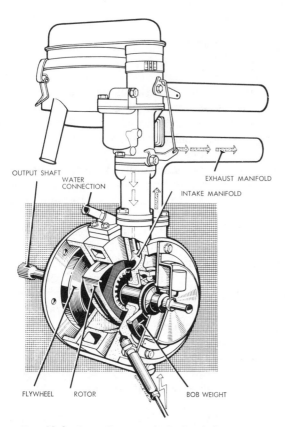

Fig. 11-2 Cross Section of NSU-Wankel Rotating
Combustion Engine Reveals Ingenious
Yet Simple Design.

As these inventors and many others worked on rotating internal combustion engines, two problems persisted: (1) the complex geometry (design) involved, and (2) sealing the power or the pressures created by the burning and expanding gases. Sealing problems in the rotating engine were not as simple to solve as those presented by the round piston in a round cylinder of a reciprocating engine.

Felix Wankel, a German engineer, was attracted to the rotating combustion engine, its problems, and its potential usefulness to man. For years, he worked in the area of developing better sealing techniques. Gradually, his expertise became known, and he set up his own engineering and research laboratory. In 1951, Wankel made contact with Dr. Ing. Walter Froede of the NSU research department. NSU is an engine manufacturer in Germany. Their efforts eventually resulted in getting rotating combustion engines out of the laboratory and into industrial production. In 1958,

Fig. 11-3 Felix Wankel with His Rotating
Combustion Engine.

the Curtiss-Wright Corporation, a company with long and broad experience in engine manufacture in the United States, became the licensee for the NSU/Wankel engine in North America. Other prominent manufacturers have joined the ranks of RC license holders:

| 1960 | Fichtel and Sachs AG | Germany |
| 1961 | Yanmar Diesel Co. Ltd. | Japan |
| 1961 | Toyo Kogyo Co. Ltd. | Japan |
| 1964 | Daimler-Benz AG | Germany |
| 1964 | Alfa Romeo | Italy |
| 1965 | Rolls-Royce Motors Ltd. | Great Britain |
| 1966 | Outboard Marine Corp. | USA |
| 1970 | General Motors Corp. | USA |
| 1970 | Suzuki Motor Co. Ltd. | Japan |
| 1971 | Toyota Motor Co. Ltd. | Japan |
| 1972 | Yamaha | Japan |

Several of these companies are currently producing RC engines for the mass market, while others are still in their developmental, testing, and limited production phases.

Curtiss-Wright has successfully manufactured and tested several versions of the Wankel engine.   In the automotive field, NSU (now Audi NSU Auto Union AG) of Germany produced the NSU Spider from 1964 to 1967 and is currently producing the RO 80 automobile. Toyo Kogyo introduced the Wankel engine in its Cosmo Sport auto of 1967 and is now producing the Mazda R-100 and Mazda RX-2.

Manufacturers producing smaller horsepower RC engines are soon to become numerous.   Fichtel and Sachs AG of West Germany is the largest producer, manufacturing RC engines which range from 6 to 20 h.p. for outboard motors, generators, pumps, lawnmowers, sailplanes, cycles, and snowmobiles. In the United states, their engines are probably most commonly seen on  snowmobiles. Yanmar Diesel Co. of Japan is marketing 20- and 45-horsepower RC outboard motors and has plans for a snow thrower, garden tractor, and other applications. Both Suzuki and Yamaha, Japanese manufacturers, are now developing Wankel-powered motorcycles. The Outboard Marine Corporation became the first United States firm to mass-produce an RC engine, introducing it in September, 1972 on their Johnson and Evinrude snowmobiles. The engine is capable of developing 35 h.p. at 5500 r.p.m. and weighs only 62 pounds.

A. The twin rotor RO-80 Engine used on the latest NSU automobiles;  B. The NSU RO-80 Engine adapted for marine application;  C. Cessna Cardinal Airplane with Curtiss-Wright RC2-60 Engine.  D. SACHS Wankel used to power a motorcycle;  E. Yanmar Rotary Outboard Motor;  F. Fichtel and Sachs Engine used to power a snowmobile.

Fig. 11-4  Some RC Engine Applications.

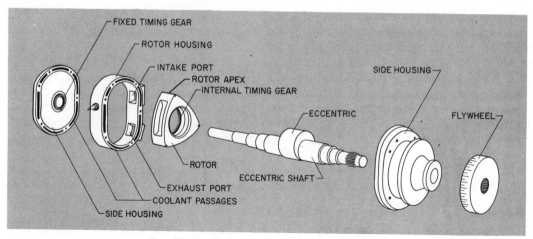

Fig. 11-5 Basic Parts of the Rotary Engine.

## HOW THEY WORK

Like the reciprocating engine, the rotating combustion engine must bring fuel into the engine, compress the fuel, ignite the fuel, allow the pressure of the burning fuel to move the rotor (piston), and allow the spent gases to be exhausted from the engine. But remember, this must be done in a rotating motion rather than a reciprocating motion.

The construction and configuration that makes this possible is a <u>rotor</u> (piston), which is a slightly rounded equilateral triangle rotating on an eccentric portion of the main drive shaft. The relationship of the eccentric bearing and the rotor radius generates the epitrochoidal shape of the housing chamber. The rotor apexes (or tips) follow the shape of the chamber as the rotor is revolved about the shaft eccentric. Remaining in constant, tight contact with the chamber walls, the rotor apexes separate the open volume between the rotor sides and the chamber into three areas which are continually enlarging and reducing as the rotor turns. The housing is provided with intake ports, spark plug, and exhaust ports located at the proper positions to take advantage of the changing volume and provide for intake, compression, power, and exhaust.

## OPERATING CYCLE

Figure 11-6 shows the operating cycle or phasing of the RC engine, which is similar to a three-cylinder piston engine since there are three sides to the rotor. This discussion of the operating principles follows the action of side AC as it finishes its exhaust phase and takes fuel into the chamber; side AB as it compresses the fuel, ignites the fuel, and begins the power phase; and side BC as it completes the power phase and begins its exhaust phase.

Positions 1, 2, 3, and 4 (numerals encircled) show the uncovering of the intake port and the increasing volume of the chamber. Fuel mixture enters the chamber, being pushed in by atmospheric pressure. The engine has a conventional carburetor and the operating principle is the same as that applied to reciprocating engines.

Positions 5, 6, and 7 show the changing geometry of the chamber during compression. As the rotor continues to turn, the fuel mixture is compressed into a smaller and smaller space. Compression ratios are designed to meet particular needs and they usually approximate those of similar sized reciprocating engines; for example, a compression ratio of 9 to 1 is used in the NSU RO 80 automobile engine. At position 7, maximum compression is attained and the spark plug fires and ignites the mixture. The spark plug tip is recessed in a hole so that the rotor can sweep by without hitting it.

Positions 8, 9, and 10 show the expanding gases exerting pressure against the face of the rotor. This is equivalent to the power stroke.

Positions **11**, **12**, and **1** comprise the exhaust phase of the cycle. As the apex passes the exhaust port, the exhaust is forced from the engine.

The design of the engine permits the rotor to travel at one-third the speed of the main drive shaft. For instance, if an RC engine has a shaft speed of 6,000 r.p.m., the rotor travels at 2,000 r.p.m. and there are 6,000 power strokes per minute. There is a power stroke for every revolution of the drive shaft. Speed ranges of 2,000 - 17,000 r.p.m. have been reached. Most small RC engines have rated speeds of 4,500 - 5,500 r.p.m.

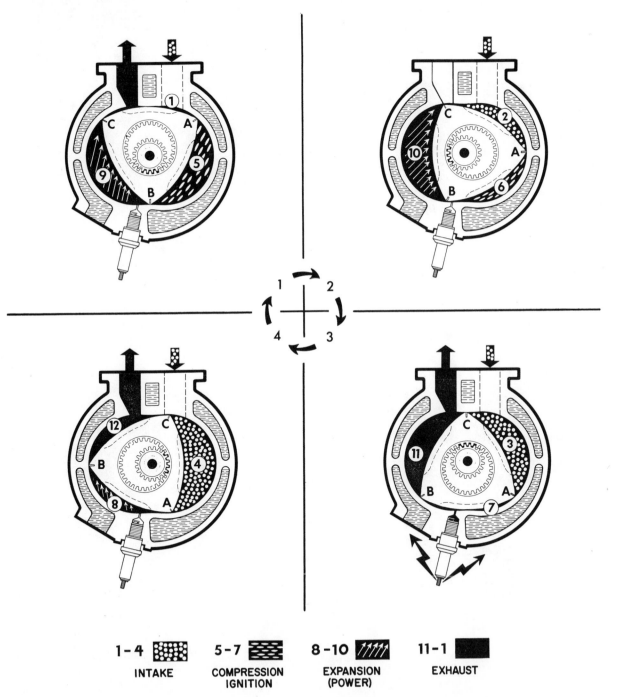

Fig. 11-6 Operating Principles of the Rotating Combustion Engine

## CONSTRUCTION OF THE ROTATING COMBUSTION ENGINE

The different makes of rotating combustion engines share the same basic operating principles and parts; however, there are variations in engineering approaches, just as there are in reciprocating engines. The following description of the Curtiss-Wright R1-60, figure 11-7, is quite typical of RC engines. Other manufacturers' specifications are interjected where appropriate.

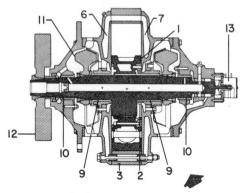

### RC-60 — Longitudinal and Cross Sections

1. Rotor With Internal Rotor Gear
2. Stationary Gear
3. Rotor Housing
4. Exhaust Port
5. Spark Plug
6. Side Housing — Drive Side
7. Side Housing — Anti-Drive Side
8. Intake Port
9. Main Bearing (Inner)
10. Main Bearing (Outer)
11. Balance Weight
12. Flywheel
13. Ignition Contact Maker

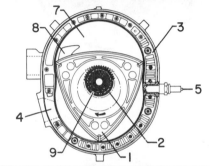

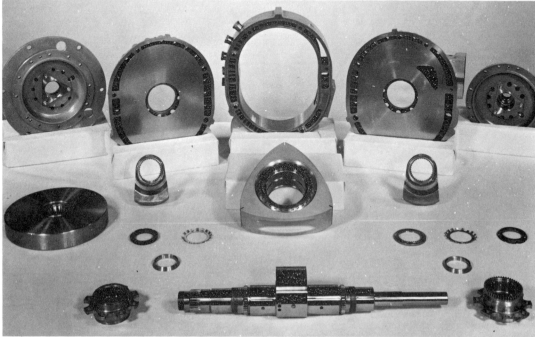

Fig. 11-7 The Curtiss-Wright Experimental Engine, RC-60.

The rotor is a hollow casting of either aluminum or cast iron, figure 11-8. The three rotor flanks are exposed to a considerable concentration of heat; therefore, cooling oil is circulated through the rotor. Oil, under pressure from the oil pump, enters the rotor through drilled passages in the main shaft, figure 11-9, picks up heat, and then is discharged back into the system. A large hole machined in the center of the rotor accommodates the eccentric of the main shaft. A ring gear is secured to the rotor and meshes with a stationary gear on one of the end housings. These gears insure that the correct relationship is followed by the engine parts as the rotor travels the epitrochoidal path.

Fig. 11-8 Hollow Construction of Rotor.

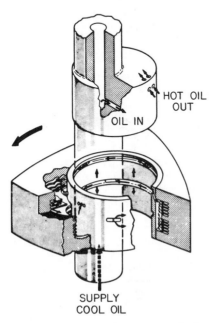

Fig. 11-9 Oil Flow Through Main Shaft, Eccentric, and Rotor.

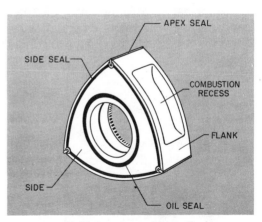

Fig. 11-10 Location of Rotor Seals.

Devising effective seals for the rotor was accomplished only after exhaustive testing and development. The rotor must be sealed on the sides and also at the three rotor apexes, figure 11-10.

The seals themselves are made of alloy cast iron which does not wear excessively nor does it cause excessive wear on the rotor housing. Light springs push the apex seals and side seals against the housing surfaces to provide an airtight seal. The apex seal may be traveling at the sliding velocity of up to 108 feet per second.

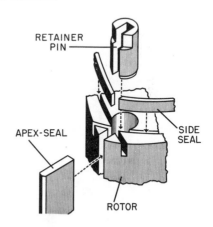

Fig. 11-11 Apex Seals and Side Seals for Rotor.

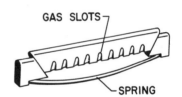

Fig. 11-12 Construction of Apex Seal Used on NSU RO-80 Engine.

Lubrication in some form must be provided, just as piston rings must be lubricated. NSU/Wankel in Germany employs a separate

oil supply delivered to the intake charge of fuel mixture. Curtiss-Wright provides lubrication by means of metering oil seal rings in the rotor itself. A rotating combustion engine consumes oil at about the same rate as a conventional reciprocating engine.

The forces that move the rotor are transmitted to the main shaft by means of an eccentric section on the shaft. The eccentric enables the rotor to follow the geometry of the housing. The main shaft is held and centered by the two end housings. One end of the shaft contains the various gear takeoffs for the engine, such as the water pump, oil pump, and distributor shaft.

Rotating combustion engines are either liquid or air cooled. In the liquid-cooled RC engines, cooling water is circulated around the main chamber housing and around the end units, figure 11-13. Special attention is given to the combustion area, figure 11-14. Combustion for each rotor flank always occurs at the same point, and an abundance of cooling media must be present at this area.

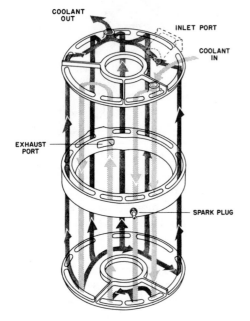

Fig. 11-13  Schematic of Housing Coolant Flow.

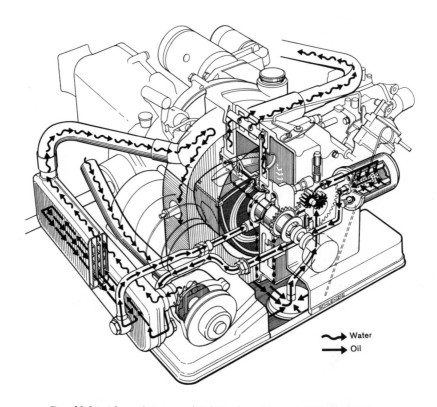

Fig. 11-14  Flow of Water and Oil Coolant Through NSU Spider Engine.

Fig. 11-15 Air-Cooled RC Engine.

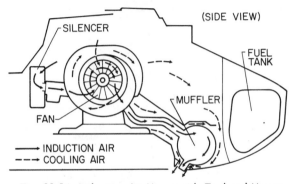

Fig. 11-16 Induction Air Mixes with Fuel and Moves
Through the Engine to Cool the Rotor. Cooling
Air is Blown Across the Radiating Fins on the Housings.

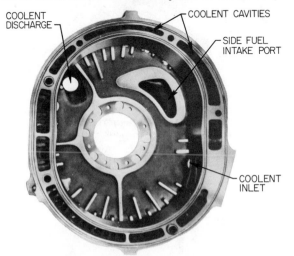

Fig. 11-17 Internal Ribbing, Side Intake Port, and
Coolant Cavities of End Housing (enclosing wall of end
housing is machined away to show internal ribbing).

Air cooling, such as in the Fichtel and Sachs AG and the Outboard Marine Corporation (OMC) RC engines, is achieved by blowing cool air across ribs or fins of the side housings and trochoid housing. The cool air is directed toward the fins by pressure fans or centrifugal blowers, figure 11-16. In areas of greatest heat concentration, the cooling ribs are more numerous, larger, and longer to provide better heat dissipation. Air-cooled RC engines have not experienced noticeable heat distortion problems. The rotor is cooled by the incoming fuel mixture which travels from the carburetor at the drive side, through triangular windows at the rotor points, to the end side housing before entering the intake ports at the periphery of the trochoid housing. This cooling technique is known as "charge cooling."

One significant change that Curtiss-Wright has incorporated into their version of the RC engine is the intake ports. The Curtiss-Wright engine has side intake ports, figure 11-17, that provide improved low-speed operation and lessen fuel consumption. The NSU/Wankel engine has peripheral intake ports located in the main housing. Both companies use peripheral exhaust ports.

The OMC engine has two intake ports to meet the need for smooth idling and full-power operation. A port on the side housing provides fuel mixture for idling. An additional intake port located on the periphery of the trochoid housing opens to allow more air flow after the first 15 degrees of throttle movement. This "power port" provides for top high-speed performance.

In the Fichtel and Sachs engines, lubricating oil is mixed with the fuel as in two-cycle engines. The ratio of oil to gasoline is 1:50 or 1:40. This method provides ample lubrication for the needle bearings or roller bearings and the side and apex seals of the rotor. The trochoid working surface is plated with a mixture of steel and bronze, while the apex seals are gray cast iron.

Lubrication in the OMC engine is accomplished by mixing oil (Evinrude or Johnson Rotary Combustion) with gasoline in an oil-to-gasoline ratio of 1:50. The OMC engine uses a tungsten carbide coating on the trochoid housing, steel apex seals, and cast iron side rotor seals; the basic castings are aluminum.

Conventional magneto ignitions and basic carburetors are used in the Fichtel and Sachs engines. The OMC engine employs a magneto-excited capacitor discharge ignition.

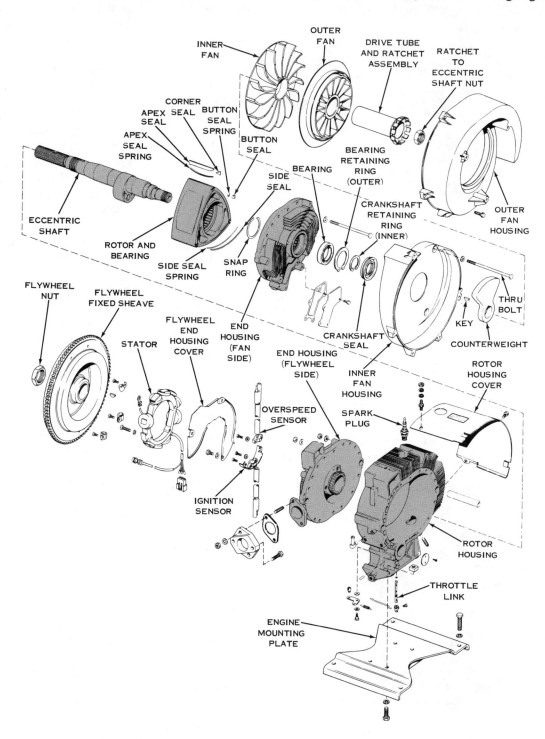

Fig. 11-18  Assembly Drawing of the OMC Rotary Combustion Engine.
(Basic parts of the engine are shaded.)

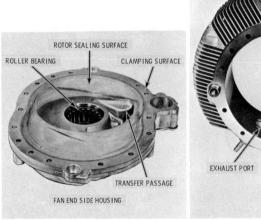
ROLLER BEARING

ROTOR SEALING SURFACE

CLAMPING SURFACE

TRANSFER PASSAGE

FAN END SIDE HOUSING

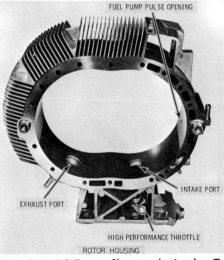
FUEL PUMP PULSE OPENING

EXHAUST PORT

INTAKE PORT

HIGH PERFORMANCE THROTTLE

ROTOR HOUSING

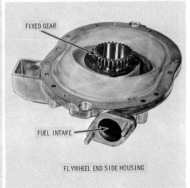
FIXED GEAR

FUEL INTAKE

FLYWHEEL END SIDE HOUSING

Fig. 11-19  Three Main Housings of the OMC RC Engine Showing the Intake, Transfer, and Porting Arrangements.

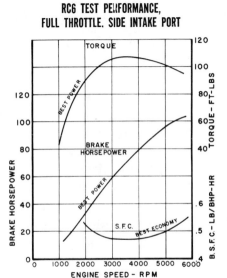

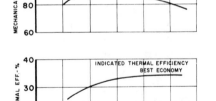

Fig. 11-20 Operating Characteristics of a Rotating Combustion Engine.

## ROTATING COMBUSTION ENGINE PERFORMANCE

The performance of rotating combustion engines compares favorably to that of reciprocating engines. Performance characteristics such as brake horsepower, thermal efficiency, and mechanical efficiency, figure 11-20, indicate the adequacy of this engine. The torque curve for the RC engine is excellent with little drop at high speed. The flow of fuel mixture, demonstrated by the volumetric efficiency of the engine, is also excellent.

RC engines are able to use fuel with a lower octane rating than piston engines of the same compression ratio. The design of the combustion area and the flow of the fuel mixture minimizes the possibility of preignition.

Gasoline may be regular grade, either leaded or unleaded.

Emissions of unburned hydrocarbons, carbon monoixde (CO), and nitrogen oxides are present in the exhaust of RC engines, just as in reciprocating engines. Hydrocarbon and CO emissions presently are comparatively high but can be lessened by having a well-tuned engine. Also, the relatively small engine size permits space for emission control devices such as a thermal reactor. Nitrogen oxide emissions are somewhat lower than those in reciprocating engines, probably because maximum temperatures are less in an RC engine. Emission control devices will enable RC engines to meet U.S. Federal and European emission standards.

Fig. 11-21  The OS/Graupner Wankel
Engine for Model Airplanes.

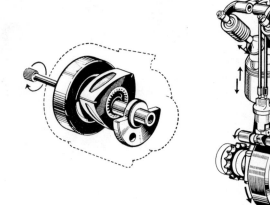

Fig. 11-22  Rotating Combustion Engines Require Fewer Parts, are Lighter
in Weight, and are More Economical to Manufacture than Reciprocating Engines.

The horsepower range of the RC engine is flexible. The Curtiss-Wright corporation constructed one single rotor engine with a 782 brake horsepower rating, as well as auto sized and small horsepower sized engines. The OS/Graupner Wankel engine powers model airplanes, figure 11-21, and produces .67 h.p. at 16,000 r.p.m. The horsepower of any basic engine can be increased by merely adding rotors in succession. A twin-rotor engine is equivalent to a six-cylinder reciprocating engine. The combination of three or four rotors and their enclosing chamber presents no construction problems, and an increase in the number of rotors offers a smoother operation.

To summarize the potential of rotating combustion engines, the following advantages are listed:

- Smooth operation with little vibration.
- High horsepower-to-weight ratio.
- Many different fuels can be used.
- Wider speed range than that of reciprocating engines.
- Excellent torque curve.
- Economical to manufacture.
- Can be produced in many different sizes.
- Fewer moving parts than reciprocating engines.

## GENERAL STUDY QUESTIONS

1. Explain the difference between rotating motion and reciprocating motion when these terms are applied to internal combustion engines.

2. What two significant problems slowed the development of rotating combustion engines?

3. Who is credited with perfecting the design for the most widely used rotating combustion engine?

4. What name is given to the geometric shape of the rotor housing?

5. What four functions must be accomplished during a complete cycle of the rotating combustion engine?

6. Does the rotating combustion engine require a unique or specially designed carburetor, ignition system, water pump, or oil pump? Explain.

7. List the key moving parts of the rotating combustion engine.

8. List several advantages of the rotating combustion engine.

## CLASS DISCUSSION TOPICS

● Discuss the role of technology in developing and manufacturing the rotating combustion engine.

● Discuss the various problems that an emerging design encounters as it becomes an established and widely used product.

● Discuss the operating characteristics of the rotating combustion engine, such as torque, volumetric efficiency, mechanical efficiency, and horsepower.

● Discuss the operating principles of the rotating combustion engine.

# LABORATORY EXPERIENCES

Many of the previous laboratory experiences apply to the RC (Wankel) engine. Using specifications for a particular RC engine model converts the appropriate laboratory experience from reciprocating to rotating combustion. For example, laboratory experience 4-5, Basic Parts of the Carburetor, satisfies both reciprocating and RC engines.

The three RC engine laboratory experiences included are the most basic and common for the student or engine owner:

- Preparing the RC Engine for Service
- Maintenance of the RC Engine
- Laying up the RC Engine for Storage

If disassembly or overhaul of an RC engine is anticipated, it is recommended that all operations be done with the aid of an applicable service repair manual and expert supervision.

## Laboratory Experience 29

### PREPARING THE RC ENGINE FOR SERVICE

OBJECTIVES

▶ To learn the correct methods of preparing an RC engine for service.

REFERENCE

- Review pages 163-174
- SACHS Wankel Engine KM 24 Manual 4016.2E Snowmobile Engine
- 1973 Evinrude and Johnson Snowmobile Service Manual 35 HP

INTRODUCTION

Before starting any engine, read and understand all instructional material; approach the engine with knowledge and technical data, not guesswork. This procedure insures correct operation and adds to the service life of the engine.

STUDENT ASSIGNMENT

You are to perform the following steps on an RC engine. Your instructor may revise or supplement certain steps to comply with the needs of available engine models; the steps below are a general guide. These steps cover the engine itself, and there may be additional points to be covered on the machine the engine is powering.

1. Check the spark plug for tightness (12-15 ft.-lbs.) Be certain the spark plug gasket is in place.

2. Check the spark plug lead; is it secure to the spark plug?

3. Using a funnel with a fine-mesh screen, fill the gasoline tank with fuel mixture, 50:1 (gas to oil). Never fill the tank while the engine is running. Use any brand-name regular gasoline, leaded or unleaded. OMC/RC engines use Evinrude and Johnson Rotary Combustion Snowmobile Lubricant or OMC Rotary Combustion Lubricant. Fichtel and Sachs engines use Sachs Rotary Piston Oil, BP Super

Outboard Motor Oil, ESSO Lub HD 30, Mobilmix TT, Mobiloil TT, or Shell-Rotella SAE 30. When mixing, partially fill the mixing container with gasoline, add lubricating oil, shake vigorously to mix, add the remaining gasoline to obtain the proper ratio, and again shake vigorously to complete the mixing.

4. New engines require a break-in period. Operate a Sachs engine at approximately half throttle under medium r.p.m.'s for the first 5 running hours. OMC engines should be operated at less than full throttle until at least one tank full of fuel has been used.

5. Understand engine safety and be familiar with all operating controls before attempting to start the engine and operate the machine.

## GENERAL STUDY QUESTIONS

1. Explain what might happen if the lubricating oil is not mixed with the gasoline.

2. What is the correct ratio of gasoline to oil?

3. List safety considerations for operating "your" engine.

4. Explain the starting procedure for "your" engine.

5. Explain the operating controls for "your" machine, such as shifting gears, choke, lights, and safety features.

Laboratory Experience 30

MAINTENANCE OF THE RC ENGINE

## OBJECTIVE

◆ To become familiar with the routine maintenance considerations of RC engines.

## REFERENCE

● Review Pages 163-174

● SACHS Wankel Engine KM 24 Manual 4016.2E Snowmobile Engine

● 1973 Evinrude and Johnson Snowmobile Service Manual 35 HP

## INTRODUCTION

An engine represents a considerable investment in money, perhaps several hundred dollars. To safeguard this investment, the engine operator must perform certain routine steps in care and maintenance. Routine care and maintenance insures the longest life possible for engine parts and may save costly repair bills.

The best source of information on engine care is the manual or instruction booklet supplied with every new engine. This information serves to acquaint the engine owner or operator with the requirements of that particular engine.

## STUDENT ASSIGNMENT

You are to perform several various maintenance activities on an RC engine. Your instructor may revise or supplement certain steps to satisfy the requirements of available engine models.

1. Remove the spark plug and clean it. Carbon deposits must be carefully removed, preferably with an abrasive blast cleaning machine. For Sachs engines, clean the plugs after every 100 hours of operation.

2. Lubricate the recoil starter as required if rewinding trouble develops. For Sachs engines, use 0.5 cc. of Anticorit oil at the grease fitting.

3. Steps 3 and 4 should be done with the engine stopped and cold. Gasoline spilled on a hot engine can explode. Remove the fuel strainer of the fuel pump and clean as required in solvent.

4. Clean the fuel strainer at the tank if one is installed.

5. Remove and clean the air cleaner as needed (for OMC engines, twice a season).

## GENERAL STUDY QUESTIONS

1. Explain the difference between preventive maintenance and repair.

2. Describe the condition of "your" spark plug.

3. What type of spark plug is recommended for "your" engine?

4. What type of air cleaner is used on "your" engine?

Laboratory Experience 31
## LAYING UP THE RC ENGINE FOR STORAGE

### OBJECTIVE

▶ To learn the requirements of engine layup for RC engines.

### REFERENCE

● Review Pages 163-174

● SACHS Wankel Engine KM 24 Manual 4016.2E Snowmobile Engine

● 1973 Evinrude and Johnson Snowmobile Service Manual 35 HP

### INTRODUCTION

Engines that are operated on a seasonal basis should have special care during their off-season storage. Persons who pay little or no attention to these requirements gamble with the functioning of their engine. To insure long, dependable engine life, follow the suggestions of the engine manufacturer.

### STUDENT ASSIGNMENT

You are to perform the following steps in laying up an RC engine for storage. Your instructor may revise or supplement the list to meet the needs of a particular engine or machine.

For SACHS engines:

1. Squirt 20 cc. (1.22 cu. in.) of oil (Shell ENSIS 30) into the carburetor inlet with the choke and throttle open. Crank the engine 5 or 6 times to spread the oil on the bearings, rotor seals, and working surfaces of the end housings.

2. One of the following anticorrosive oils should be applied to the outside surfaces:

> Anticorit 5 or Messrs FUCHS D-6800
>
> Mobil MIL-L-644B
>
> Shell ENSIS Fluid 260
>
> ESSO Rust Ban 395

3. Drain the fuel system of the engine.

For OMC engines:

1. Drain the fuel tank, using a siphon hose.

2. Operate the engine to consume the fuel remaining in the carburetor.

3. Remove the spark plug.

4. Insert 1 teaspoon of OMC Rotary Combustion Oil into the engine through the spark plug hole. Move the eccentric shaft one revolution. Insert a teaspoon of oil to the second chamber and again turn the shaft one revolution. Repeat for the third chamber. Now crank the engine several times to distribute the oil. Replace the spark plug.

5. Apply OMC Accessory Engine Cleaner to the engine.

6. Clean or replace the fuel pump filter screen.

7. After removing the air cleaner element, clean or replace it.

8. Perform additional storage requirements by consulting the manufacturer's instruction book for your snowmobile.

## GENERAL STUDY QUESTIONS

1. What can happen to gasoline during long periods of storage?

2. Can engine layup be accomplished by the average owner?  If it can, what information sources can be employed?

# APPENDIX

## RECIPROCATING ENGINE TROUBLESHOOTING CHART

### ENGINE FAILS TO START OR STARTS WITH DIFFICULTY

| Cause | Remedy |
| --- | --- |
| No fuel in tank | Fill tank with clean, fresh fuel. |
| Shutoff valve closed | Open valve. |
| Obstructed fuel line | Clean fuel screen and line. If necessary, remove and clean carburetor. |
| Tank cap vent obstructed | Open vent in fuel tank cap. |
| Water in fuel | Drain tank. Clean carburetor and fuel lines. Dry spark plug points. Fill tank with clean, fresh fuel. |
| Engine over-choked | Close fuel shutoff and pull the starter until engine starts. Reopen fuel shutoff for normal fuel flow. |
| Improper carburetor adjustment | Adjust carburetor. |
| Loose or defective magneto wiring | Check magneto wiring for shorts or grounds; repair if necessary. |
| Faulty magneto | Check timing, point gap, and if necessary, overhaul magneto. |
| Spark plug fouled | Clean and regap spark plug. |
| Spark plug porcelain cracked | Replace spark plug. |
| Poor compression | Overhaul engine. |

### ENGINE KNOCKS

| Cause | Remedy |
| --- | --- |
| Carbon in combustion chamber | Remove cylinder head or cylinder and clean carbon from head and piston. |
| Loose or worn connecting rod | Replace connecting rod. |
| Loose flywheel | Check flywheel key and keyway; replace parts if necessary. Tighten flywheel nut to proper torque. |
| Worn cylinder | Replace cylinder. |
| Improper magneto timing | Time magneto. |

## ENGINE MISSES UNDER LOAD

| Cause | Remedy |
|---|---|
| Spark plug fouled | Clean and regap spark plug. |
| Spark plug porcelain cracked | Replace spark plug. |
| Improper spark plug gap | Regap spark plug. |
| Pitted magneto breaker points | Clean and dress breaker points. Replace badly pitted breaker points. |
| Magneto breaker arm sluggish | Clean and lubricate breaker point arm. |
| Faulty condenser (except on Tecumseh Magneto) | Check condenser on a tester; replace if defective. |
| Improper carburetor adjustment | Adjust carburetor. |
| Improper valve clearance (four-stroke cycle engines) | Adjust valve clearance. |
| Weak valve spring (four-stroke cycle engines) | Replace valve spring. |
| Reed fouled or sluggish (two-stroke cycle engines) | Clean or replace reed. |
| Crankcase seal leak (two-stroke cycle engines) | Replace worn crankcase seals. |

## ENGINE LACKS POWER

| Cause | Remedy |
|---|---|
| Choke partly closed | Open choke. |
| Improper carburetor adjustment | Adjust carburetor. |
| Magneto improperly timed | Time magneto. |
| Worn piston or rings | Replace piston or rings. |
| Lack of lubrication (four-stroke cycle engine) | Fill crankcase to proper level. |
| Air cleaner fouled | Clean air cleaner. |
| Valves leaking (four-stroke cycle engine) | Grind valves. |
| Reed fouled or sluggish (two-stroke cycle engine) | Clean or replace reed. |
| Improper amount of oil in fuel mixture (two-stroke cycle engine) | Drain tank; fill with correct mixture. |
| Crankcase seals leaking (two-stroke cycle engine) | Replace worn crankcase seals. |

## ENGINE OVERHEATS

| Cause | Remedy |
|---|---|
| Engine improperly timed | Time engine. |
| Carburetor improperly adjusted | Adjust carburetor. |
| Air flow obstructed | Remove any obstructions from air passages in shrouds. |
| Cooling fins clogged | Clean cooling fins. |
| Excessive load on engine | Check operation of associated equipment. Reduce excessive load. |
| Carbon in combustion chamber | Remove cylinder head or cylinder and clean carbon from head and piston. |
| Lack of lubrication | Fill crankcase to proper level. |
| Improper amount of oil in fuel mixture | Drain tank; fill with correct mixture. |

## ENGINE SURGES OR RUNS UNEVENLY

| Cause | Remedy |
|---|---|
| Fuel tank cap vent hole clogged | Open vent hole. |
| Governor parts sticking or binding | Clean, and if necessary, repair governor parts. |
| Carburetor throttle linkage, throttle shaft and/or butterfly binding or sticking | Clean, lubricate, or adjust linkage and deburr throttle shaft or butterfly. |

## ENGINE VIBRATES EXCESSIVELY

| Cause | Remedy |
|---|---|
| Engine not securely mounted | Tighten loose mounting bolts. |
| Bent crankshaft | Replace crankshaft. |
| Associated equipment out of balance | Check associated equipment. |

## ROTATING COMBUSTION ENGINE TROUBLESHOOTING CHART *

Troubleshooting to determine the cause of any operating problem may be broken down into the following steps:

a. Obtaining an accurate description of the trouble

b. Preliminary inspection

c. Use of Trouble Check Chart to analyze engine performance

An accurate description of the trouble is essential for troubleshooting. The owner's comments may provide valuable information which will serve as a clue to the cause of the problem.

### Preliminary Inspection

1. Engine turns over freely
2. Spark at spark plug
3. Carburetor adjusted properly
4. Power port butterly closed completely at idle
5. Air cleaner clean and properly installed
6. Air intake clean and not restricted
7. Cooling fan intake not restricted and fan air exit under muffler not restricted
8. Proper fuel and oil in tank
9. Static air leak check within limits

### STARTING

1. Hard to start or won't start

   a. Low static air leak check

   b. Old fuel, water in fuel, or restricted fuel passages

   c. Choke not working properly

   d. Primer not working properly

   e. Carburetor low-speed needle not adjusted correctly

   f. Bad spark plug

   g. No spark

   h. Air cleaner or intake blocked or restricted

   i. Clogged fuel line or filter

   j. Engine flooded

   k. Faulty or missing gaskets on intake systems

2. Engine turns over extremely easy

   a. Low static air leak check

   b. Spark plug loose

   c. Cracked or broken engine castings

3. Engine starts, but stops immediately

   a. Fuel pump not working

   b. Carburetor low-speed system blocked or out of adjustment

   c. Fuel Filter clogged

   d. Choke not working properly

4. Engine won't turn over

   a. External parts assembled wrong causing interference

   b. Rotor assembled upside down, gears not meshing

   c. "J" gap plug installed instead of surface gas type

   d. No gasket under surface gap plug

   e. Bearings seized

   f. Rotor cracked or broken

   g. Engine castings cracked or broken

5. Weak spark or no spark

   a. Faulty charge coil

   b. Faulty sensor coil

   c. Faulty power pack

   d. Grounded ignition switch or wire

   e. Flywheel not magnetized

   f. Faulty ignition coil or leads

   g. Ignition switch not working

### STARTING - MANUAL STARTER

1. Manual starter pulls out, but starter does not engage flywheel

b. Excess or incorrect grease on pawls or spring

c. Pawls bent or burred

d. Pawls frozen (water) in place

2. Starter rope does not return

a. Recoil spring broken or binding

b. Starter housing bent

c. Loose or missing parts

3. Clattering manual starter

a. Friction spring bent or burred

b. Starter housing bent

c. Excess or incorrect grease on pawls or spring

d. Dry starter spindle

STARTING - ELECTRIC STARTER

1. Starter cranks too slowly

a. Weak battery

b. Loose or corroded connections or ground connection

c. Faulty starter solenoid or solenoid wiring

d. Worn armature brushes or spring

e. Faulty field or armature (shorted or open windings)

2. Starter will not crank engine

a. Weak battery

b. Loose or corroded connections or ground

c. Broken wire in harness or connector

d. Faulty ignition key switch

e. Faulty starter solenoid or solenoid wiring

f. Moisture in starter motor

g. Broken or worn brushes or broken brush spring

h. Faulty field or armature (shorted or open windings)

i. Starter does not engage with engine because drive gear is not free on helix.

3. Starter will not disengage flywheel ring gear

a. Drive gear is not free on helix (debris must be removed)

b. Lubricate helix

RUNNING - LOW SPEED

1. Low-speed miss

a. Incorrect gas - lubricant ratio

b. Incorrect idle adjustment

c. Loose or broken ignition coil wires

d. Spark plug terminal loose

e. Weak coil

f. Loose electrical connections

g. Power port butterfly not closed completely

h. Bad or missing gaskets around intake manifold

i. Choke not operating correctly

j. Low static air leak check

RUNNING - HIGH SPEED

1. High-speed miss

a. Overspeed sensor improperly adjusted

b. Water in fuel

c. Weak spark

d. Arcing around ignition coil or leads

e. Bad spark plug

f. Low static air leak check

g. Carburetor inlet needle sticking

2. Poor acceleration, top rpm is low

a. Incorrect gas - lubricant ratio

b. Old fuel

c. Fuel hose plugged or kinked

d. Fuel filter restricted

e. Bad fuel pump

f.  Pulse line to fuel pump restricted

g.  Loose or broken high-tension lead

h.  Weak coil

i.  Bad power pack

j.  Carburetor passageways restricted

k.  Power port butterfly not opening completely

l.  Overheating

m.  Low static air leak check

n.  Fuel tank vent restricted or blocked

## RUNNING - HIGH AND LOW SPEED

1.  Engine overheats

a.  Incorrect gas - lubricant ratio

b.  Improper engine assembly

c.  Cooling fins blocked by foreign material

d.  Cooling fan intake restricted

e.  Cooling air exit restricted

f.  Dirty air filter

g.  Air intake restricted

h.  Intake air box leaking, getting air from under shroud

2.  Engine seizes (stops suddenly)

a.  No oil in gas

b.  seized rotor or main bearing

c.  Broken rotor or stationary gear

d.  Cracked or broken engine castings

* Courtesy of Outboard Marine Corp.

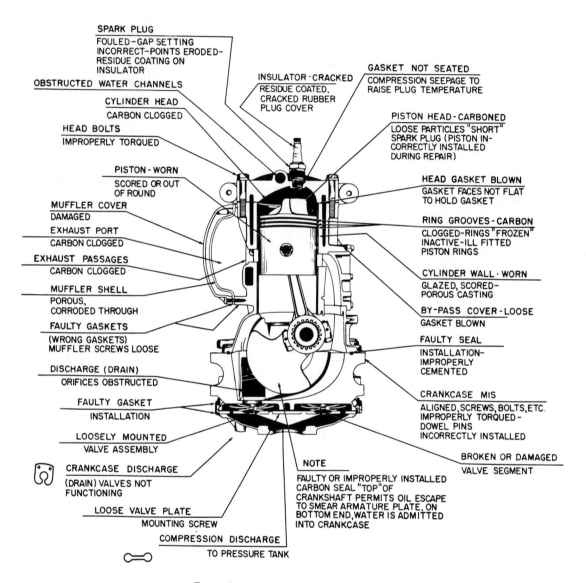

SPARK PLUG
FOULED – GAP SETTING
INCORRECT – POINTS ERODED –
RESIDUE COATING ON
INSULATOR

OBSTRUCTED WATER CHANNELS

CYLINDER HEAD
CARBON CLOGGED

HEAD BOLTS
IMPROPERLY TORQUED

PISTON – WORN
SCORED OR OUT
OF ROUND

MUFFLER COVER
DAMAGED

EXHAUST PORT
CARBON CLOGGED

EXHAUST PASSAGES
CARBON CLOGGED

MUFFLER SHELL
POROUS,
CORRODED THROUGH

FAULTY GASKETS
(WRONG GASKETS)
MUFFLER SCREWS LOOSE

DISCHARGE (DRAIN)
ORIFICES OBSTRUCTED

FAULTY GASKET
INSTALLATION

LOOSELY MOUNTED
VALVE ASSEMBLY

CRANKCASE DISCHARGE
(DRAIN) VALVES NOT
FUNCTIONING

LOOSE VALVE PLATE
MOUNTING SCREW

COMPRESSION DISCHARGE
TO PRESSURE TANK

INSULATOR – CRACKED
RESIDUE COATED,
CRACKED RUBBER
PLUG COVER

GASKET NOT SEATED
COMPRESSION SEEPAGE TO
RAISE PLUG TEMPERATURE

PISTON HEAD – CARBONED
LOOSE PARTICLES "SHORT"
SPARK PLUG (PISTON IN-
CORRECTLY INSTALLED
DURING REPAIR)

HEAD GASKET BLOWN
GASKET FACES NOT FLAT
TO HOLD GASKET

RING GROOVES – CARBON
CLOGGED – RINGS "FROZEN"
INACTIVE – ILL FITTED
PISTON RINGS

CYLINDER WALL – WORN
GLAZED, SCORED –
POROUS CASTING

BY-PASS COVER – LOOSE
GASKET BLOWN

FAULTY SEAL
INSTALLATION –
IMPROPERLY
CEMENTED

CRANKCASE MIS
ALIGNED, SCREWS, BOLTS, ETC.
IMPROPERLY TORQUED –
DOWEL PINS
INCORRECTLY INSTALLED

BROKEN OR DAMAGED
VALVE SEGMENT

NOTE
FAULTY OR IMPROPERLY INSTALLED
CARBON SEAL "TOP" OF
CRANKSHAFT PERMITS OIL ESCAPE
TO SMEAR ARMATURE PLATE, ON
BOTTOM END, WATER IS ADMITTED
INTO CRANKCASE

Fig. A-1 Power Head Diagnosis Chart.

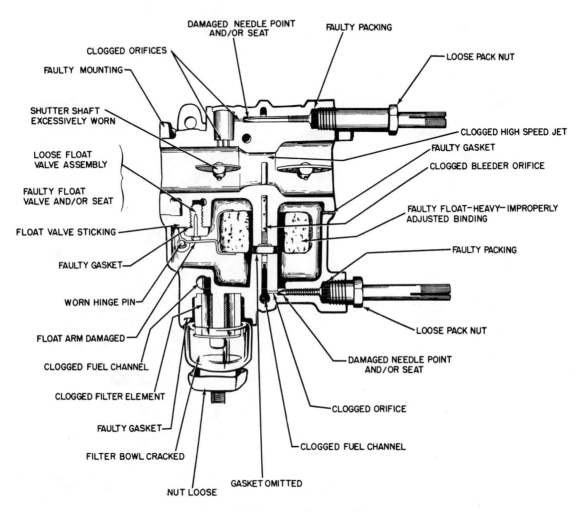

Fig. A-2 Carburetion Diagnosis Chart.

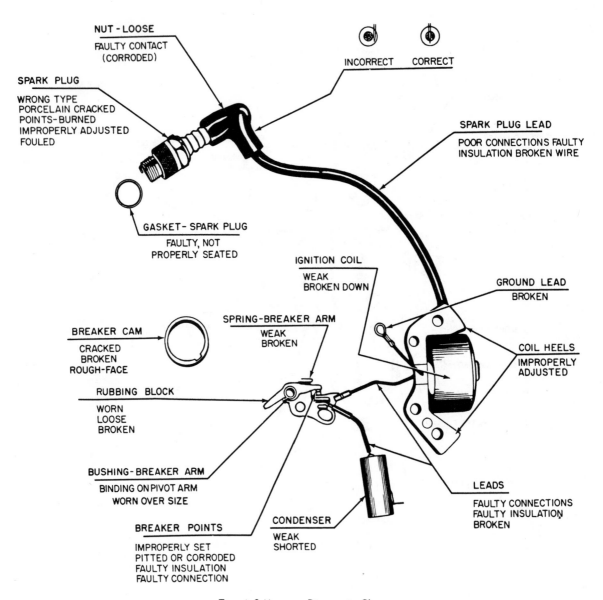

**NUT - LOOSE**
FAULTY CONTACT
(CORRODED)

INCORRECT    CORRECT

**SPARK PLUG**
WRONG TYPE
PORCELAIN CRACKED
POINTS - BURNED
IMPROPERLY ADJUSTED
FOULED

**SPARK PLUG LEAD**
POOR CONNECTIONS FAULTY
INSULATION BROKEN WIRE

**GASKET - SPARK PLUG**
FAULTY, NOT
PROPERLY SEATED

**IGNITION COIL**
WEAK
BROKEN DOWN

**GROUND LEAD**
BROKEN

**BREAKER CAM**
CRACKED
BROKEN
ROUGH - FACE

**SPRING - BREAKER ARM**
WEAK
BROKEN

**COIL HEELS**
IMPROPERLY
ADJUSTED

**RUBBING BLOCK**
WORN
LOOSE
BROKEN

**BUSHING - BREAKER ARM**
BINDING ON PIVOT ARM
WORN OVER SIZE

**LEADS**
FAULTY CONNECTIONS
FAULTY INSULATION
BROKEN

**BREAKER POINTS**
IMPROPERLY SET
PITTED OR CORRODED
FAULTY INSULATION
FAULTY CONNECTION

**CONDENSER**
WEAK
SHORTED

Fig. A-3 Magneto Diagnosis Chart.

Acknowledgments

Publications Director
    Alan N. Knofla

Editor-in-Chief
    Marjorie Bruce

Sponsoring Editor
    Fred W. Smith

Revision
    George E. Stephenson

Production Director
    Frederick Sharer

Production Specialist
    Lee St.Onge
    Jean Le Morta

Illustrations
    Anthony Canabush
    Michael Kokernak

Manufacturers and government agencies have supplied information in the form of instruction books books on basic principles, pamphlets, booklets, and photographs. Without these sources of firsthand information, the research and writing of this book would have been difficult, if not impossible.

The author wishes to acknowledge the following companies and organizations which have supplied material and information: Automotive Electric Association, Bolens Products Division Food Machinery and Chemical Corporation, Buick Motors Division General Motors Corporation, Cedar Rapids Engineering Company, Chrysler Corporation, Cushman Motor Works, Inc., Delco Remy Division General Motors, E. Edelmann and Company, Forster Brothers, Gravely Tractors, Inc., Holley Carburetor Company, Internal Combustion Engine Institute, Lawn Mower Institute, Inc., Marvel-Schebler Products Division Borg Warner Corporation, Mustang Motor Products Corporation, Northrop Corporation, Oliver Outboard Motors, Outboard Motor Manufacturers' Association, Propulsion Engine Corporation, Quick Manufacturing, Inc., Thompson Products, Toro Manufacturing Corporation, Waukesha Motor Company, West Bend Aluminum Company, Westinghouse Electric Corp., Whizzer Industries, Inc. Wright Saw Division Thomas Industries, Inc.

Particular thanks is due to those companies and government agencies which have supplied many of the illustrations that are found in the text. Specific contributions are listed below.

AC Spark Plug Division, General Motors Corporation, Flint, Michigan — figures 7-25 and 7-26

Aluminum Company of America, PIttsburgh, Pa. — figure 3-7

American Oil Company — figure 4-17

Audi NSU Auto Union, 7107 Neckarsulm, German Federal Republic — Figures 11-1, 11-2, 11-3, 11-4, 11-6, 11-14, 11-21, 11-22

Briggs-Stratton, Milwaukee, Wisconsin — figures 3-5, 3-17, 3-24, 3-25, 4-3, 4-4, 4-5, 4-9, 4-10, 4-24, 4-28, 5-7, 7-9, 7-19, 8-7, 8-8, 8-9, 9-13, 9-20, 9-21, 9-22, 9-28, 9-30, 9-31

Champion Spark Plug, Toledo, Ohio — figures 4-21, 4-22, 4-23, 7-24, 8-2, 8-3, 8-4, 8-5

Clinton Engines, Clinton, Michigan — figures 3-6, 3-8, 3-14, 3-16, 3-27, 4-1, 4-2, 5-4, 8-12, 8-13, 8-14, 8-15, 8-16, 8-17, 9-1, 9-2, 9-5, 9-6, 9-7, 9-8, 9-9, 9-10, 9-11, 9-12, 9-23, 9-24, 9-25, 9-27, 9-34

Curtiss-Wright Corporation, 1 Passaic St., Wood-Ridge, N.J. 07075 — Figures 11-7, 11-8, 11-9, 11-11, 11-13, 11-17, 11-20

Ethyl Corporation — figure 4-20

Evinrude, Milwaukee, Wisconsin — figure 6-10

Fairbanks-Morse, Chicago, Illinois — figures 7-8, 7-10, 7-11, 7-13, 7-14, 7-20, 7-22

Johnson Motors, Waukegan, Illinois — figures 3-3, 3-13, 4-6, 4-7, 4-13, 4-19, 5-13, 6-7, 6-8, 6-9, 7-12, 7-21, Appendix figures A-1, A-2, A-3, and front cover photo

Kiekhäfer Corporation, Fond du Lac, Wisconsin — figures 3-16, 9-17, 9-26, 9-32, 9-33, 9-35, 9-36, 9-37

Kohler Company, Kohler, Wisconsin — figure 3-15

Lauson  Power Products Dept., Division of Tecumseh Products Company, Grafton, Wisconsin — figures 4-26, 4-27, 5-6, 5-10, 5-11

Lawn-Boy Company, Galesburg, Illinois — figures 3-4, 6-2, 6-4, 9-4

Lincoln-Mercury Division, Ford Motor Company, Dearborn, Michigan — figures 3-1, 6-5, 6-6, 6-8, 8-6

McCulloch Company, Los Angeles, California — figure 5-12

Mobil Oil Corp., 150 E. 42nd St., New York, New York — figures 11-5, 11-10, 11-12, 11-15

Outboard Marine Corp., 100 Pershing Rd., Waukegan, Ill. 60085 — figures 11-16, 11-18, 11-19

Perfect Circle Company, Hagerstown, Indiana — figures 3-9, 3-10, 3-11, 9-29

Standard Oil Company of New Jersey, New York, New York — figures 3-19, 3-20, 3-22, 4-19, 5-5, 6-1

Tecumseh Products Company, Grafton, Wisconsin — figures 3-12, 3-23, 3-26, 3-28, 3-29, 4-16, 4-22, 7-23, 8-10, 8-11, 9-14, 9-15, 9-16, 9-19

Wico Electric Company, West Springfield, Massachusetts — figures 7-16, 7-17, 7-18

Wisconsin Motor Corporation, Milwaukee, Wisconsin, — figures 4-25, 5-8, 5-9, 6-3

Zenith Carburetor Division, Bendix Corporation, Detroit, Michigan — figures 4-14, 4-15

# INDEX